ACCELERATING THE LITERACY PERFORMANCE OF BILINGUAL STUDENTS

Also Available

Developing Reading Comprehension: Effective Instruction for All Students in PreK–2
Katherine A. Dougherty Stahl and Georgia Earnest García

Expanding Reading Comprehension in Grades 3–6: Effective Instruction for ALL Students
Katherine A. Dougherty Stahl and Georgia Earnest García

ACCELERATING
the Literacy Performance of Bilingual Students

Evidence-Based Instruction in Grades K–6

GEORGIA EARNEST GARCÍA

THE GUILFORD PRESS
New York London

A Division of Guilford Publications, Inc.
www.guilford.com

Printed in the United States of America

This book is printed on acid-free paper.

Last digit is print number: 9 8 7 6 5 4 3 2 1

Library of Congress Cataloging-in-Publication Data is available from the publisher.

ISBN 978-1-4625-5601-4 (paperback)
ISBN 978-1-4625-5602-1 (cloth)

About the Author

Georgia Earnest García, PhD, is Professor Emerita in the Department of Curriculum and Instruction at the University of Illinois at Urbana–Champaign. She has held appointments at the Center for the Study of Reading, the RAND Reading Study Group on Skillful Reading, and the National Literacy Panel on Language Minority Children and Youth. Prior to obtaining her doctorate, she was a Peace Corps volunteer, bilingual education teacher, English teacher, and ESL/EFL teacher. Dr. García has authored or coauthored several books as well as numerous book chapters and journal articles. After retiring, she served on the Educational Testing Service's Dual Language Assessment Team and the WestEd Reading Content Team, which updated the Reading Assessment Framework for the 2026 National Assessment of Educational Progress. Dr. García was inducted into the Reading Hall of Fame in 2019. She continues to collaborate with bilingual teachers and schools and to conduct and publish research on the literacy development, instruction, and assessment of bilingual students.

Acknowledgments

I want to thank Dr. Lisa Domke, Dr. Chaehyun Lee, and Ms. Olga Halpern for reviewing chapters in the book. I am very grateful for their expertise and time. In addition, I want to thank Dr. Jason Stegemoller for sharing his expertise on Spanish reading. I also want to thank the many teachers, students, and administrators with whom I have worked over the years. Your observations, insights, concerns, and questions helped to inform this book.

Preface

The aim of this book is to substantially improve the literacy instruction and performance of different types of bilingual students at the elementary level: current emergent bilingual students (i.e., English learners or English language learners); former emergent bilingual students—emergent bilingual students who exited from bilingual or English-as-a-second-language (ESL) instruction and who are now in all-English classrooms; students in dual-language (DL) classrooms—emergent bilingual students who speak the same minority language and majority speakers who speak English; and students who speak English as a second language (L2) but who always have been in all-English classrooms. When I refer to them all, I call them bilingual students. This book is written for preservice teachers, inservice teachers, literacy personnel, school administrators, teacher educators, and policymakers.

Between spring 2019 and spring 2021, most bilingual students did not receive in-person instruction because their school districts had moved to remote-distance learning to prevent COVID-19 from spreading (Sugarman & Lazarín, 2020). In fact, all but two states in the United States forbade in-person schooling between 2020 and 2021. During this time, the type of remote-distance learning that schools implemented required students to have access to the internet and to computers, tablets, and/or smartphones. Sadly, many bilingual students did not have internet access or the required equipment (i.e., computers and similar devices) to participate. And those who did have access to the internet and the necessary equipment often did not understand what they were supposed to do. A survey conducted in California during the spring of 2020 revealed that one-third of the state's bilingual families did not understand how to employ distance learning with their children (Williams & Marcus, 2021).

When bilingual students did participate in remote-distance learning, they completed packets of written work and spent much of their time watching the teacher, other students, and/or videos online. Few bilingual students received the type of interactive instruction and feedback needed to advance their language and literacy development in the home or first (L1) language and second (L2) language (Najarro, 2021; Sugarman & Lazarín, 2020; Williams & Marcus, 2021).

The number of emergent bilingual students who participated in federally required assessments in 2021 compared to 2019 (Najarro, 2021) also was low, making it difficult to interpret the pandemic and postpandemic assessment data for them. Due to school closures, the federal government waived the federal assessment requirements for emergent bilingual students during 2019–2020, resulting in fewer students participating in the required language proficiency and literacy assessments.

Nonetheless, the data available showed that, postpandemic, the English language and literacy performance of emergent bilingual students was lower or did not substantially improve compared to prepandemic. For example, one of the more popular English language proficiency assessments, the World-Class Instructional Design and Assessment (WIDA, 2023a), reported that in 2021, compared to 2019, the speaking scores of emergent bilingual students declined in general, with major drops in scores for first and sixth graders (Najarro, 2021). Analysis of the 2022 reading comprehension test scores for a national sample of emergent bilingual students on the National Assessment of Educational Progress in English reading (Nation's Report Card, 2022) showed that the average test score for emergent bilingual fourth graders in 2022 was the same as in 2019, although it was still significantly lower than that of the English speakers. Given that the 2022 average reading test score for fourth-grade English speakers significantly dropped between 2022 and 2019, we should not applaud the finding for emergent bilingual students.

This book is written in response to the instructional and assessment situation during the pandemic. It emphasizes research-based instruction designed to promote and accelerate the L1 and L2 language development and literacy of bilingual students.

Chapter 1 introduces readers to the different types of bilingual students in the United States, the types of specialized education programs provided for them, and information about their academic performance. Chapter 2 presents the theoretical insights and theories that guide current research and instruction designed to develop and improve the language and literacy performance of bilingual students. *Translanguaging*—bilingual individuals' use of their complete linguistic repertoires (O. García, 2009)—and translanguaging pedagogy (O. García, Johnson, & Seltzer, 2017) are explained in Chapter 2.

Chapter 3 shares the techniques and instructional approaches that teachers of bilingual students employ to make their L2 instruction comprehensible. The chapter also briefly reviews the L2 language teaching approaches that have been historically used. Much of the chapter focuses on content-based language teaching, which characterizes the instruction currently implemented in one-way and two-way dual-language programs.

Chapter 4 describes instructional activities that will promote bilingual students' oral language and literacy development. The activities include those that are appropriate for beginning L1 and L2 learners and those appropriate for more advanced L1 and L2 learners. The chapter also includes a brief review of the implications involved in employing the Science of Reading with emergent bilingual students.

Chapter 5 describes how bilingual teachers should select and use different types of narrative and expository texts with bilingual students—stories, fables, narrative nonfiction, expository texts, picture books, chapter books, multicultural texts, and dual-language books. How to identify and employ narrative and expository text structures and graphic organizers to improve bilingual students' reading comprehension and learning is explained.

Chapters 6 and 7 focus on beginning reading. In Chapter 6, the role of L1 instruction and beginning L1 reading instruction in Spanish and in languages other than English, such as Arabic and Chinese, are discussed. Chapter 7 focuses on beginning reading instruction in English. It also includes comprehension strategies that should be taught to beginning readers and writers in the L1 and L2.

Chapter 8 emphasizes reading comprehension instruction for bilingual students in grades 2 and above. Comprehension strategies for instruction in the L1 and L2 are presented, along with descriptions of instructional programs implemented and tested with bilingual students.

Chapter 9 focuses on bilingual students' writing instruction in L1 and L2. It covers instruction for beginning writers and more advanced writers in elementary school. Among other instructional topics, the chapter explains invented spelling, modeled writing, and how to use an adapted version of the writer's workshop with bilingual students.

Chapter 10 discusses the vocabulary and academic language development of bilingual students. How to select words for explicit vocabulary instruction and how to provide bilingual students with explicit vocabulary instruction are explained. The chapter also defines academic language and explains how it should be taught to bilingual students.

Chapter 11 emphasizes disciplinary literacy instruction for bilingual students in grades 3 to 6. Examples of disciplinary literacy programs already implemented and evaluated with bilingual students are presented. Guidelines are provided for teachers' development of their own disciplinary literacy programs in science and history/social studies for bilingual students.

Chapter 12 discusses authentic and formative assessments, summative assessments, and interim assessments. Assessment biases that adversely affect the language and literacy evaluation of bilingual students are discussed. The chapter ends with an explanation of the importance of using a comprehensive assessment system with bilingual students. Finally, the Conclusion reviews what bilingual teachers should emphasize in their instruction and how they should organize it so that bilingual students' literacy and academic performance are accelerated in grades K through 6.

All chapters begin with guiding questions that you and your students should be able to answer after reading each chapter. Throughout the book, vignettes, dialogues, tables, and figures that illustrate key points are provided. Given that 75% of emergent bilingual students are Spanish speakers (U.S. Department of Education, 2022), most of the L1 examples focus on Spanish, with occasional examples from other L1 languages.

I hope that you enjoy reading and using the book as much as I enjoyed writing it. Feedback from you, along with questions, always are welcome. You can reach me at *georgiaearnestgarcia@gmail.com*.

Contents

Purchasers of this book can download and print larger versions of select materials at *www.guilford.com/garcia-forms* for personal use or use with students (see copyright page for details).

CHAPTER 1

Introduction to Teaching Emergent Bilingual and Dual Language Students

GUIDING QUESTIONS

- Who are emergent bilingual students?
- Why are specialized educational programs required for emergent bilingual students?
- What are the most effective educational programs for emergent bilingual students?
- Why are additive bilingual instructional settings more advantageous than subtractive bilingual instructional settings?
- Why is it important to identify former emergent bilingual students?
- Who are the bilingual students in two-way dual-language programs?

Ms. Malone, the multilingual and multicultural coordinator for the Newsom School District, is meeting with three sets of parents today. The first couple—Mr. and Mrs. García—are from Mexico. They arrived in the United States 6 years ago, and just moved from Texas to Illinois. They have three children: a 3-year-old, a 6-year-old, and an 8-year-old. Mr. García works in construction, while Mrs. García takes care of the house and watches the children. Although Mr. García speaks some English, Spanish is the language spoken in the home because Mrs. García primarily speaks Spanish.

The second couple—Mr. and Mrs. Fonseca—are from Honduras and arrived in the United States a month ago. The father has been accepted into a master's degree program in engineering at the local university. His wife does not have a work permit and will stay at home.

The father, who speaks English and Spanish, tells Ms. Malone that they speak Spanish at home. They have two children: a 5-year-old and a 9-year-old.

The third couple—Mr. and Mrs. Pham—are from Vietnam. They have been in the United States for 6 months. Mrs. Pham works part-time in a nail salon, while Mr. Pham is a cook in a Vietnamese restaurant owned by a relative. They speak enough English to do their jobs, but they speak Vietnamese at home. They have three children: a 6-year-old, an 8-year-old, and a 10-year-old.

School district personnel tested all the children in English. They identified them as emergent bilingual students because they speak their home languages but need to learn English in school.

Ms. Malone recommends that Mr. and Mrs. García and Mr. and Mrs. Fonseca enroll their 5- and 6-year-old children in the district's Spanish–English two-way dual-language (DL) program, which only begins in kindergarten and first grade. She tells them that DL education is one of the most effective bilingual education programs offered in the United States.

She recommends that the Garcías' and the Fonsecas' 8- and 9-year-old children be placed in the district's one-way Spanish–English DL program because the children have never been in a two-way DL program and have limited proficiency in English. In the one-way DL program, they will be with other emergent bilingual students who speak Spanish and who are learning English. Bilingual teachers fluent in Spanish and English will teach them by using both languages throughout elementary school.

Ms. Malone explains to the Phams that the district does not have a sufficient number of Vietnamese-speaking children to offer a two-way or one-way DL program for Vietnamese-speaking children. Therefore, she recommends that the Pham children attend Culver School, which has a Transitional Program of Instruction (TPI). In this program, the Pham children will receive English-as-a-second-language (ESL) instruction for 90 minutes each day, 45 minutes of instruction in Vietnamese 4 days each week, and the rest of their daily instruction in all-English classrooms.

All the parents are confused. They do not understand why their children will not be placed in all-English classrooms right away. They think that this is the best way for their children to learn and speak English immediately. As you read this chapter, think about what Ms. Malone will tell each set of parents.

This chapter introduces you to the different types of bilingual students discussed in this book and to the educational programs that serve them. First, the book introduces you to a major focus of the book, emergent bilingual students—students who know a minority language at home and who are in the process of acquiring a new language, English, at school (O. García & Kleifgen, 2018; O. García, Kleifgen, & Falchi, 2008). Next, the specialized programs that the federal government has approved for the instruction of emergent bilingual students are presented. Then, the academic performance of emergent bilingual students is discussed. In the next two sections, two other types of bilingual students—former emergent bilingual students and bilingual students in two-way DL programs—are described. The chapter closes with concluding remarks.

EMERGENT BILINGUAL STUDENTS

O. García et al. (2008) coined the term *emergent bilingual students* to refer to students who speak a minority language at home and who are learning English at school. This is a much more positive term than some of the other terms that historically were used. For example, the United States government has referred to students who do not know English as limited-English proficient (LEP) students, limited-English-speaking students, English language learners (ELLs), and, most recently, English learners (ELs) (Every Student Succeeds Act [ESSA], 2015). These terms are considered deficit because they do not acknowledge that the students already know a language other than English. To counter deficit terms, the term *emergent bilingual students* is used throughout this book rather than other terms such as ELLs or ELs. Some educators currently use the term *multilingual students* to recognize the multiple languages and dialects that students may know. However, because this book explicitly focuses on students' acquisition of two languages, regardless of dialectal variation, it uses the term *emergent bilingual students*.

Demographic statistics indicate that the number of emergent bilingual students who attend United States public schools continues to increase. According to the Condition of Education (Hussar et al., 2020), 5 million emergent bilingual students attended public schools in 2017 compared to 3.8 million in 2000. They represented slightly over 10% of public school students. The majority of them were enrolled in elementary school.

Approximately 75% of emergent bilingual students are Spanish speakers (United States Department of Education, 2022). Other languages spoken by emergent bilingual students include (in alphabetic order): Arabic, Brazilian, Chinese, Haitian Creole, Hmong, Korean, Nepali, Polish, Portuguese, Russian, Samoan, Somali, Swahili, Tagalog, Urdu, and Vietnamese, among others. Although the largest numbers of emergent bilingual students live in California, New York, Texas, Arizona, and Illinois, they increasingly are found in other states throughout the United States.

TYPES OF EDUCATIONAL PROGRAMS APPROVED FOR EMERGENT BILINGUAL STUDENTS

A large percentage of emergent bilingual students (97%) participate in language programs specifically designed for them (United States Department of Education, 2022). Currently, 46 states provide some type of bilingual education program for emergent bilingual students at the elementary level (Rutherford-Quach et al., 2021). A bilingual education program includes home or first-language (L1) instruction and English as a second language (ESL) or English instruction.

Some of the states that previously outlawed bilingual education (such as California and Massachusetts) now allow bilingual education (A. García, 2020). When bilingual education was unavailable in California and Massachusetts, the academic performance of emergent bilingual students did not improve, but substantially decreased or stayed the same.

Just placing emergent bilingual students in all-English classrooms is illegal (Ovando & Combs, 2018). Although some emergent bilingual students succeed when they are only placed in all-English classrooms, most do not. To characterize this situation, many bilingual educators refer to the placement of emergent bilingual students in the all-English classroom as submersion or sink or swim. Although schools cannot place emergent bilingual students in all-English classrooms, parents have the legal right to do so.

Legal Basis for Specialized Programs

Two federal court cases provide the legal basis for the United States government's requirement that states that receive federal funds provide specialized programs for emergent bilingual students: *Lau v. Nichols* (1974) and *Castañeda v. Pickard* (1981). In *Lau v. Nichols*, parents of Chinese-speaking students in San Francisco filed a lawsuit against the San Francisco United School District for violating their children's rights because the school district did not provide instructional help for their children to acquire English. The United States Supreme Court ruled that providing non-English-proficient Chinese students with the same or identical education as native-English-speaking students did not constitute equal education according to the Civil Rights Act of 1964. The Court required the San Francisco School District to take positive steps to overcome the educational barriers that the non-English-speaking Chinese students faced. However, it was beyond the Court's responsibilities to specify what the school district had to do.

The Civil Rights Division of the United States Department of Education outlined in the Lau Remedies what states and school districts had to do to provide equal education for non-English-speaking students (K–12) in school districts that received federal funds (see Lau Remedies, *web.stanford.edu*, 2022). As the first remedy, school districts had to determine the extent to which children entering the school district spoke a language other than English in the home. Second, based on the children's language proficiency status, the school district had to provide them with appropriate services. Lastly, when there were 20 or more emergent bilingual students who spoke the same minority language in a school district, district personnel had to develop and place the children in an approved bilingual education program.

The first two remedies remain in effect today, but the third remedy, which required bilingual education, was changed in 1981 to include other types of services. The Fifth Circuit Court in the United States ruled in *Castañeda v. Pickard* (1981) that school districts' program choices had to meet a three-part test, which expanded district options. The three-part test includes the following:

1. The chosen program has to be "recognized as sound by some experts in the field or . . . considered . . . a legitimate experimental strategy";
2. "the programs and practices . . . [are] reasonably calculated to implement this theory effectively" (i.e., there are adequate resources and personnel); and
3. the program succeeds, after a legitimate trial, in producing results indicating that students' "language barriers are actually being overcome" (*www2.ed.gov*, Office for Civil Rights).

When Congress reauthorized the Elementary and Secondary School Act in 2015, known as the Every Student Succeeds Act (ESSA), several new requirements were established for the education of emergent bilingual students. Now, states must use standardized or uniform criteria within the state to identify emergent bilingual students and include a measure of English proficiency for emergent bilingual students when evaluating the academic quality of the school district.

Types of Approved Specialized Programs

Table 1.1 shows the different types of programs that the federal government currently approves for emergent bilingual students at the elementary level. Brief descriptions of each program are provided below.

TABLE 1.1. Approved Programs for Emergent Bilingual Students

Program type	Language groups	Length of time	Language focus
Developmental or maintenance bilingual education	Same L1 group	K–5/6	L1 and ESL
English as a second language (ESL)	Variety of L1 groups or same L1	Part-time and full-time	ESL
One-way dual-language (DL) education	Same L1 group but different proficiencies in L1 and English	K–5/6	L1 and English
Structured/Sheltered English immersion (AZ & MA)	Variety of L1 groups or same L1	Part-time or full-time	ESL
Transitional bilingual education (TBE)	Same L1 group	Early exit: 3–4 years; late exit: K–5/6	L1 and ESL
Transitional program of instruction (TPI, IL)	Different L1 groups	K–5/6	L1, ESL, all-English
Two-way immersion (TWI) or two-way dual-language education (DL)	Same L1 group and English speakers	K–5/6; sometimes through middle school	L1 and English

Note. L1 = home or first language other than English; AZ = Arizona; MA = Massachusetts.

Developmental/Maintenance Bilingual Education

In Developmental/Maintenance Bilingual Education, certified bilingual teachers fluent in the L1 and English teach emergent bilingual students from the same L1 throughout elementary school. The students receive L1 and ESL instruction, with instruction in the L1 continuing throughout elementary school but decreasing as students acquire English. The aim of the program is to help the students become bilingual and biliterate.

ESL Instruction

When there are insufficient numbers of emergent bilingual students from the same minority language to warrant a bilingual education program (usually 20 or more students), school districts still have to provide the students with some type of English language services, usually ESL instruction. ESL instruction for elementary-age students may include explicit English instruction (see Lems, Miller, & Soro, 2017) and/or sheltered English instruction (Echevarria et al., 2017), in which teachers scaffold emergent bilingual students' access to the school curriculum by using ESL techniques. Some of the ESL techniques include teachers' pacing the speed of their talk in English according to the students' English performance levels, and accompanying their English instruction, oral book reading, and use of videos with gestures, illustrations, realia, physical demonstrations, and modeling. Chapter 3 describes how to shelter or support bilingual students' second-language (L2) instruction.

Emergent bilingual students may participate in full-time or part-time ESL instruction. During part-time instruction, an ESL teacher may pull students out of the all-English classroom for ESL instruction or participate in the all-English classroom by pushing into the classroom. In push-in ESL instruction, the ESL teacher supports the instruction and learning of emergent bilingual students by employing ESL techniques to make the classroom teacher's instruction comprehensible.

One-Way DL Education

In one-way DL education, which lasts throughout elementary school, the students are from the same minority language group but often vary in their L1 and English proficiencies. They are taught by certified bilingual teachers and immersed in L1 and English content instruction throughout elementary school. The students acquire the two languages by using them with each other and their bilingual teachers for social and academic purposes. The goals are for the students to become bilingual and biliterate. This is the program that Ms. Malone recommended for the Garcías' and the Fonsecas' 8- and 9-year-old children.

English Immersion Programs

Several states authorized English immersion programs for emergent bilingual students. These are programs that emphasize instruction in the English language.

In 2000, the state of Arizona passed a law that required students newly classified as emergent bilingual students to attend a Structured English Immersion classroom for at least 4 hours each day during their first year of classification (Mo, 2019). In Arizona's version of Structured English Immersion, emergent bilingual students received explicit instruction in the English language, with an emphasis on "phonology (pronunciation—the sound system of a language), morphology (the internal structure and forms of words), syntax (English word order rules), lexicon (vocabulary), and semantics (how to use English in different situations and contexts)," in addition to explicit English reading and writing instruction (Arizona Department of Education, 2014, p. 4). Sadly, the expectation that emergent bilingual students in Arizona would become English proficient after participating in Structured English Immersion for one year was unrealistic. In response to the poor performance of emergent bilingual students in Arizona, the Arizona State Board of Education (2014) made several changes to how Structured English Immersion is now implemented.

In 2002, the Massachusetts State Board of Education (2022) approved a different version of English Immersion for its emergent bilingual students, which it called Sheltered English Immersion. In Massachusetts, teachers with special training in sheltered English teach classrooms in which emergent bilingual students are integrated with English speakers. The teachers employ ESL techniques to make the school's curriculum in English comprehensible for emergent bilingual students. Teachers occasionally use students' L1, but it is not a standard feature of the Massachusetts Sheltered English Immersion Program. In 2019, Massachusetts also allowed transitional bilingual education and two-way dual-language education (Mitchell, 2019), described below.

Transitional Bilingual Education

One of the first programs that the federal government approved for emergent bilingual students was transitional bilingual education (TBE). In TBE, bilingual teachers (proficient in the L1 and English), who are certified in bilingual education and early childhood and/or elementary education, teach the elementary curriculum to students who speak the same minority language. The teachers begin with L1 instruction, slowly increasing the amount of ESL instruction. The aim of the program is to move the emergent bilingual students into all-English classrooms as soon as possible. Programs that last 3 years or less are called early-exit TBE programs. Programs that continue beyond 3 years are called late-exit TBE programs.

Transitional Program of Instruction

In Illinois, when schools do not have 20 or more students from the same minority language group in attendance, the school district has to provide a part-time or full-time Transitional Program of Instruction (TPI) (Illinois State Board of Education, 2022). In a TPI, a certified bilingual or ESL teacher provides the students with ESL instruction, and a proficient speaker of the L1 provides them with as much L1 instruction as possible. If no L1 speakers are available to serve as teachers, then the school does not have to provide L1 instruction. When students are in a part-time TPI, they also will receive instruction from a certified teacher in an all-English classroom. This is the type of program that Ms. Malone recommended for the Pham children, who speak Vietnamese at home.

Two-Way DL Education

In two-way DL education (sometimes referred to as two-way immersion education), half or more of the students speak the same minority language and half or less are English speakers (Howard et al., 2018). The two language groups are integrated into the same classrooms and taught in both languages by certified bilingual teachers throughout elementary school. In some states and school districts, DL education continues through middle school. The goals of the program are to help the two groups of students to become bilingual, biliterate, bicultural, and high achieving. Students acquire the languages by using them for social and academic purposes, and they are taught the required state curriculum. They often do not receive explicit language instruction in either language. Although the most popular DL programs are for Spanish speakers and English speakers, two way-DL also includes other language groups such as Arabic-English; French-English; Mandarin-English; and Navajo-English, among others. In this book, English speakers in DL programs are referred to as English-speaking DL students or English-dominant students.

Two of the more popular two-way DL programs are 90–10 and 50–50 (United States Department of Education, Office of English Language Acquisition, 2015). In 90–10 DL programs, starting in kindergarten and/or first grade, the students receive 90% of their instruction in the minority language and 10% in English, with the instructional percentages in the two languages changing until they are 50–50 in fourth grade. In 50–50 programs, the students receive 50% of their instruction in each language during all the elementary grades. Enrollment in a two-way 90–10 Spanish–English DL program is what Ms. Malone recommended for the Garcías' and the Fonsecas' 5-year-old and 6-year-old children.

Although you might think that the English performance of emergent bilingual students would improve with more English instruction, this is not necessarily the case. Several researchers reported that emergent bilingual students in 90–10 DL programs met their state English proficiency standards and academic standards much quicker than those in 50–50 DL programs (Acosta, Williams, & Hunt, 2019). Researchers explained that emergent bilingual students do well in DL programs when they continue to learn in their L1 throughout the elementary grades; socialize with English speakers, who provide them with L2 resources and models; and are in classrooms in which their language and culture are supported (Lindholm-Leary & Hernández, 2011).

THE ACADEMIC PERFORMANCE OF EMERGENT BILINGUAL STUDENTS

The assessment of emergent bilingual students is covered in more detail in Chapter 12. Here, however, it is important to realize that employing English tests developed for English speakers in the United States to evaluate the academic performance of emergent bilingual students is problematic. The authors of the Standards for Educational and Psychological Testing (American Educational Research Association [AERA], American Psychological Association [APA], & National Council on Measurement for Education [NCME], 1999, 2014) warned that the accuracy of such assessments with emergent bilingual students was likely to be compromised because it was difficult to know how much of their English test performance was due to their limited English proficiency or to their performance in the domain being tested. For example, although the average reading comprehension test score for a sample of emergent bilingual fourth graders in 2019 on a national reading test in English—the National Assessment of Educational Performance (NAEP)—was significantly lower (219) than the average score (224) for a sample of nonbilingual fourth graders (National Center for Education Statistics, 2020), the reason for the low scores of the emergent bilingual students—their low English proficiency or their English reading comprehension, or a combination of the two—is not known.

Evaluations of Bilingual Students' Academic Performance

In response to the difficulty involved in interpreting the performance of emergent bilingual students on English assessments, researchers have sought alternate ways to evaluate their academic performance. Collier and Thomas (2017) conducted longitudinal analyses of the length of time it took emergent bilingual students to perform at grade level in English. They found that when emergent bilingual students were in DL programs from K/first grade through fifth/sixth grades, it took at least six years before they performed at grade level on English tests. If students did not have the opportunity to learn in their L1, but participated in some ESL instruction, then it often took them 7 to 10 years of participation in United States schools, with many of them never attaining grade-level performance in

English. Collier and Thomas explained that one reason it took emergent bilingual students so long to perform at grade level in English was that native-English speakers continued to learn new content, accelerating the knowledge assessed on English tests, while emergent bilingual students still were developing their English proficiency. They reported that their findings showed that to keep pace with the learning of native-English speakers, emergent bilingual students needed to learn new material through their L1 as they developed their English proficiency.

Other researchers conducted comparative evaluations of the academic performance of emergent bilingual students in all-English classrooms, bilingual education programs, and ESL programs. Their findings revealed that Spanish-speaking emergent bilingual students in two-way DL programs outperformed Spanish-speaking emergent bilingual students on English reading tests in all-English classrooms and other types of bilingual and ESL programs (Slavin & Cheung, 2005; Steele et al., 2017; United States Department of Education, Office of English Language Acquisition, 2015). For example, in a comparative statistical analysis of 17 studies, Rolstad, Mahoney, and Glass (2005) reported that emergent bilingual students who participated in bilingual education programs benefited more than those who participated in ESL or Structured English Immersion. Also, within bilingual education programs, those who participated in DL programs had higher test scores than those who participated in early-exit TBE programs.

Additive Bilingualism Compared to Subtractive Bilingualism

Additive bilingualism occurs when students add a new language to their existing languages. In contrast, subtractive bilingualism occurs when students lose a language as they acquire a new language (Lambert, 1981). One reason that emergent bilingual students in DL programs attain higher academic performances than students in early-exit TBE programs and all-English or ESL classrooms may be the additive nature of DL programs. Additive instructional settings generally are more motivating for bilingual students than subtractive settings. They facilitate the construction of strong bilingual identities and provide bilingual students with the opportunity to use all that they know and can do when learning academic content (see Chapter 2).

FORMER EMERGENT BILINGUAL STUDENTS

In the past, when emergent bilingual students attained grade-level performance in English or were exited from bilingual education, they no longer were described as emergent bilingual, and their performance data were included in the data for English-speaking students. There were two consequences: Schools no longer adapted their instruction and/or assessments for the students, and information about their progress and grade-level performance was lost. Recently, the federal government recognized the lost data problem. It now requires that states with federal funding continue to collect data for former English learners (the term that the federal government uses) for 2 to 4 years after they have been exited from specialized services (United States Department of Education, 2016).

BILINGUAL STUDENTS ENROLLED IN TWO-WAY DL PROGRAMS

Two types of bilingual students are enrolled in two-way DL programs: emergent bilingual students who speak the same minority language and students who speak English—the United States societal language. The aims of DL programs are for both types of students to become bilingual, biliterate, and high achieving (Howard et al., 2018).

Although both types of students benefit from participating in two-way DL programs (Steele et al., 2017), educators implementing the programs need to make sure that they do not privilege or prioritize the performance of students from English-speaking families compared to that of students from language-minority families. Several researchers reported that it was not unusual for English to dominate DL curricular decisions and for students from English-speaking families to demand and receive more attention from the DL teachers than students from Spanish-speaking families (Cervantes-Soon et al., 2017; Cortina, Makar, & Mount-Cors, 2015).

CONCLUDING REMARKS

As a former bilingual education, ESL, and English-as-foreign-language teacher, I can attest to the fact that working with emergent bilingual students is very rewarding. Emergent bilingual students and their families usually are very appreciative of the support that their teachers provide them. A motivational factor is that, with appropriate instruction, the ongoing progress that emergent bilingual students make in school is fairly easy to see.

When working with emergent bilingual students, it is important to remember that although they are acquiring another language, English, they already have developed some competence and knowledge in their L1. The best way to help them learn in United States schools is by tapping into their L1 knowledge and competence as they acquire English. Just placing emergent bilingual students at the elementary level in all-English classrooms is illegal in the United States unless the students' parents reject the specialized services. Also, it is important to remember that former emergent bilingual students still need instructional support when they are exited from specialized programs and placed in all-English classrooms. If you are implementing a DL program, then you need to safeguard that you are not privileging or prioritizing the performance of students from English-speaking families compared to those from language-minority families. Lastly, I hope that you enjoy teaching and working with bilingual students and bilingual teachers as much as I do.

Theories and Theoretical Insights Relevant to Bilingual Students and Bilingual Education

GUIDING QUESTIONS

- What are the implications of the sociolinguistic and sociocultural perspectives for teaching bilingual students?
- How does L2 acquisition differ from L1 acquisition?
- What is the silent period?
- What are the definitions of basic interpersonal communication skills (BICS) and cognitive academic language proficiency (CALP)?
- What is Cummins's interdependence hypothesis?
- What is translanguaging?
- Why is culturally responsive instruction important for bilingual students?

Ms. Gilroy is a new first-grade teacher at a school that has a Transitional Program of Instruction (TPI). Tuan Pham from Vietnam, who was introduced in Chapter 1, is in her class. Ms. Gilroy is concerned because when Tuan speaks English on the playground, he sounds fluent. For instance, when it was his turn to go down the slide, he said, "My turn, my turn. You get off." However, in the classroom, he rarely speaks English. When Ms. Gilroy asked Tuan to introduce himself to the class, he only said, "My name, Tuan." Unlike the other students in her class, he did not say where he was from or how many brothers and sisters he had. Ms. Gilroy asked Mr. González, who administers the English language proficiency test to new students, about what she had observed. He told her that she might have witnessed examples of BICS and CALP. She wondered what he meant.

The purpose of this chapter is to review the major theories and theoretical insights about bilingual children's L1 and L2 acquisition, bilingualism, biliteracy development, translanguaging, and school performance. Scholars develop theories to explain phenomena and human behavior. When researchers empirically test the theories and contradictory or new findings emerge, theorists often adapt or change the theories to take into account the contradictory or new findings. Thus, theories and theoretical insights, including those presented here, often are subject to adaptation or change. To account for any changes or adaptations in theories and insights, under each major heading, the theories and insights are presented chronologically, with the oldest ones presented first.

SOCIOLINGUISTIC AND SOCIOCULTURAL VIEWS OF LANGUAGE, LEARNING, AND LITERACY

Sociolinguistic Views of Language

Sociolinguists attest that all children naturally, and without formal instruction, acquire the oral language that surrounds them and through which they interact with other humans (Halliday, 1978; Saville-Troike, 2006; Wolfram, 1991). They also believe that every language is functional; that is, every language meets the communicative needs of its populace. No one language or dialect is superior to another (Adger, Wolfram, & Christian, 2007). Languages change, and language variation is normal. The languages that children acquire vary according to the cultural contexts and roles they enact in the contexts.

Rather than viewing language as a discrete set of vocabulary words and grammatical rules to master, scholars who employ sociolinguistic perspectives view language as a communicative process that humans develop through their use with other people (Lems et al., 2017). Based on empirical studies of his young son's language development, Halliday viewed language learning as acquiring "social and cultural practice[s]" (as cited in Thwaite, 2019, p. 43). Halliday stated that "language is the main channel through which the patterns of living are transmitted to him, through which he learns to act as a member of a 'society' . . . and to adopt its 'culture' " (Halliday, 1978, p. 9). Because languages are how humans become members of a society, they are key parts of human identity. In addition, languages play a key role in students' learning. According to Halliday, students learn language(s); they learn about language(s); and they employ language(s) to learn.

Sociocultural Views of Learning

Vygotsky (1978) believed that conversations between adults and children were the origins of language and thought because speech emerged in social interactions, and thought was internalized speech. He proposed that children's learning was facilitated when expert others exposed them to knowledge or tasks that were slightly beyond their current knowledge or capabilities. He called the zone in which this learning occurred the zone of proximal development, or the ZPD, symbolized by i + 1.

In a recent review of research and theories about learning, the National Academies of Sciences, Engineering, and Medicine (2018) supported sociocultural views of learning when they concluded that

> All learners grow and learn in culturally defined ways in culturally defined contexts. While humans share basic brain structures and processes, as well as fundamental experiences such as relationships with family, age-related stages, and many more, each of these phenomena are [sic] shaped by an individual's precise experiences. Learning does not happen in the same way for all people because cultural influences are influential from the beginning of life. (p. 2)

According to Bennett (2023), sociocultural learning theorists locate learning within communities, where "recurring patterns of . . . activity . . . foster the development of knowledge, sense-making, and modes of behaving that are particular to . . . a classroom, school, family, disciplinary community, or cultural group" (p. 85). It is important to remember that these cultural patterns of practice influence how children learn and use language.

Sociocultural Views of Literacy

Scholars such as Street (2003) and Gee (1991) hold sociocultural views of literacy in which literacy practices are not just cognitive and linguistic processes, but social and political practices reflective of the cultures and societies in which they have been developed and the people who employ them. How people develop their literacy practices, what they develop, when and how they employ them, and their engagement are all influenced by the cultural and political contexts in which the practices develop and are enacted. The sociocultural view of literacy also acknowledges the power differentials in society that adversely affect the literacy acquisition and use of people marginalized by the larger society.

The resources (background knowledge, language[s], experiences, skills, etc.) students bring to their reading and writing are socioculturally acquired and influence their literacy performance and assessment (Bennett, 2023). Researchers reported that differences in groups' cultural schemata or background knowledge often resulted in their interpreting reading passages differently. Those who brought the same cultural knowledge and experiences as the author performed better on comprehension measures than those who brought different cultural knowledge and experiences (David & Norazit, 2000; G. E. García, 1991; Steffensen, Joag-Deve, & Anderson, 1979).

L1 ACQUISITION

L1 acquisition usually refers to the first language that children acquire and display between birth and age 3 (Saville-Troike, 2006). Within the bilingual literature, the L1 is referred to as the home, native, or first language.

Most language educators accept that humans' L1 acquisition is innate and universal. However, they combine this assumption with the sociolinguistic insight that young children acquire the language they hear in the environment in which they are immersed (Krashen, 1981; Saville-Troike, 2006). Krashen argued that young children do not acquire the language that surrounds them through instruction, but rather by figuring out what is meant by those who use it. He considered L1 acquisition to be a natural event that did not require instruction or rule learning.

Although young children are not explicitly taught their L1, they do spend a considerable amount of effort, attention, and time (prebirth to about 5–6 years) developing it. Researchers documented that while in the womb babies listen to the language spoken in the environment outside of the womb and favor the language sounds of their mothers over other language sounds not heard while they were in the womb (Klass, 2017; Saville-Troike, 2006).

Language Proficiency

According to linguists, acquiring proficiency in a language requires development of the following components (Lems et al., 2017):

- **Phonology, phonological awareness, and phonemes:** Phonology refers to the sounds that characterize a language and that constitute words in a language; phonological awareness refers to the ability to recognize and manipulate the sounds in a language; and phonemes are the individual sounds of a word.
- **Syntax:** the organization of words.
- **Morphemes:** the smallest units of words that carry meanings. Single words can be morphemes, such as *cat* and *the*. Bound morphemes have to be combined with words, such as the plural *s*.

- **Vocabulary:** words with meanings.
- **Discourse structures:** the varied ways in which words and syntax are organized to convey meaning.

Hymes pointed out that language proficiency also includes communicative competence (1972a, 1972b). Communicative competence means that students know how to use a language appropriately in different social contexts according to the varied roles they play.

Communicative Competence

Canale and Swain (1980) identified four competences that make up communicative competence: linguistic (grammar, vocabulary, and syntax), sociolinguistic (how to use the language appropriately), discourse (how to organize the language), and strategic competence (e.g., how to enter, leave, and repair conversations). Pragmatics, or the knowledge of what a speaker implies and what a listener infers in a particular language and social context, also is part of communicative competence.

L2 ACQUISITION

L2 can refer to one or more additional languages. It usually is the language that individuals acquire after developing their L1, unless they are acquiring two languages at the same time, as in the case of simultaneous bilinguals.

Stages of L2 Language Acquisition

Krashen and Terrell (1983) hypothesized that individuals acquiring an L2 usually go through five stages of language acquisition: preproduction, early production, speech emergence, intermediate fluency, and advanced fluency. Hill and Björk (2008) proposed that the preproduction stage usually lasts 0–6 months; the early production stage lasts 6 months–1 year; the speech emergence stage, 1–3 years; the intermediate fluency stage, 3–5 years; and the advanced fluency stage, 5–7 years to attain. However, if the L2 learner does not have a strong base in their L1, then it may take the learner 7–10 years to attain advanced fluency. It is important to acknowledge that these time periods are approximate. According to Grosjean (2010), bilinguals develop their languages according to their purposes for using them and their audiences.

The Silent Period

When L2 learners are in the preproduction stage, they may go through a silent period where they listen to the L2 but do not speak it. This is a time when the L2 learner is observing L2 use. The silent period may last 6 weeks to a year (Lems et al., 2017). Although not every L2 learner goes through a silent period, many do. Teachers are advised not to force L2 learners to speak when they are in the silent period.

Receptive and Productive Competences

When teacher educators discuss the scope of L2 teaching, they usually refer to students' communicative competence and receptive and productive competences (Lems et al., 2017). Receptive competence refers to students' listening and reading performance in a particular language, whereas productive competence refers to their speaking and writing performance in a language. Although there is no definitive research on the issue, features of L2 receptive competence are thought to precede L2 productive competence (Lems et al., 2017; Lindholm-Leary, 2001); that is, listening competence is thought to precede speaking competence, and reading competence is thought to precede writing competence.

Contrastive Analysis

Contrastive analysis involves comparing the linguistic features of two languages. In the 1950s and 1960s, proponents of contrastive analysis theory hypothesized that how well learners acquired an L2 depended on the similarity of linguistic features between the L1 and L2 (Lems et al., 2017). However, empirical research did not support the predictive nature of contrastive analysis.

Today, contrastive analysis is used to understand the L2 difficulties that students may have when their L1 and L2 differ in certain linguistic features (Lems et al., 2017). For instance, when an ESL teacher asked me to work with a small group of Spanish speakers on their oral English reading, and I asked one of the students to read a sentence posted on the whiteboard ("He will go to the store"), the students in the group expressed their concern. Due to the differences in Spanish and English phonology, they knew that the child would mispronounce *will* as *wheel*. Because he had difficulty pronouncing the *i* in *will*, to know if he understood what he orally read, I asked him to explain what the sentence said in English or Spanish. He demonstrated that he knew what *will* meant, but he could not pronounce the English word correctly.

Comprehensible Input

Krashen (1985) proposed that L2 acquisition occurs in a fashion similar to L1 acquisition. For example, when learners are exposed to meaningful L2 interactions and comprehensible input, their L2 acquisition is subconscious and does not involve thinking about or enacting language rules. Krashen defined meaningful interactions as authentic communication opportunities and comprehensible input as language that is just beyond the learner's current comprehension or i + 1. He used "i" to refer to the L2 learner's current level of L2 proficiency and +1 to represent additional language input just beyond the learner's current comprehension. Although comprehensible input and Vygotsky's (1978) ZPD both use "i + 1," they mean different things.

Interactionist Theories

Other researchers proposed an interactionist theory of input and output (Long, 1981; Long & Porter, 1985; Pica, 1987). According to these theorists, L2 learners improve their L2 when they interact with native speakers of the L2 and negotiate their use of the L2. For example, L2 learners may negotiate what they say so that the native-speaker understands it and/or the native speaker may negotiate what they say so that L2 learners understand it. Strategies that native speakers use to make their speech comprehensible when conversing with L2 learners include repetition, paraphrasing, and increasing wait time, among others (Saville-Troike, 2006).

Comprehensible Output

Swain and Lapkin (1995) hypothesized that to become proficient in an L2, L2 learners needed opportunities for comprehensible output. Comprehensible output occurs when students notice they have made an error in their L2, and they adjust their speech to improve their communication. This usually occurs when L2 learners are speaking with native speakers of the L2, which could be a teacher or other students.

Swain (2000) developed the comprehensible output theory partially in response to the experiences of native English-speaking students in Canada who were taught in French immersion classrooms during elementary school. In the French immersion classrooms, native French-speaking teachers taught the students, but the students only were in classrooms with other English speakers. Their academic performance in English was the same as that of native English-speaking students who were in all-English classrooms. Although their French was proficient, they made nonnative-like errors in their grammar, vocabulary, and speech.

Monitor Hypothesis

One reason why Krashen thought it was better for L2 learners to be immersed in an L2 context with native speakers of the L2, rather than receiving formal instruction in the L2, was the monitor hypothesis. According to Krashen (1982), when L2 learners think about or enact language rules, they are monitoring their language output. This is a conscious effort, which Krashen called the monitor hypothesis. To monitor their L2, learners have to know the language rule, focus on form, and have sufficient time to think about the rule and apply it. Krashen hypothesized that when L2 learners employ the monitor, their L2 fluency would be adversely affected.

Affective Filter Hypothesis

Another Krashen (1982) hypothesis is the affective filter hypothesis, When the affective filter, or learners' anxiety about acquiring or learning a language, is low, then it is easier for them to acquire the language. When the affective filter is high, it is more difficult for learners to acquire the language.

Motivation

Researchers talk about the importance of motivation for L2 acquisition. Lems et al. (2017) described four types of motivation that characterize individuals' L2 motivation: integrative, instrumental, assimilative, and intrinsic. Integrative motivation occurs when L2 learners learn the L2 so they can join the L2 society but still maintain their L1 identity. Instrumental motivation characterizes when L2 learners want to acquire the L2 for specific purposes, such as, for a job, or to communicate with an L2 relative. Assimilative motivation is when L2 learners desire to become a member of the L2 society. Intrinsic motivation describes L2 learners who pursue a task to obtain it. In the case of L2 learning, they want to learn another language. When L2 teachers tap into what motivates students, they often facilitate their L2 learning.

THEORIES AND INSIGHTS SPECIFIC TO BILINGUAL STUDENTS AND BILINGUAL EDUCATION

Bilingualism

Bilingual experts do not think that being bilingual means that individuals have identical, native-like proficiencies in their languages (Gort, 2019; Grosjean, 2010). Instead, in contrast to monolinguals (people who know only one language), bilinguals know and use more than one language. However, their language proficiencies and use of the languages may vary.

Biliteracy

Biliteracy is when students read and write in more than one language. Biliteracy is not expert monolingual (single language) literacy development in each language. Bilingual researchers define biliteracy as a unique construct that reflects bilinguals' abilities to think, read and/or write in two or more languages to various degrees (Edelsky, 1986; Gort, 2019; Moll et al., 2001). Hornberger (1990) presents a broader definition of biliteracy. She contends that it involves "any and all instances in which communication occurs in two (or more) languages in or around writing" (p. 213).

The extent to which bilingual students display biliteracy may well depend on the nature of the learning environment. According to Moll et al. (2001), when students are encouraged to think, respond, and learn in both their languages, then an optimal environment for biliteracy has been created. Hornberger (1989) developed a continuum of biliteracy to explain how biliteracy development can be affected by numerous factors, including, among others, the bilingual development of the learners, the linguistic features of the languages, the micro-macro social contexts, the media, the content of texts, and the power differentials of diverse groups within society.

Simultaneous versus Sequential or Successive Bilinguals

Some of the theories about bilingual students vary according to whether the students are simultaneous bilinguals or sequential or successive bilinguals. Simultaneous bilinguals are children who become proficient in two or more languages before they are four or five years old (Bauer, 2000). Their language acquisition processes are thought to be similar to L1 acquisition processes (Gort, 2019). By the time the children are two years of age, simultaneous bilinguals usually "know which language to speak to whom and in [which] situation" (Gort, 2019, p. 230).

Sequential or successive bilinguals are children who first become proficient in their L1, then, after they are four or five years old, become proficient in an additional language. Most L2 theorists focus on sequential or successive bilinguals. This book also emphasizes sequential or successive bilinguals.

Basic Interpersonal Communication Skills versus Cognitive Academic Language Proficiency

Cummins (1981) proposed an explanation for why some sequential or successive bilingual students, such as Tuan (the student from Vietnam in the chapter vignette), speak their L2 fairly well in social settings but have difficulty using it in academic settings. He differentiated between bilingual students' development and use of basic interpersonal communication skills (BICS) and cognitive academic language proficiency (CALP). BICS are the L2 oral skills that bilingual students demonstrate on the playground or while shopping or traveling, while CALP are the L2 academic skills needed in the classroom. Another name for BICS is social language, while another name for CALP is academic language. Cummins hypothesized that students developed BICS quickly, after only 1–3 years of L2 immersion or instruction, but needed 4–7 years of bilingual or L2 instruction or immersion to develop CALP.

Several scholars critiqued Cummins's differentiation of bilingual students' language skills into BICS and CALP as being oversimplified or supporting a skill-based view of literacy and language, which ignored the social and political nature of language and literacy (Valdés, 2004; Wiley, 1996). Cummins (2008) responded to the critics by stating that his purpose was to highlight that language proficiency was not a unitary construct. He was concerned that too many bilingual students were being misplaced in special education. He reported that he developed BICS and CALP to highlight that bilingual students' demonstration of language proficiency could vary according to the nature of the tasks they were asked to perform. Beginning L2 learners usually demonstrated higher L2 language proficiency when they performed tasks that were context embedded or supported, but demonstrated lower L2 language proficiency when they performed tasks that were context-reduced or had fewer supports.

Cross-Linguistic Transfer

Cummins (1981) also developed several theories to explain how humans can use what they have learned or acquired in one language while working or thinking in another language. The key point here is that bilinguals can utilize a lot of information acquired in one language without having to relearn it in another language. Cummins and others called this ability cross-linguistic transfer although a number of researchers questioned how the transfer mechanism actually worked in the brain (Genesee, Geva, Dressler, & Kamil, 2006).

The Interdependence Hypothesis

According to Cummins's interdependence hypothesis (1981, 2000), once students develop a conceptual base in one language, they should be able to transfer knowledge and skills from the conceptual base to another language, with two caveats. First, they need to be adequately exposed to the other language, and second, they have to be motivated to use it.

Cognitive Underlying Proficiency and Structural Underlying Proficiency

Not everything transfers, however. To differentiate between what transfers and what does not transfer, Cummins (1981) proposed an iceberg metaphor. Below the water is the cognitive underlying proficiency (CUP), or the knowledge and skills that can be used in more than one language. Above the water are the structural underlying proficiencies (SUPs), or the knowledge and skills that require separate learning and experiences in each language. For example, when children learn to read, CUP involves the overall understanding that reading in an alphabetic language—a language in which letters represent sounds, such as English, Spanish, or French—involves figuring out the sound–symbol correspondence of the specific language. Once acquired, this understanding does not have to be relearned in another alphabetic language. However, the actual implementation of this understanding or knowing how to decode in each language does have to be learned. The latter is the structural underlying proficiency or SUP.

Threshold Hypothesis

Several researchers (Alderson, 1984; Cummins, 1976) proposed that before bilingual students could effectively transfer knowledge or skills acquired in one language to another language, they first needed to develop a certain level of proficiency in the weaker language. Clarke (1980) coined the term *short circuit hypothesis* to characterize what happens when good L1 adult readers with limited L2 proficiency read in the L2, but do not use the high-level strategies for reading comprehension that they acquired during L1 reading. Durgunoğlu (2002) hypothesized that bilingual children who were strong L1 readers, but weak L2 readers, probably needed to improve their L2 oral proficiency. However, little is known about the level of L2 proficiency needed for optimal transfer.

Monolingualism and Monoglossic Pedagogy versus Translanguaging and Translanguaging Pedagogy

Monolingualism and Monoglossic Instruction

Until recently, many bilingual educators thought that the best way to help emergent bilingual students become bilingual and biliterate was for them to receive separate instruction in each language for set periods of time (Heller, 1999). The instruction in each language was based on what was known about the monolingual development and instruction of expert speakers of the respective language. Accordingly, this type of instruction has been called monoglossic instruction. Martin-Beltrán (2010) reported that supporters of monoglossic instruction argued that when students received simultaneous instruction in two or more languages, they were likely to become confused, depend on the language they knew best, and/or not be motivated to acquire another language.

Two movements within bilingual education helped to change this thinking: the field's focus on translanguaging practices (O. García, 2009) and the success of DL education programs (see Chapter 1). As part of a language-revitalization project in Wales, Williams (1994) coined the Welsh term for translanguaging to characterize how Welsh instructors employed both Welsh and English to help students in Wales acquire and use Welsh, which had become a lost language.

Translanguaging Practices

Proponents of translanguaging (Canagarajah, 2011; O. García, 2009) reject the view of bilinguals as "two monolinguals in one body" (Gravelle, 1996, p. 11; Grosjean, 1982). Instead, they propose that bilinguals, compared to monolinguals, employ unique language practices to communicate, make meaning, share experiences, and transmit knowledge. O. García and Lin (2017a) explain that "bilingual children have one complex and extended repertoire of linguistic features . . . ," which are "not simply two bounded [or named] languages" (p. 14) Translanguaging includes several practices that previously were viewed negatively, such as code-mixing (moving between languages within a sentence) and code-switching (moving between languages at sentence boundaries), which now are viewed positively.

It is important to acknowledge that García and Lin (2017a) do not discount the interdependence hypothesis, which explicitly discusses the roles of the L1 and L2 (Cummins, 1981). O. García and Lin clarified this point: "There is almost universal agreement among scholars that the language practices of bilinguals are interdependent and that enhancing the child's home language practices will surely result in more academic competence in a new language" (p. 13).

Empirical research has demonstrated bilingual students' spontaneous use of oral and written translanguaging practices. For instance, Lee and I (Lee & García, 2020) reported that Korean American first graders employed oral translanguaging to communicate in their Korean heritage first-grade classroom. In heritage classrooms, students are taught in their home languages about the country that they or their parents immigrated from and how to read and write in the home language. Heritage language schools usually are private, and students' parents fund them. The Korean

American students in the Lee and García study attended all-English schools during the school week and the Korean heritage school on Saturdays.

The Korean American first graders orally translanguaged for four purposes: "sociolinguistic (. . . according to the social context), metalinguistic (when they demonstrated and applied their understanding of language), metacognitive (when they thought about and evaluated their knowledge of language through inner speech), and sociocultural (when they applied culturally oriented language)," such as reference to family members (Lee & García, 2020, p. 8). The following transcript shows how the Korean heritage teacher and a Korean American first-grader employed translanguaging for a sociolinguistic purpose. The teacher translanguaged when she asked the first grader if she helped another student to read in English. When the student answered, she repeated the English words that her Korean heritage teacher had used. Then, when the teacher asked her how she helped the student, first in Korean, then in English, the student replied in English. Translanguaging is underlined in the transcript.

> TEACHER: 아 친구가 영어 책 잘 못 읽어서 그럼 English reading 도와줘? (Oh, your friend is not good at reading in English, so do you help her with English reading?)
>
> RENA: 응. 나 매일 내 친구 English reading help 해줘.(Yes, I help her with English reading every day.)
>
> TEACHER: 어떻게 도와줘 (How do you help her?) How do you help her?
>
> RENA: Sometimes she picks up [an] English book, and I help her. (Lee & García, 2020, p. 10)

Godina and I (G. García & Godina, 2017) documented how fourth-grade Latinx bilingual students employed translanguaging to explain their reading comprehension of texts in English and Spanish. The bilingual students paraphrased, summarized, and translated in Spanish what they had read in English and vice versa. In the example below, a fourth grader and I translanguaged when we discussed her comprehension of an English text:

> TEXT: Although the whale's ears are only two tiny holes in the skin, they can hear underwater sounds from as far away as 1,000 miles.
>
> GEORGIA: ¿Por qué te sorprendió? (Why were you surprised?)
>
> STUDENT: Porque no pensaba que las ballenas podían oír de lejos con los oídos chiquitos (Because I didn't think that whales could hear so far away with such small ears). (G. García & Godina, 2017, p. 293)

Several researchers have shown how bilingual elementary students employ translanguaging while writing (Lee & García, 2021; Velasco & García, 2014). In a diary entry written for her Korean heritage classroom, a Korean American first grader wanted to identify three wishes but did not know how to write twin in Korean. On an audio-recording, Lee, the Korean teacher, heard the child say to herself in Korean (translated to English), "I don't know how to write the word *twin* in Korean. I know how to say it in Korean but don't know how to write [it]. . . . I will write it in English then!" (Lee & García, 2021, p. 11). Instead of changing her writing, she translanguaged to complete it.

Translanguaging Pedagogy

Translanguaging pedagogy refers to bilingual teachers' use of translanguaging to teach bilingual students (O. García et al., 2017). O. García and Lin (2017b) acknowledge the tension that exists between bilingual educators who emphasize developing bilingual students' separate or named languages (i.e., L1 and L2) versus those who support translanguaging and who do not discuss named languages. They advise that bilingual educators combine the two positions, "allocat[ing] separate spaces for the named languages although softening the boundaries between them" at the same time that they "provide an instructional space where translanguaging is nurtured critically" (p. 127). Chapter 3 provides specific examples of translanguaging pedagogy.

CULTURALLY RESPONSIVE APPROACHES TO EDUCATION

Culturally responsive instruction involves the implementation of curricula, instruction, and classroom practices that emphasize the histories, values, and practices of students from diverse backgrounds in contrast to the values, practices, and experiences of monolingual, native-English-speaking, middle-class students (Banks, 2019). Translanguaging practices clearly are part of culturally responsive education. When school personnel collaborate to help immigrant children and children of immigrants develop a sense of school belonging (DeNicolo, Yu, Crowley, & Gabel, 2017), then they are instantiating a type of culturally responsive instruction. DeNicolo and her colleagues cite Goodenow and Grady's (1993) argument that a sense of school belonging occurs when immigrant children and children of immigrants feel "personally accepted, respected, included and supported by others" at school (p. 61).

In the United States, the values, language, history, and behavior of the Anglo (non-Hispanic white), English-speaking middle class still dominate the curriculum and instruction of many minority students (Au, 2016; Banks, 2019). This occurs even though more students of color were enrolled in United States public schools in 2021 than Anglo students (National Center for Education Statistics, 2023d). Sometimes, school personnel are aware of this hegemony; other times they are not. Hegemony refers to the dominant societal and linguistic group's control or influence over other groups.

Aims of Culturally Responsive Instruction

One aim of culturally responsive instruction is to make sure that school personnel are aware of the mainstream biases that operate in public schools and classrooms. Hernandez (2000) coined the term *the hidden curriculum* to reference the unrecognized biases evident in the ways of interacting and speaking at school and in the school curriculum.

An equally important aim of culturally responsive instruction is to diversify teachers' curriculum, instruction, language, and behavior so that the historical and current experiences, values, language(s), and behavior of minority students are recognized and included. Moll (2001) points out that including multicultural literature in the curriculum is one way for teachers to diversify their curriculum. Others encourage teachers to learn as much as possible about the diverse groups in their classrooms (Au, 2016; Stahl & García, 2015, 2022). When there are multiple linguistic or cultural groups in a teacher's classroom, Au recommends that the teacher promote "two contrasting worldviews:" one that reflects the "mainstream values of competition and individual achievement" and the other that reflects the values of many United States minority groups, such as "cooperation and group well-being" (p. 38). Stahl and García (2015) suggest that educators cultivate an "I wonder stance" so that when parents or students from a minority group do not respond as they expected, the educators identify what they expected, compare it to what occurred, and consult several people familiar with the minority culture (p. 25).

A Sense of School Belonging

In a review of research on how immigrant children (documented and undocumented) and children of immigrants respond to United States schools, DeNicolo and her colleagues (DeNicolo et al., 2017) explain the importance of school personnel helping immigrant children and children of immigrants develop a sense of school belonging. DeNicolo et al. hypothesize that when children attain a sense of school belonging, their academic performance in United States schools will increase.

To attain a sense of school belonging, DeNicolo et al. (2017) recommend that school personnel employ *cariño conscientizado*—a pedagogy based on *cariño*, or authentic care, and Freire's (1970) concept of critical consciousness. Authentic care draws from the Mexican view of what it means to be *bien educado* or well educated (e.g., have good manners) and to be morally, socially, and personally responsible for your thoughts and actions (Valenzuela, 1999, p. 23). To implement authentic care, teachers need to understand their students, access their students' resources or cultural funds of knowledge (González, Moll, & Amanti, 2005), and employ critical consciousness.

Cultural Funds of Knowledge

Cultural funds of knowledge refer to the types of knowledge and skills that working-class parents and community members share with children (Gonzalez et al., 2005). In response to educators' complaints that the families of the Latinx children in their classrooms were not educating them as requested, González and her colleagues trained teachers to work as ethnographers to document how families viewed education and the work that they and their children did in the local Latinx community. They discovered that the families valued education but viewed it as part of developing a moral person (Valenzuela, 1999). They also found that, among other skills, the families used mathematics when cooking; mathematics and economics when selling candies; and physics and mechanical knowledge when repairing bicycles. The researchers then worked with the teachers to invite family members to share their skills with the students in their classrooms and to incorporate and reference the skills in their classroom instruction.

Critical Consciousness

Critical consciousness is implemented when educators recognize and counter racist and hegemonic policies that adversely affect their students (DeNicolo et al., 2017). To initiate critical consciousness, school personnel need to work with local immigrant communities to revise the school curriculum so that diversity is considered an asset and immigrant children and children of immigrants are centered in the curriculum in terms of instructional practices that include their cultural funds of knowledge (González et al., 2005).

CONCLUDING REMARKS

Proponents of sociolinguistic views of language negate the idealized views of standard languages, which societies often hold. They consider all dialects and language variations to be viable and functional. Therefore, schools should not discriminate against nonstandard versions, but should instead value the dialects and languages that students bring with them to school. Because the languages or dialects that a student speaks is part of the student's identity, it is especially important for teachers and school personnel to respect them.

The culturally based nature of language, learning, and literacies means that teachers and educational personnel should become informed about their students' languages, cultural backgrounds, literacies, and histories. When doing so, teachers need to take an emic or relativistic perspective; that is, they need to view cultural differences from the students' and communities' perspectives, not from their own or the larger society's perspectives (G. García, 1992). A number of researchers (Au & Jordan, 1981; Heath, 1983; Valdés, 1996) have documented the different ways that students from diverse backgrounds (i.e., children who are not Anglo and/or from the middle and upper class) interpret the world, interact, speak, and write compared to the dominant groups in society. When schools and teachers emphasize the ways that Anglo, middle- or upper-class, native-English-speaking children are raised and interact, they discriminate against other groups of children. School personnel can counter such hegemonic practices by implementing culturally responsive instruction and *cariño conscientizado* (DeNicolo et al., 2017).

When working with bilingual children, educational personnel need to understand bilingualism, biliteracy, and key theories about bilingual children's language and literacy development, instruction, and academic performance. Because there usually is a lag between theory development and changes in instructional practices, educational personnel will have to do their best to stay informed. For instance, translanguaging, one of the most recent theoretical constructs, is just beginning to influence how bilinguals are taught. As educators of bilingual children, educational personnel will need to do their best to keep up with new research findings, theories, and theoretical insights.

Second-Language (L2) Teaching Approaches to Advance Bilingual Students' Learning

GUIDING QUESTIONS

- What is sheltered L2 instruction?
- What are the strategies for making L2 instruction comprehensible?
- How can use of the L1 support bilingual students' L2 language and academic learning?
- How can translanguaging aid bilingual students' L2 language and academic learning?
- What is the rationale for content-based language approaches?
- What are the similarities and differences between specially designed academic instruction in English (SDAIE) and the sheltered instruction observation protocol (SIOP)?
- Why is it helpful to post and review language and content objectives for content-based L2 lessons?
- What is English language development instruction?
- What type of L2 instruction should occur in dual-language classrooms?

Mr. Cramer taught a fifth-grade all-English classroom. Several bilingual students who recently exited from an early-exit transitional bilingual education (TBE) program were in his classroom. He was excited about showing his students a video on the women's suffrage movement, which resulted in passage of the 14th amendment to the Constitution approving women's right to vote. He thought the video would provoke a lot of conversation among his students.

> However, he was disappointed that none of the former emergent bilingual students participated in the whole-class discussion. When he asked the early-exit TBE teacher if they were shy, she asked him how he had prepared the students for the video and if he had scaffolded it by using ESL techniques. He was surprised to hear that the former emergent bilingual students still needed ESL techniques.

If you have bilingual students in your classroom who are not highly proficient or fluent in the language you are using for instruction, similar to the fifth-grade former emergent bilingual students in Mr. Cramer's class, then it is very likely that they will benefit from the use of L2 techniques to make your instruction comprehensible. The students could be emergent bilingual students, former emergent bilingual students, or dual-language students. It is especially important to use L2 techniques when you teach content in a language that not all your students fully understand. The good news is that the L2 support you provide to bilingual students will not disadvantage those students who are fluent in the instructional language. In fact, the L2 support should enhance their comprehension of your instruction. Because L2 techniques usually support or scaffold bilingual students' L2 learning, they are called sheltered instruction.

MAKING STUDENTS' L2 INSTRUCTION COMPREHENSIBLE

All teachers of current and former emergent bilingual students should know how to use L2 techniques to shelter or support their instruction. They also should know how to access and employ their students' L1 knowledge and translanguaging.

Sheltered L2 Instruction

When you employ L2 techniques to make your instruction comprehensible, you are "sheltering" your instruction because you are scaffolding students' comprehension (Krashen, 1981). Sheltered instruction occurs when teachers support bilingual students' comprehension of L2 talks, videos, audio recordings, teacher read-alouds, interactive teacher read-alouds, and instruction.

To effectively shelter an L2 video, audio-recording, teacher read-aloud, talk, instruction, or text, you first need to view, listen, or read the material. Then you need to chunk it into units that your students can comprehend. Next you need to decide what you will use to illustrate the key points in the material and how you will assess your students' comprehension of the material.

In the vignette presented at the beginning of this chapter, Mr. Cramer, the fifth-grade teacher, neglected to find out how much the former emergent bilingual students already knew about the women's suffrage movement and women's rights in the United States before showing the video. Asking all the fifth graders to share what they knew about the two topics first in small groups, then in the whole class, would have informed him about what they already knew about the topics and would have activated their background knowledge. To prepare his students for the video, he could have given them a written timeline or summary of what they were going to see in simplified (i.e., modified) English. Next, Mr. Cramer needed to shelter the students' comprehension of the video by dividing it into comprehensible units. Many academic videos are 30–45 minutes in length, which is too long for many L2 learners to follow and comprehend. Chunking and showing the video for 10–15 minutes for each viewing is more realistic. Then, Mr. Cramer should have decided what he wanted his students to learn from each section of the video and what supports (e.g., illustrations/photos, short audiorecordings, physical action, video captions) he could use to aid his students' comprehension. After gathering and preparing the supports, he needed to decide how he was going to check his students' comprehension and what he would do if they did not comprehend important parts of the video. Mr. Cramer also needed to allow his students to come up with their own ideas and contributions as long as they accurately reflected or extended what was in the video. Lastly, before showing the video, he needed to make sure that his students already knew how to participate in student discussion in the whole-group setting. If you think sheltering a lesson is a lot of work, you are correct. It takes time and effort to plan and shelter L2 content lessons.

Fortunately, you do not have to do all of the above for every lesson. The L2 strategies that you employ will vary according to the lesson's focus and to what your students already know and can do in the L1 and L2. The World-Class Instructional Design and Assessment (WIDA) provides guidance on how to teach language arts, mathematics, science, and social studies to bilingual students in English (WIDA, 2020) and Spanish (WIDA, 2013, 2023b) according to the students' grade levels and language proficiencies in English or Spanish. You should also implement L2 principles derived from the ESL literature.

L2 PRINCIPLES FROM ESL LITERATURE

- Integrate reading, writing, listening, and speaking in your L2 presentations or talks.
- Use multiple modalities for your L2 instruction; in addition to speaking, reading, and writing, draw, gesture, act out, model, show realia, and complete hands-on activities.

- Chunk the instruction into comprehensible sections.
- Provide appropriate wait time for student responses.
- Check frequently for student comprehension by employing multiple modalities; that is, have your students show you what they understand by speaking, writing, drawing, acting out, and completing hands-on activities.
- For beginning L2 students, "slow down your [L2] speech, clearly enunciate, use known or pretaught vocabulary," and pause frequently (Stahl & García, 2022, p. 27).
- When possible, employ themed instruction across more than one content area, so that students will have multiple contexts for the same background and vocabulary knowledge.

For example, if you are teaching your students about electricity, you could show them two written columns on a whiteboard with space underneath them. One column heading would be "What we *think* we know about electricity" and the other heading would be "What we *now* know about electricity" (Ogle, 1986). I recommend that you read aloud each of the column headings, show your students examples of electricity (e.g., light bulbs, hair dryers and electric razors, electric appliances), explain the headings, and then have your students chorally read the headings. Then, find out what your students already know about electricity by asking them to orally share what they think they know. Write their ideas on the whiteboard under "What we *think* we know."

Next, be sure to say, write, and post a child-friendly definition of electricity so that all your students can hear and see the definition. Then, ask your students to orally read the definition. Next, tell your students that several students are going to demonstrate examples of electrical current. Tell them that afterward, you will ask the class to share what they saw, and so they will need to take notes on what they observe. Model how you want them to take notes. Have the students turn electric lights and appliances on and off and/or activate electrical circuits via "Snap Circuits," a commercial product that can be purchased. Then, have your students work in partners to write and/or draw what they saw demonstrated about electricity. In pairs have your students write and post their answers to "What we *now* know about electricity" on the whiteboard (Ogle, 1986). Orally review their answers, being sure to correct erroneous information. Then, collect their writing or drawings to see how well they understood what was demonstrated and to plan your next lessons.

L1 Use

When teaching in the L2, you should tap into bilingual students' relevant L1 knowledge (i.e., their background knowledge, cultural experiences, and conceptual and vocabulary knowledge). There is considerable empirical evidence to validate Cummins's interdependence hypothesis (1981), in which he predicted that bilingual individuals could use much of what they knew or learned in their L1 while learning in another language. For instance, when bilingual students know a concept that is identical in their L1 and L2, then they just need to know the L2 vocabulary label to access the concept; they do not need to be taught the concept in their L2. For example, bilingual students should be able to use what they know about earthquakes in one language when working in the other language.

However, when there are operational differences in language or cultural contexts, then you need to teach them the differences. For example, if they understand how electricity works in their L1, then they do not need to relearn how electricity works in their L2, but they will need to know that in the United States we use 110–120V (60 Hz), while most other countries use 220–240V (50 Hz). Because of the voltage differences, when you travel from the United States to other countries and take small appliances purchased in the United States with you (e.g., a hair dryer or electric razor), you often have to take and use a voltage converter in the other countries.

Yes–No Vocabulary Test to Estimate L1 Knowledge

A quick way to estimate what bilingual students already have learned in their L1 is to give them a yes–no vocabulary test for a content area topic (Anderson & Freebody, 1983). In a yes–no test, you list L1 content-area words for a topic your class is studying and have the students check "yes" for the L1 words they know and "no" for the L1 words they do not know. Then, you can teach them the L2 labels for the known concepts, and spend more time teaching them the L2 words for unknown concepts in both languages.

L1 Preview and Review

You also can use the L1 to preview and review what students are learning or reading in their L2 (Mercuri & Musanti, 2021). For previews, you can provide bilingual students with brief oral and/or written summaries in their L1 for L2 talks, readings, and videos. The L1 previews help them to activate the appropriate background knowledge and to anticipate what will be presented in their L2. If you do not know all the L1s of your students, you will need to ask for help from L1 adult speakers or older L1-speaking students at your school to develop L1 previews.

For reviews, assign students from the same L1 but of different L2 proficiency levels to work in pairs or small groups. Ask them to work together to complete L1 surveys or to write brief L1 summaries of what they learned. Let them speak in their L1, L2, and/or translanguage while completing the survey or writing the summaries. If you do not understand the L1, you should ask the student with the highest L2 proficiency level to briefly summarize in a conference with you or during the whole-class setting what the students learned and did not learn or understand.

Use of L1 and Dual-Language Texts

Some texts are printed in several languages. Assigning students to read a text in their L1 before reading the same text in their L2 may aid your students' L2 comprehension. Another possibility is to ask students to read dual-language texts in which the same content is provided in the L1 and L2. When you have students read texts in their L1 and L2 or dual-language texts, it is important for you to hold discussions with your students about what they read in the L2, so that you can evaluate how well they understood the L2 material. (Chapter 5 presents more information on the use of dual-language texts with bilingual students.)

Small Groups of L1 Speakers of Varied L2 Proficiencies

When you assign students to work in small groups, it often is helpful to put three to five students from the same L1, but of different L2 proficiencies, in the same groups. Then, you should let the students choose the language in which they want to perform the assigned task. If the students choose to use the L1, and you do not know it, you should ask the student who is most proficient in the L2 to explain to you and to the rest of the class what they decided or accomplished in the small group. Frequently, when you allow students to use their L1 during small-group work, they will participate more extensively than when they are required to use the L2.

Use and Acceptance of Translanguaging

According to their book on translanguaging pedagogy, O. García et al. (2017) define translanguaging classrooms as "any classroom in which students may deploy their full linguistic repertoires, and not just the particular language" (p. 1). They explain that a translanguaging pedagogy involves teachers leveraging or "us[ing] to maximum advantage, the language practices of their bilingual students and communities while addressing core content and language development standards" (p. 2). O. García et al. (2017) emphasize that teachers can employ a translanguaging pedagogy in any classroom in which bilingual students are enrolled: bilingual (transitional or DL) classrooms, ESL, or all-English classrooms.

Some examples of translanguaging practices include translating and what used to be called code-mixing and code-switching. For instance, a bilingual Latina fourth grader translanguaged when she translated an

English text into Spanish, employed code-mixing (underlined) to figure out *blanket*, and used an English word (*atmosphere*) in her Spanish translation of the text:

> TEXT: Those clouds are a special part of the planet's blanket of air, its atmosphere.
>
> MARISA: Las nubes eran una parte especial del planeta, *cobija, blanket, cobija* de aire, de *atmosphere* (G. García & Godina, 2017, p. 290).

To support the L2 development of bilingual students, O. García et al. (2017) recommend that teachers facilitate their bilingual students' academic learning by encouraging them to utilize "linguistic practices [translanguaging] for academic contexts; making space for students' bilingualism and ways of knowing; [and] supporting students' bilingual identities and socioemotional development" (p. 7). In concrete terms, this means the following:

- Let bilingual students translanguage to show what they understand in their L2.
- Let bilingual students translanguage to "discuss, negotiate, and . . . write down connections" (p. 9).
- Let bilingual students translanguage to share "their learning in both languages" (p. 9).
- Let bilingual students translanguage to engage with and comprehend complex L2 texts.

Similarly, as teachers of bilingual students, you should translanguage to facilitate your students' L2 learning. For instance, if you are conducting an interactive teacher read-aloud (see Chapter 4), and your students do not know a key vocabulary word, telling your students what the word means in their L1 often is the quickest way to proceed with the read-aloud. My colleague and I (G. García & Lang, 2023) described how second-grade teachers in a two-way DL program (Spanish–English) strategically employed translanguaging during their science instruction, which was supposed to be in Spanish, because they did not have Spanish science texts. They introduced topics in Spanish, read the available materials in English, and then employed Spanish to discuss what was read in English.

LANGUAGE-BASED INSTRUCTIONAL APPROACHES

Several language-based instructional approaches have been implemented for L2 and foreign language teaching in the United States. The most popular historical approaches are grammar-translation, audiolingual, and communicative language teaching.

Grammar-Translation Approach

When I first learned Spanish in high school, the most popular method for teaching foreign languages was grammar translation. Lems et al. (2017) explain that grammar-translation instruction typically involves reading an L2 text and translating it to English, with an emphasis on learning syntactic rules and L2 vocabulary. Although students may learn the L2 grammar and vocabulary and how to read and write in the L2, they usually do not develop proficient speaking or listening skills. This is the type of instruction that university students often receive when they have to pass a foreign language test as part of their PhD degree.

Audiolingual Approach

The instructional approach that I received during Peace Corps training was audiolingual. When they assessed my Spanish, I could not understand proficient oral Spanish or speak it very well even after I had taken three years of Spanish in high school and a year in college. The Peace Corps language instructors improved my Spanish by having me listen to audiotapes of people speaking Spanish and memorize and participate in dialogues. They evaluated my oral progress according to the speed with which I spoke and my use of correct pronunciation. They did not provide me with a grammar book or any rules for using Spanish, which I found frustrating. Once I stopped trying to figure out the grammar rules, and memorized and responded to the dialogues, my Spanish-speaking and -listening comprehension substantially improved.

Communicative Language Teaching

When I began my PhD program in bilingual education, the foreign and L2 language teaching courses that I took emphasized the communicative language teaching approach (Savignon, 1983). This approach focuses on communication according to the social roles that learners will enact when using the language. Lems et al. (2017) explain that students learn to comprehend and produce oral and written language, but in context; that is, they learn to use the language for specific communicative purposes according to their purpose for acquiring it. For instance, if students plan to live in an L2 setting, then their instruction will focus on the language they need for the daily tasks they will perform in the setting. Communicative language instruction usually focuses on speaking and listening, but it also includes relevant reading and writing tasks for specific roles and settings. Saunders and Goldenberg (2010) explain that language use is emphasized more than language form or knowledge. Accurate pronunciation is not emphasized.

To implement communicative language teaching, instructors create and employ oral communicative tasks that require interaction among their students and themselves, along with the use of authentic, not contrived, texts. Brandl (2009) recommends that teachers develop communicative tasks based on students' personal experiences. The tasks involve role-playing, interviews, group work with assigned participant roles, opinion-sharing, scavenger hunts, and/or the completion of partially completed tasks. Communicative language teaching is still in vogue today, especially in foreign language and ESL classrooms in the United States.

CONTENT-BASED LANGUAGE APPROACHES

Critics of the language-based approaches point out that emergent bilingual students need an ESL approach that helps them to acquire social and academic English at the same time that they learn the grade-level United States curriculum in English (Chamot & O'Malley, 1987; Echevarria, Vogt, & Short, 2004). Academic English refers to the specific vocabulary, syntax, and procedural language (e.g., identify the main idea; explain why . . .) employed in content areas, such as literacy, mathematics, science, and social studies. Emergent bilingual students cannot afford to wait to develop sufficient English proficiency before being taught academic content in English. The content-based approaches combine students' L2 learning with their content learning, so that students do not delay their content or curricular learning until they attain a high level of L2 proficiency. Although content-based approaches emphasize acquiring a language by using it for authentic social and academic purposes (Halliday, 1993), teachers' lesson planning still needs to pay attention to their state's English language development standards for emergent bilingual students and content-area standards for all students.

Several content-based language approaches have been developed and implemented. Historically, the most popular ones are the cognitive academic language learning approach, (CALLA; Chamot & O'Malley, 1987); specially designed academic instruction in English, (SDAIE; California Department of Education, 1993); and the sheltered instruction observation protocol (SIOP; Echevarria et al., 1999, 2004, 2017). Each of these approaches is described next.

CALLA

Chamot and O'Malley (1986) explained that they developed CALLA as a supplemental ESL content-based approach to aid intermediate and advanced ESL students in their transition from bilingual or ESL instruction to all-English grade-level content instruction. They designed CALLA to help ESL students move from communicative language instruction, which typically was emphasized in their ESL instruction, to academic instruction, which they would encounter in grade-level, all-English, content classrooms, such as, mathematics, science, and social studies.

According to Chamot and O'Malley (1987), CALLA is a cognitively oriented approach to bilingual students' academic language and learning that includes three components: (1) English language development, which focuses on the academic and procedural language that bilingual students need for learning content instruction in English; (2) content-based ESL instruction, which focuses on "the concepts, facts, and skills" to be taught in each subject area (p. 233); and (3) special learner strategies, which help students to connect what they are learning with their background knowledge and to remember what they are learning. It includes students' comprehension and application of metacognitive, cognitive, and social affective strategies. Metacognitive strategies refer to students' evaluation of what they know; cognitive strategies are mental thinking strategies or processes; and social affective strategies refer to strategies that involve student motivation and emotions.

CALLA content-based lesson planning, implementation, and evaluation have five phases: "preparation, presentation, practice, self-evaluation, and expansion" (Chamot & Robbins, 2005, p. 10). For instance, preparation includes identifying the lesson purposes or objectives, accessing or providing students with the appropriate background knowledge, developing the required vocabulary; and motivating students to learn the material. The presentation stage includes the use of a variety of methods to "present new information; the model[ing of] processes explicitly, [the explanation of] learning strategies, [and making] connections to students' prior knowledge" (p. 10). Practice involves "hands-on/inquiry-based activities, . . . different cooperative learning [configurations], authentic content tasks, [and student employment of] learning strategies" (p. 11). Self-evaluation occurs when "students reflect on their own learning, . . . evaluate themselves, . . . [and] assess their own strategy use" (p. 11). In expansion, teachers encourage students "to apply" what they are learning to their "own lives," to "make connections between their language [knowledge] and content [knowledge]," to relate what they are learning in the L2 to what they know in the L1, and for "parents to contribute to [student] learning" (p. 11). The presentation stage includes the use of a variety of methods to "present new information; the 'model[ing of] processes explicitly, [the explanation of] learning strategies, [and making] connections to students' prior knowledge" (p. 10). Practice involves "hands-on/inquiry-based activities, . . . different cooperative learning [configurations], authentic content tasks, [and student employment of] learning strategies" (p. 11). Self-evaluation occurs when "students reflect on their own learning, . . . evaluate themselves, . . . [and] assess their own strategy use" (p. 11).

In 2023, you still can find information on the internet about implementing CALLA, along with CALLA lesson plans. CALLA does not substitute for grade-level content-area instruction, but presents bilingual students with "a sample of high priority content topics that develop academic language skills appropriate to the subject area at the student's grade level" (Chamot & O'Malley, 1987, p. 235). Effective use of CALLA often requires collaboration between bilingual education or ESL teachers and content-area teachers.

SDAIE

My understanding of SDAIE is that when California voters outlawed bilingual education in 1998, the California Department of Education approved SDAIE as a way to improve the academic and English language performance of emergent bilingual students enrolled in all-English classes (California Department of Education, 1993). However, I was unaware of SDAIE until I gave a talk on teaching bilingual students, and a member of the audience asked me if I was familiar with SDAIE. Now that I know more about SDAIE, I suspect that some of my talk's instructional recommendations duplicated some of the SDAIE instructional strategies. SDAIE combines ESL strategies with effective teaching and learning strategies for all students.

The purpose of SDAIE is to provide emergent bilingual students who have attained the "intermediate stage of English fluency" with instruction on the grade-level curriculum in all-English classrooms (Nickolaisen, n.d., p. v). According to Genzuk (2011), SDAIE emphasizes the development of emergent bilingual students' knowledge in content areas, with learning the English language as a desired by-product. SDAIE aims to facilitate emergent bilingual students' academic content learning in English and their interaction with native-English speakers.

SDAIE includes ESL strategies, expository or informational text strategies, and general learning strategies designed to make content-area instruction in regular all-English classrooms comprehensible to bilingual students (Genzuk, 2011). In addition, SDAIE advises teachers to lower the affective filter of emergent bilingual students (i.e., reduce their stress) through cooperative learning, partner work, small-group work, games, and hands-on experiences (Nickolaisen, n.d.). Instead of error correction, SDAIE recommends teacher modeling, restatement of correct language, and teacher expansion of students' utterances.

MAJOR SDAIE FEATURES (NICKOLAISEN, N.D.)

- "Contextualizing the lesson" or use of verbal and nonverbal supports (visuals, graphic organizers, gestures, physical action, and drama) to convey the lesson's meaning (p. vi).
- "Tapping prior knowledge" (p. vi).
- "Modifying the use of a text" by providing text summaries before instruction, and highlighting a text's use of headings, subheadings, bold type, and pictures to communicate its meaning (p. vi).
- "Creating a positive affective domain" by implementing hands-on activities, games, and pair and small-group work (p. vi).
- "Teaching study skills," providing student practice on summarizing and paraphrasing texts, and using graphic organizers (p. vi).

In terms of teachers' oral language, SDAIE encourages teachers to exaggerate their use of intonation ("the stress, pitch, and . . . phrasing") to highlight "key vocabulary and key concepts"; to slow down their speech; to vary their voice volume; and to include pauses (Nickolaisen, n.d., p. ix). Teachers also are instructed to employ simple sentences and to rephrase important concepts. They are encouraged to repeat key information and vocabulary, as well as to use choral and shared reading, along with echo reading. (Choral and shared reading are defined in Chapter 4.) In echo reading, the students repeat what the teacher reads, duplicating as much as possible the speed and fluency that the teacher demonstrates.

Unfortunately, teacher implementation of SDAIE in California schools did not substantially improve the English academic and language performance of emergent bilingual students (Parrish et al., 2006). The expectations that SDAIE would work with all emergent bilingual students, and that all teachers would be trained in SDAIE and successfully implement it in their all-English classrooms, might have been unrealistic. When California voters approved bilingual education in 2016, primary or home language instruction became part of SDAIE. As of 2023, SDAIE includes primary language instruction, English language development instruction, and mainstream instruction.

SIOP

The SIOP model initially was developed by Echevarria et al. (1999), with support from the federal Center for Research on Education, Diversity, and Excellence (CREDE) and the Center for Applied Linguistics (CAL), to help middle-school and high school teachers facilitate the academic content and English learning of emergent bilingual students. Since its origin, SIOP has been adapted for early childhood education, the elementary grades, and DL classrooms. Teachers can implement SIOP in bilingual classrooms, DL classrooms, ESL classrooms, and all-English classrooms.

SIOP provides a detailed way for teachers to design and implement content-based English lessons for emergent bilingual students. The lesson planning and implementation involve eight interrelated parts, with instructional strategies for each part. The eight parts are lesson "preparation, building background, comprehensible input, strategies, interaction, practice/application, lesson delivery, and review/assessment" (Echevarria et al., 2004, p. 58). For instance, the strategies for lesson preparation include the following:

- Identifying and writing content and language objectives so that they are child-friendly.
- Making sure that the concepts taught are age appropriate.
- Providing supplemental material to make the taught material comprehensible and engaging.
- Adapting material so it is comprehensible for the different language proficiencies in the class.
- Providing "meaningful activities that integrate lesson concepts (e.g., interviews, letter writing, simulations, models) with language practice opportunities for reading, writing, listening, and/or speaking" (Echevarria et al., 2004, p. 58).

A unique feature of SIOP is teachers' identification of student-friendly content and language objectives for each lesson. The content objectives usually reflect state standards for the specific content areas, while the language objectives identify the specific language knowledge and/or skills that students need for participation in the content areas. Teachers are encouraged to share the content and language objectives with their students by posting them so that students can see them, to read the objectives aloud, to ask students to orally read them aloud, and to review the objectives throughout the lesson. Toward the end of the lesson, it is recommended that you ask your students if the objectives were met.

SIOP CONTENT AND LANGUAGE OBJECTIVES FOR A UNITED STATES CIVIL WAR LESSON

Content Objective: Identify two causes of the Civil War in the United States

Lesson Objectives:

1. With your partner, write a paragraph about one of the reasons that the North fought the South during the United States Civil War.

2. Begin the paragraph with a topic sentence.
3. Provide three supportive details in the paragraph.

When I taught bilingual and ESL teachers how to use SIOP, it was not easy for them to identify content and language objectives, but once accomplished, the objectives helped them to plan lessons so that emergent bilingual students developed their English and content-area knowledge simultaneously. When they asked their students if they had attained the objectives, they were surprised to discover that third through sixth graders were able to evaluate whether the lessons met the content and language objectives. The teachers thought the two objectives helped them and their students to stay focused on their instructional aims.

Planning and implementing a SIOP lesson take considerable time because SIOP includes content-based language strategies and effective teaching strategies. The SIOP checklist for lesson planning and implementation has 30 features on it (Echevarria et al., 2004, pp. 209–210). To help teachers use SIOP, CAL provides SIOP professional staff development for administrators and teachers, along with sample SIOP lesson plans.

Three weaknesses of SIOP are the amount of time that it takes to design and implement a SIOP lesson, the limited use of students' L1 in the SIOP lessons, and the SIOP's limited focus on multicultural education and students' cultural funds of knowledge (González et al., 2005). When I taught SIOP, I showed my teachers how to include the L1, multicultural education, and cultural funds of knowledge in their lesson planning, and I asked them to do so.

EXPLICIT L2 INSTRUCTION

English Language Development Instruction

Whether emergent bilingual students will acquire English best through formal English instruction or through participation in content-based language approaches or in DL classrooms that provide authentic opportunities for English learning still is controversial and is a question that has not been well researched (Saunders & Goldenberg, 2010). Several researchers argue that even when emergent bilingual students participate in content-based or DL classrooms, they still will benefit from separate and explicit English language development (ELD) instruction (Dutro, Nuñez, & Short, 2016; Gersten et al., 2007). Dutro et al. (2016) and Saunders and Goldenberg (2010) recommend that DL teachers incorporate explicit English language instruction into their content-area instruction so that students can acquire English grammatical features that nonnative L2 speakers typically do not acquire through immersion instruction. Gersten et al. (2007) do not discuss the placement of ELD instruction in a particular program, but they support the provision of explicit ELD instruction to emergent bilingual students on a daily basis, starting in the primary grades. To my knowledge, none of these authors has proposed separate instruction in the partner language for English-dominant DL students.

Proponents of explicit ELD instruction indicate that this type of instruction can occur as part of a bilingual program or a content-based language approach, or as a component of a DL program (Dutro et al., 2016; Saunders & Goldenberg, 2010). They recommend that ELD be taught as a separate instructional unit for about 30–45 minutes daily. They suggest that it include emergent bilingual students of the same English proficiency levels, so that the ELD instruction is targeted for them. Saunders and Goldenberg (2010) recommend that English be the primary language employed during ELD instruction with strategic use of the L1.

According to Dutro and her colleagues (2016), ELD instruction should include "systematic ELD" and "integrated ELD" instruction. Systematic EDL instruction is formal, explicit ESL instruction. It should follow a "scope and sequence of language skills," or a linguistic continuum, so that there are no gaps in what students are taught and learn (Dutro et al., 2016, p. 55). It includes differentiated objectives to match emergent bilingual students' diverse levels of English proficiency. For instance, for beginning learners of English who move from minimal "receptive or productive English to a basic use," Dutro and her colleagues recommend that an objective is for the students to "move from nonverbal to single-word or short-phrase responses to longer oral responses" (p. 53). Your state's English language development standards provide guidance for your students' ELD instruction.

Integrated ELD instruction is instruction that helps emergent bilingual students to comprehend what they are taught in English in language arts, mathematics, history/social studies, science, art, and technical subjects. When teachers are designing integrated ELD instruction, they should work backward from a standard to identifying the "cognitive and linguistic demands of the performance task" (Dutro et al., 2016, p. 56). The cognitive task should be the same for all language proficiency levels, but the language instruction to accomplish the task should vary by proficiency level (p. 69). Students also need opportunities to practice the specific oral and written language they are learning. The practice tasks should require the students to accurately and appropriately employ the specific "language features" that were taught (Dutro et al., p. 62).

According to Saunders and Goldenberg (2010), during ELD instruction, teachers should provide their students with explicit feedback, correcting any errors. They point out that research evidence shows that prompting students to use correct language forms rather than simply restating the correct forms or recasting what they said is the most effective type of feedback.

L2 INSTRUCTION IN TWO-WAY DL CLASSROOMS

In two-way DL immersion classrooms, the focus is on teaching content and languages simultaneously. The aims are for DL students to acquire their L2 and to further develop their L1 by using the languages to communicate with their teacher(s) and each other as they learn the academic content emphasized in the grade-level curriculum (Howard et al., 2018). In the two-way, Spanish–English DL programs that I observed (90–10 and 50–50), teachers are not told to implement any type of language-based instructional approach or content-based instructional program. In recognition of this situation, CAL sponsored the development of SIOP for two-way immersion (TWI) classrooms, which it calls the two-way immersion observation protocol (TWIOP) model (Howard, Sugarman, & Coburn, 2006).

The TWIOP Model

The TWIOP model (Howard et al., 2006) is similar to the SIOP model except that it includes a number of additions and modifications. Four additions are

- the coordination of instruction in the two languages,
- an emphasis on cross-linguistic transfer,
- an increased focus on cross-cultural awareness, and
- the explicit teaching of how DL students should interact with their peers in cooperative groups.

To promote the coordination of instruction, thematic instruction is recommended (Howard et al., 2006). In thematic instruction, an academic theme in one or more content areas (such as literacy and social studies and/or science) is emphasized across both languages, and students are expected to use what they learned in one language and academic domain to aid or approach their learning in the other language and academic domain. For instance, in one of the 50–50 DL schools in which I conducted research, the first-grade teachers implemented thematic instruction about explorers and exploration during their English and Spanish literacy instruction and social studies instruction in Spanish (G. García & Lang, 2023).

In terms of the other additions, Howard and her colleagues (2006) explain that to implement cross-linguistic transfer, instruction in the two languages should be complementary or build on each other, but they should not duplicate each other. To promote cross-cultural awareness, teachers should establish, post, and share cultural objectives, which should be implemented in the DL lessons. The last addition is the explicit teaching of strategies to facilitate the work of the two language groups in cooperative groups, such as teaching students how to provide wait time and to use gestures and slower speech for beginning L2 learners.

A number of modifications are also recommended for some of the SIOP strategies (Howard et al., 2006). For SIOP strategies 1 (content objectives) and 2 (language objectives), TWIOP teachers are encouraged to develop and implement content and language objectives in each language so that they overlap. For SIOP strategy 14 (use of learning strategies, such as predicting, summarizing, categorizing, and self-monitoring), Howard and her colleagues recommend that teachers emphasize that the strategies are not language specific; students should be provided with opportunities to use the strategies in both languages. For SIOP strategy 15 (use of scaffolding techniques consistently throughout the lesson), they recommend that TWIOP teachers teach their students how to provide scaffolding and modeling for their L2 peers.

Similar to SIOP, TWIOP still recommends that teachers keep their DL instruction in the two languages separate. However, SIOP strategy 20 has been changed to the following: "As appropriate, allow students to clarify key concepts in L1 for strategic purposes with an aide, peer, or L1 text" (Howard et al., 2006, p. 13). SIOP strategy 29 now has been changed to ensure cross-linguistic transfer of vocabulary knowledge; it recommends that "core vocabulary" be reviewed during instruction "in each language" (p. 15). Strategy 30 includes reviewing core concepts in each language. A caveat for strategies 29 and 30 is that vocabulary and key concepts should not be "reintroduced" in each language but reviewed in each language (p. 16). For strategy 32, similar assessments should be used in each language, and the assessment results should be "shared across languages" with partner instructors who teach in the other language (Howard et al., 2006, p. 17). Because implementing the TWIOP requires teacher planning and coordination across the content areas and languages, Howard et al. (2018) recommend that district and school administrators provide DL teachers with paid opportunities to plan and coordinate their DL instruction.

Recommended DL Instruction without TWIOP

Prior to the pandemic, I spent six years working with DL teachers and administrators in a 90–10, Spanish–English DL program and a 50–50 Spanish–English DL program. Neither program employed the TWIOP. However, both DL programs implemented their own versions of content-based language teaching in English and Spanish. I also provided recommendations for improved instruction and assessment to the administrators and teachers in both programs. I present these recommendations below because other DL teachers and students will likely benefit from them.

The first recommendation is to provide DL teachers with professional staff development on how to shelter their instruction and employ SIOP content and language objectives. The next recommendation is for the DL teachers to provide thematic instruction across academic domains, such as social studies, science, and literacy, and in the two instructional languages. Another recommendation is to increase the use of think-pair-share and student-led small-group discussion, so that students from the two language groups increase the amount of time that they interact with each other and discuss open-ended, engaging topics in each language. An additional recommendation is to accept student translanguaging and to encourage the DL teachers to employ strategic translanguaging so that the DL students improve their learning. Another recommendation is to provide time for explicit L2 language instruction in English and the partner language on grammar and vocabulary. Lastly, DL teachers should employ ongoing formative literacy assessments (see Chapter 12), so that they understand what individual students can and cannot do in each language and across their languages.

CONCLUDING REMARKS

I previously collaborated with administrators and teachers in two Spanish–English dual-language programs (one was 90–10, and the other was 50–50) and was surprised to discover that neither program employed a specific content-based language approach or trained their teachers on how to shelter students' instruction in English or Spanish. The expectation was that the DL students would learn what they needed to say or comprehend in the L2 by being immersed in the DL context—hence, the program name two-way DL immersion.

Prior to the pandemic, one of the first-grade DL teachers in the 90–10 DL program confessed to me that she explicitly taught the English-dominant students how to ask to go to the bathroom in Spanish because they did not know how to appropriately conjugate the verb *poder* (can or be able to) to say "¿Puedo ir al baño?" (Can I go to the bathroom?) Instead, they were repeating what they heard her say, "Puedes ir al baño" (You can go to the bathroom), which she found annoying. She was surprised at how quickly they learned to use the correct question. She then asked me if I thought it was okay for her to teach the Spanish-dominant students how to say, "May I go to the bathroom" in English. I said, "Yes." Sometimes, explicit language instruction saves time and should be used.

Learning how to provide sheltered L2 instruction and how to implement content-based language approaches both take time. One way to reduce the required time is for teachers of bilingual students in the same grades to share the lesson planning workload. Also, remember that you do not have to shelter everything that is taught in the L2. What you shelter and how long you spend sheltering the L2 depends on whether students know the concepts in their L1, the difficulty of the L2 task, and the complexity of the L2. You may not know Italian, but if you know another romance language, you probably can figure out the phrase that I am using to close this chapter without any sheltering of it: "Buona fortuna!"

CHAPTER 4

Instructional Activities to Promote Bilingual Students' Oral Language and Literacy Performance

GUIDING QUESTIONS

- Why are rhymes and songs useful for teaching bilingual students?
- How can shared reading promote the oral language and literacy performance of bilingual students?
- What are the benefits of interactive teacher read-alouds for bilingual students?
- Why should teachers let bilingual students translanguage when discussing texts?
- How does student discussion about texts aid bilingual students' oral language and literacy development?

Ms. Smith is the assistant principal at Charles Elementary School, which has a two-way Spanish–English DL program (K–6). Ms. Smith was visiting the DL classrooms at the school. She was surprised to see one of the fourth-grade DL teachers, Mr. Peters, read aloud *Charlotte's Web* (White, 1952) in English to his fourth graders. She thought the book was way too difficult for the emergent bilingual students in his class. Also, Ms. Smith purposefully had chosen to observe Mr. Peters's English literacy instruction because she did not speak or understand Spanish. So, she did not understand why he encouraged his students to translanguage, or use all their linguistic resources, when they answered his questions and asked questions about the book. She thought that during English instruction, he and his students were only supposed to use English. After reading Chapter 4, what would you tell Ms. Smith about why Mr. Peters read *Charlotte's Web* and encouraged his students to translanguage when they answered and asked questions?

IMPORTANCE OF ORAL LANGUAGE DEVELOPMENT

When classrooms with bilingual students in them are silent or quiet, educators should be concerned. Bilingual students' oral language and literacy development is promoted when they hear and speak their languages, not when they are quiet. This is one reason why the remote-distance learning that bilingual students received during the pandemic was not the best way to promote their language and literacy development.

However, just listening and speaking in a language is not enough for bilingual students to develop their languages and biliteracy. Chapter 2 explained the importance of comprehensible input (Krashen, 1985), comprehensible output (Swain & Lapkin, 1995), and student–student and student–teacher interaction (Long, 1981; Long & Porter, 1985). To create comprehensible input, teachers need to employ oral language and written language just beyond what their students currently understand. To promote comprehensible output, they need to provide bilingual students with the opportunities to use oral or written language for authentic purposes just beyond what they currently can do. Students of different language proficiencies also need opportunities to work together and to communicate with each other.

One way to move your students just beyond their capability is to rely on Vygotsky's (1978) zone of proximal development. To do this, you first should employ formative assessment to examine what your students can do. Formative assessment is ongoing, completed by you, the classroom teacher, and reveals how your students' approach and complete key classroom instructional activities (see Chapter 12). Next, push your students slightly to the +1 stage by aiding their performance with scaffolding or support when necessary.

The activities presented in this chapter provide all types of bilingual students—emergent bilingual students, former emergent bilingual students, DL students, and bilingual students in all-English classrooms—with opportunities for comprehensible input, output, and interaction. Many of these activities can be used in grades K–6. However, it is likely that your expectations for what students can do, and the content presented in the activities, will change according to the grade level you teach.

GRADUAL RELEASE OF RESPONSIBILITY

The instructional activities in this chapter emphasize the gradual release of responsibility (GRR; Pearson & Gallagher, 1983; Stahl & García, 2015, 2022). The GRR highlights the importance of teachers' implementing instructional activities that include teacher-modeling or teacher-directed instruction; collaborative instruction in which both the teacher and students are active participants but with the teacher as the major director; teacher-guided instruction in which the teacher guides the students to become independent practitioners; and lastly, student-directed activities in which students act independently. If your instruction moves from teacher-directed to more student-directed activities, then you are making sure that you provide your students with active involvement in their oral and literacy development rather than passive involvement. Chapter 8 provides more information on how to implement the GRR.

INSTRUCTIONAL ACTIVITIES

Choral Language Activities: Rhymes and Songs

Rhymes and songs are excellent ways to introduce a new language or to get bilingual students to use an L2. They emphasize the sounds, vocabulary, and syntax of a particular language. A rhyme's use of repeated words, words that rhyme, and rhythm facilitates bilingual students' oral participation even when students do not know all the words or remember them all. Three popular English rhymes are: "Five Little Monkeys"; "Hickory, Dickory Dock"; and "Twinkle, Twinkle Little Star." If you search for the rhymes online, you will find videos with the words, illustrations, and gestures or actions for each of the rhymes on YouTube (youtube.com), which you can share with your students. The videos help to shelter the rhymes by making them comprehensible for L2 learners. Over time, many of the English rhymes have been turned into songs.

Like rhymes, songs often include repeated words, words that rhyme, and rhythms. However, a song is sung, whereas a rhyme is spoken. Songs include music and melodies, which enhance students' participation, especially when they do not know all the words. Table 4.1 lists some of the English songs, along with Spanish translations, which have been effectively used with bilingual students. Although some of the English songs were developed for young children, many of them can be used with older children. If you search for the songs online, you will find videos of people singing some of them on YouTube. You also can use popular songs by singers such as Marc Anthony, Shakira, Taylor Swift, or Rihanna; just be sure to read the lyrics first to make sure they are appropriate for your students.

When teaching a new rhyme or song, teachers should initiate it but should invite their students to chime in or chorally participate as the students become familiar with the rhyme or song. The shared nature of the choral response encourages bilingual students to participate even when they do not understand the meanings of the words or cannot participate independently. An individual student's performance usually is hidden when a class or group recites rhymes or sings songs, reducing the anxiety that students may feel when working with a new language. Repeated use of the rhymes and songs helps your students to become familiar with them.

L2 Techniques

Posting the written version of a rhyme or song, providing illustrations for key words or parts of the rhyme or song, and pointing to the illustrations and words while you and your class say the rhyme or sing the song will shelter or support your bilingual students' understanding of the rhymes

TABLE 4.1. English Songs and Spanish Translations

Song	Gestures	K–2 students	Older students (3–6)	Spanish translation
The ABC Song		x	x	
BINGO	x	x	x	x
Five Green Speckled Frogs	x	x		x
Good Morning	x	x	x	x
Head, Shoulders, Knees, & Toes	x	x	x	x
Hokey, Pokey	x	x	x	x
I Am a Rock			x	x
If You're Happy and You Know It	x	x	x	x
I Still Haven't Found What I'm Looking For			x	x
Itsy-Bitsy Spider	x	x		x
My Favorite Things			x	x
Old MacDonald Had a Farm		x		x
She'll Be Coming 'Round the Mountain		x	x	x
Wheels on the Bus	x	x		x

and songs. Accompanying the rhymes and songs with physical gestures helps your students to learn the meanings of the words and to remember them.

Rhymes and Songs to Develop Literacy

Rhymes and songs also can aid bilingual students' literacy development (Cunningham, 2017). According to Reading Rockets (*www.readingrockets.org*), reciting rhymes is a literacy activity because it helps students to hear the sounds and syllables in words. Singing songs helps students to develop phonological (sound–symbol awareness), syntactic (grammatical) and vocabulary knowledge. Some of the English songs, such as, the ABC song and the BINGO song, specifically emphasize literacy skills.

Rhymes and Songs in Languages Other than English

When you are teaching in a language other than English, I encourage you to use rhymes and songs originally written in the respective language because they will reflect that language better than a translation from English. For example, syllables are an important linguistic feature in Spanish, and teachers often use rhymes to teach them. A popular Spanish rhyme that teachers employ to teach syllables is about making chocolate, a children's drink in Latin America and Spain (translation in parentheses): "Bate, bate, chocolate" (Beat, beat, chocolate). There are several versions of this rhyme with different lyrics.

BATE, BATE, CHOCOLATE

Bate, bate chocolate (Beat, beat, chocolate)
Con arroz y con tomate. (With rice and with tomato.)
Uno, dos, tres, CHO! (One, two, three, CHO!)
Uno, dos, tres, CO! (One, two, three, CO!)
Uno, dos, tres, LA! (One, two, three, LA!)
Uno, dos, tres, TE! (One, two, three, TE!)
Cho-co-la-te!

(Unpublished Latin American folk rhyme)

Many of the Spanish rhymes have been put to music, turning them into songs. Table 4.2 lists Spanish songs that you can use when teaching in Spanish or when teaching the Spanish language.

TABLE 4.2. Original Spanish Songs

Song title	Young students (K–2)	Older students (3–6)
A mi burro	x	
El barquito chiquito	x	
Los pollitos dicen	x	
Me voy, me voy		x
Que llueva	x	
Rueda, rueda, rueda	x	
Sol solecito	x	
Un elefante se balanceaba	x	
Vivir mi vida		x
Yo contigo, tu conmigo		x

Morning Message

Many elementary teachers begin the school day with a morning message. The morning message is an oral language and literacy activity. When students are in kindergarten or first grade, the teacher usually writes the morning message on a whiteboard. In the message, she or he often identifies the day of the week and the focus of the school day. Figure 4.1 shows Spanish and English versions of a morning message that a first-grade bilingual teacher (Spanish–English) could use with first graders. Sometimes, teachers use the morning message to deal with difficult or emotional topics. For instance, a fifth-grade DL teacher used it to announce that she would miss school for several days because her daughter was very ill. She asked her students to help her substitute.

In kindergarten and first grade, before the students enter the classroom, the teacher usually has the morning message posted on a whiteboard or computer screen. Once the students are seated, the teacher points to the words as he or she reads the morning message aloud. This helps to promote students' sound–symbol correspondence. Next, the teacher has the students read aloud the message with him/her, what we call a choral reading, while pointing to each word. The choral reading supports those students who may not be able to read each word independently. It helps to develop the students' sound-symbol recognition, decoding and fluent oral reading.

In grades 1–6, you can write the morning message as your students watch you do it, or your students can write the morning message. Whoever writes the message should read the message aloud while pointing to each

Hoy es el lunes, el 11 de abril, 2022. Primero, vamos a leer y escribir. Despues, trabajarémos en el jardín escolar.

Today is Monday, April 11, 2022. First, we are going to read and write. Then, we will work in the school garden.

FIGURE 4.1. Morning message in Spanish and English.

word. Then, the author should lead a choral reading of the message by asking everyone to read with him or her while pointing to each word. The morning message usually involves about 10 minutes of classroom time.

L2 Techniques

If you do not think your students will understand all the words in the message, then you should use L2 techniques to contextualize their meaning. For Figure 4.1, as you read the message, you could point to the date on a posted calendar or to the respective day on a posted list of days of the week; pantomime or show illustrations of what is meant by reading and writing; and show photos of students working in the school garden. See Chapter 3 for more information on how to shelter or support your students' L2 comprehension.

Biliteracy Instruction

The morning message also provides an opportunity for biliteracy instruction. You first should present the written message in one language. Then after making the written message comprehensible and having the class chorally read it, you could present the same written message in the other language—known as the partner or nontarget language in DL classrooms—by following the same procedures. Next, I suggest that you spend time discussing and showing how the two languages differ. For instance, in Figure 4.1, you could point out how the days of the week are written differently in Spanish and English, and how the adjective comes before the noun in Spanish, but after the noun in English. With older students, you also could discuss how future is expressed in two different ways in both languages.

Translanguaging Opportunity

When your students write the morning message, they may draw on all their linguistic resources, or translanguage, to compose it. Because translanguaging is a language practice characteristic of bilingual individuals, you should accept and encourage it. In the following example, Juan Miguel employed translanguaging to explain that his mother broke her arm: "Ayer (yesterday), after school, mí mamá, se cayó (my mother fell) and broke her arm. We took her to the hospital. Ahora (now), she has a cast en el brazo (on her arm)."

Culturally Responsive Activity

When the morning message is open to student contributions, and language-minority students share community actions or cultural events that affect them, then it has the potential to become a culturally responsive activity. Freire and Valdez (2017) defined culturally responsive activities as those that created or reflected awareness of sociopolitical forces that affected language-minority students or that emphasized their cultural competence. A DL principal, with whom I collaborated, had his teachers implement morning messages in Spanish at his DL school in K–5 classrooms for 20 minutes every day. He told me that he mandated Spanish to try to offset the imbalance in language use that sometimes occurs in Spanish–English DL programs, when English and English-dominant students are privileged over Spanish and Spanish-dominant students (Cervantes-Soon et al., 2017).

Shared Reading

Shared reading occurs when teachers invite their students to read a text along with them. Often, students do not read the text at exactly the same time as the teacher but repeat parts of it. In echo reading, students read a chunk of text after the teacher reads it, such as a paragraph or page (Stahl & García, 2015). When the teacher repeatedly reads the same text, then students may spontaneously join the reading, performing a choral reading. I observed this happen in a bilingual (Spanish–English) kindergarten. The teacher and her kindergartners enacted shared reading when they read laminated cards with brief stories on them that the teacher had made for her syllable instruction in Spanish.

The idea of shared reading is based on Holdaway's (1982) concept of the Shared Book Experience, which requires a teacher to read an oversized book with enlarged print and illustrations to the entire class. In shared reading, students need to see the book or print being read. You can show them the oversized book as you read it aloud, post a computer image of the text in the book on a whiteboard or classroom wall, or provide copies of the book being read to individual students or pairs of students. Shared reading can be done with stories and informational texts and should occur in both languages. It helps bilingual students to develop their print awareness, reading fluency, vocabulary, and text comprehension. It usually takes about 10–20 minutes of instructional time.

Interactive Teacher Read-Alouds

For interactive teacher read-alouds (and teacher read-alouds), you orally read a book to your students, while you show them the book illustrations and employ L2 techniques to make the book reading comprehensible for those students who are not proficient in the book's language. However, in contrast to teacher read-alouds, during interactive teacher read-alouds, your students actively participate as you read the book aloud. For example, your students may interrupt the reading to ask questions or to answer questions that you or other students ask. You can conduct the interactive teacher read-aloud with the whole class or small groups of students. In the primary grades (K–2), the interactive teacher read-aloud should last about 15 minutes, and in the intermediate grades (3–6) about 30 minutes (Stahl & Garcia, 2015, 2022).

Interactive teacher read-alouds (and teacher read-alouds) allow you to orally read texts that are beyond your bilingual students' current reading performance. By doing so, you introduce your students to ideas, syntax, and vocabulary beyond their current performance levels. When you read books that your state standards recommend or require, you are providing your students with access to common knowledge and literacy experiences expected for the grade you teach. For example, when Mr. Peters read the book *Charlotte's Web* (White, 1952) in the vignette at the start of this chapter, he was exposing his students to a text that commonly is used in third or fourth grade in the United States. When you employ either type of teacher read-aloud with the entire class, you help to promote a literacy community in which you are providing all your students with access to the same books, building their common background knowledge and literacy experiences.

For both types of teacher read-alouds, you should select and read the books and texts you are going to use ahead of time to make sure that they will interest and engage your students, to practice your oral reading, and to plan how you will conduct the teacher read-aloud and utilize the books and texts. You also want to access students' prior knowledge about the author, genre or type of text, text structure or text organization, and key topics or ideas in the text before beginning either type of teacher read-aloud. If your students do not have key knowledge about the text, then you need to provide it. After conducting the read-aloud, you should make the book that you read available for your students to read on their own.

It is important to read aloud both narrative (i.e., fiction, plays, and poetry) and expository or informational texts to bilingual students. When selecting texts, be sure to choose texts that will interest and engage your students. Sometimes teachers use texts that relate to a current topic in science and/or social studies. Connecting the teacher read-aloud to students' content-area instruction usually gives students the appropriate background knowledge to comprehend the text. For more information on how to do this, see Chapter 11.

Benefits of Interactive Teacher Read-Alouds for Bilingual Students

Bilingual students will benefit more from interactive teacher read-alouds than from teacher read-alouds The interactive teacher read-alouds require them to actively participate rather than passively listen to what is read. In addition, teachers can monitor their comprehension when students answer and ask questions. The example below provides a partial transcript of a simulated interactive teacher read-aloud in a Spanish–English DL third-grade classroom with a short book, *The Paper Bag Princess* (Munsch, 1980). The teacher, Ms. Martin, begins the interactive teacher read-aloud in English, but she encourages her students to translanguage when answering her questions, which facilitates their participation. Translations are in parentheses.

Example: Interactive Teacher Read-Aloud of *The Paper Bag Princess* (Munsch, 1980) with DL Third Graders

[Ms. Martin asks her third graders what they know about princesses in fairy tales. She posts their ideas on a whiteboard.]

GINA: They are very beautiful.

TOMÁS: Lots of times they are in trouble.

GERALDO: A prince saves them.

GABRIELA: Son ricas. (They are rich.)

[Ms. Martin begins to read the book, *The Paperbag Princess.* She stops after she has read the first page and shows her students the illustration on the second page. She asks them what they think.]

ALFREDO: Es como lo dijimos. (It is like what we said.)

[After reading the third page and showing the illustration on the fourth page, she asks the students to tell their partners what they think will happen next and to write their ideas in their notebooks. Then, she asks several of them to share their ideas.]

GERMÁN: Creo que gritó para Prince Ronald que le ayudara. (I think she shouted for Prince Ronald to help her.)

ELIZABETH: I think she tried to hide somewhere because she didn't have clothes.

MS. MARTIN: As you hear more of the story, decide if your ideas are correct or incorrect.

[Next, Ms. Martin reads page 5.]

MS. MARTIN: Based on what I've read, were your predictions correct?

JUAN: No, because she didn't ask for Prince Ronald's help.

JULIE: She found a paper bag and wore it.

ENRIQUE: No entiendo lo que pasó cuando dice que el dragón dejó "horses' bones." (I don't understand what happened when it says that the dragon left "horses' bones.")

MS. MARTIN: Good point, Enrique. The book doesn't really tell us what happened. It says, "He was easy to follow, because he left a trail of burnt forests and horses' bones." You have to make an inference or educated guess about what happened. Who thinks they know what the author meant?

[Several students answer Ms. Martin. Then, she reads pages 6–20].

MS. MARTIN: OK, talk to your partner about words that you think describe the princess. Write the words in your notebooks.

MS. MARTIN: Now choose a word, and tell us why you think it describes the princess.

HERIBERTO: She's brave. She was not afraid of the dragon.

IRENE: I think she's inteligente (intelligent) cuz' she trick [*sic*] el dragón (the dragon).

MS. MARTIN: OK, work with your partner to think of words that describe the dragon. Write the words in your notebooks.

L2 Techniques

If you are doing the interactive teacher read-aloud or teacher read-aloud in a language that your students do not know well, then you need to employ L2 techniques to make what you are reading comprehensible to them. For example, you can employ the students' stronger language to preview what you are going to read, and after reading the book in the weaker language, employ their stronger language to review what you just read. Also, encouraging your students to discuss the book or answer your questions by translanguaging (i.e., use all their linguistic resources) typically will result in more classroom participation. Lastly, asking your bilingual students to share their responses or answers to teacher questions in pairs or small groups in their L1 or L2 before sharing them with the entire class usually results in higher levels of student participation. When bilingual students are given the opportunity to rehearse what they are going to say, they usually participate more.

Shared Writing and the Language Experience Approach

Shared writing occurs when you coauthor a text with your students. You should write the text on a whiteboard or on a large flip chart so that all your students can see what you are writing. As you write the text, you ask your students to provide you with information. For example, with both narrative (fiction) and expository (informational) text, you should ask them to give you a title.

The language experience approach (Ashton-Warner, 1963; Stauffer, 1965) is a type of shared writing in which your students help you, the teacher, to write a text about an experience they had or a topic they learned about. This approach is beneficial for bilingual students because it draws on common background knowledge and provides them with content vocabulary. At the same time, the teacher can show students how to spell and write their thoughts in their L1 or English. A DL second-grade teacher with whom I collaborated often employed the language experience approach when she taught science in Spanish because she had very few Spanish informational texts available for her students to read or for her to read aloud. She introduced the science topics through mini-lessons. During the mini-lessons, she read aloud to the students the written material available in Spanish, often supplementing it with material written in English that was not covered in the Spanish materials or material that she had learned through her own online research. Then, on subsequent days, when she had her students recap what they had heard her read or discussed on the previous days, she had them participate in the language experience approach by dictating a text to her. For example, when summarizing what they had learned about hormigas (ants), her second graders dictated the following:

> "Comen lo que está en el piso." (They eat what is on the floor.)
> "Tienen 6 patas." (They have six legs.)
> "Tienen 2 ojos compuestos." (They have two compound eyes.)
> . . . .
> "Son insectos." (They are insects.) (Lang, 2019, p. 144)

Many times, teachers write the dictated texts in paragraphs. After completing the text, the students reread the text aloud. When teachers have aides or parent volunteers, they can ask them to type the text and duplicate it, so that all the students have a written version to illustrate and read independently.

Implementation of the Science of Reading with Emergent Bilingual Students

The Science of Reading (SOR) promotes English reading instruction that emphasizes specific methods for teaching "phonological awareness, phonics and word recognition, fluency, vocabulary and oral language comprehension, and text comprehension" (Jiban, 2022). Although some of the SOR instruction includes rich literacy activities (e.g., teacher read-alouds), it also includes isolated rule learning, drill instruction, and adherence to an instructional sequence of phonics instruction (Northwest Education Association [NWEA], 2023). In addition, students read decodable texts, which include words with letter–sound correspondences explicitly taught to students (see Chapter 5). To improve students' text comprehension, proponents of the SOR advise teachers to read aloud complex texts to their students in whole-class settings and to provide scaffolding, as necessary, to help students comprehend the texts.

Implementation of the SOR with emergent bilingual students can be both positive and negative. Based on an empirical review of L2 literature, Shanahan and Beck (2006) concluded that when L2 students received explicit English decoding instruction, they decoded English texts as well as native-English speakers. In a study with second-grade and fourth-grade bilingual Latinx students (G. García et al., 2021), my colleagues and I found that the teachers' use of whole-class, interactive teacher read-alouds, along with the GRR (Pearson & Gallagher, 1983), effectively presented the students with cognitive strategies, which they later applied to their reading comprehension (see Chapter 8).

However, implementing the SOR with emergent bilingual students can be problematic, especially when the instruction is not adapted for bilingual students (see Chapter 7). Although the L2 students in the Shanahan and Beck (2006) review decoded English texts as well as native-English speakers, their comprehension of English texts was significantly less. A major problem is that the Simple View of Reading, the theory that underlies the SOR (NWEA, 2023), is not a strong predictor of emergent bilingual students' English reading comprehension.

Simple View of Reading

The Simple View of Reading states that decoding, or the use of sound–symbol correspondence to figure out written English words when reading aloud, and language comprehension (historically referred to as listening comprehension) predict the English reading comprehension of native English-speaking students (Gough & Tunmer, 1986; Hoover & Gough, 1990). The assumptions here are that when students decode English words, they hear the words they orally read, and they recognize what they mean because they are in their oral vocabulary, resulting in reading comprehension.

Several reading researchers critiqued the Simple View of Reading and the Science of Reading for being too simplistic (Cervetti et al., 2020; Duke & Cartwright, 2021; Hiebert, 2023). For example, Hiebert pointed out that what accounts for beginning readers' effective English reading is their automatic recognition of letter–sound patterns in words, not their rule learning. To improve students' recognition of letter–sound patterns in words, she reported that students need to encounter lots of words through frequent reading. She warned that decodable texts do not expose students to the number of words necessary for them to develop their recognition of letter–sound patterns.

Quantitative studies showed that the Simple View of Reading predicted the English reading comprehension of native English speakers when they read simple texts for which they had the requisite background, syntactic (grammatical), and vocabulary knowledge (Stahl & García, 2015). However, it did not predict native English speakers' comprehension of more complex texts in English, which involve a range of background knowledge, complex rhetorical structures, and unfamiliar vocabulary (Stahl & García, 2022).

The Simple View of Reading is not a good predictor of the English reading comprehension of emergent bilingual students because bilingual students do not always know the meanings of the English words they can decode (Shanahan & Beck, 2006). Also, a *strong* predictor of K–2 emergent bilingual students' English reading—their L1 reading performance (G. García, 2000)—is not included in the Simple View of Reading.

Erroneous Critiques of Guided Reading Instruction

Some SOR advocates (Jiban, 2022; NWEA, 2023) critique a popular small-group instructional reading method that often is used with bilingual students—guided reading instruction (Fountas & Pinell, 2011)—which I discuss in more detail in the next section. Although whole-class instruction can be effectively used with bilingual students, it ignores the range of differences and experiences that are likely to characterize emergent bilingual students in a single classroom (see Chapter 12). In contrast, small-group reading instruction can help teachers to differentiate their instruction. Therefore, when you teach bilingual students, I recommend that you include both types of instruction.

During guided reading, teachers often introduce a phonics or reading strategy, unfamiliar vocabulary or syntax, and they listen to individual students mumble or whisper read (i.e., softly read aloud to themselves) leveled texts (see Chapter 5), documenting and supporting the student's oral reading, while the other students in the group read to themselves or do other group work (Fountas & Pinnell, 2011).

It is important to realize that some of the Science of Reading critiques of guided reading are erroneous. For instance, several critiques stated that students in guided reading did round-robin oral reading, instead of individual whisper or mumble reading, which also is done in SOR instruction (Jiban, 2022; NWEA, 2023). The critiques also implied that students read simple texts (Jiban, 2022; NWEA, 2023). However, in guided reading, students read instructional texts, which are more complex and challenging than the decodable texts required in the SOR (Hiebert, 2024).

Teacher-Led Small-Group Reading Instruction

Guided Reading

Guided reading involves a small-group meeting between the teacher and four or five students who read at a similar instructional level (Fountas & Pinnell, 2010, 2011; Stahl & García, 2015). Instructional level is a student's highest reading level when they receive aid from the teacher. Because students are developing as readers, the groups are temporary; the group membership should change as each student's reading development changes.

Guided reading in English is appropriate for bilingual students in grades K–3, but it does not pose sufficient challenges for students in grades 4–6 unless they are beginning readers (Stahl & García, 2015). Guided reading in Spanish usually occurs in grades K–2. If students in grades 3–6 are beginning Spanish readers, then guided reading in Spanish is appropriate for them.

To begin guided reading, the teacher first introduces the students to the text they are going to read, often through a brief picture walk (Fountas & Pinnell, 2011). During the small-group meeting, the teacher listens to each student softly read aloud (e.g., mumble read) an instructional text (Stahl & García, 2015). The aim of the mumble read is for the student to decode the words accurately, to read with fluency, and to understand what is read. The teacher provides each student with feedback on the mumble read. While the student mumble reads, the other students in the group read another text independently or complete related work. After each student mumble reads, the teacher may present a reading comprehension strategy for the students to use and/or teach unknown vocabulary.

Guided reading typically occurs on a daily basis for a total of 45–60 minutes, with each guided reading group meeting for about 15–20 minutes. While the teacher works with a small group of readers, the other students in the class rotate through different activities for about 15–20 minutes each. Possible activities include reading to themselves or with a partner; listening to and reading a story on the computer; writing about what they read, heard read, or saw in a video or on the computer; writing about their own topics; and participating in a vocabulary center, where students work on decoding, syllables, new vocabulary, and/or cognates.

Stahl and I (2015) encourage you to meet with students in guided reading groups according to their reading performance. You should meet daily with K–1 students who read below grade level; with grade-level readers in grades 2 (in Spanish/English) and 3 (in English) two or three times each week; and with high-performing readers in grades K–2 in Spanish and K–3 in English twice a week. For students in grades 3 (in Spanish) and 4 (in English) and above who are fluent and accurate decoders, we recommend that you implement small-group and whole-group reading comprehension instruction instead of guided reading instruction.

Small-Group Reading Instruction

One way to accelerate your students' reading performance is to meet periodically with small groups of students who read similarly to present them with new reading strategies or techniques, to review their reading comprehension and use of new vocabulary, and to help them interpret and analyze literature. When my daughter was in third grade, she received high grades for reading. However, during the previous summer, I required her to read independently for 30 minutes on Monday–Thursday. After she read, I asked her questions about the texts she was reading and soon realized that she was skimming the texts for plot, not reading them closely. When I mentioned this to her third-grade teacher, he was surprised, but admitted that he really did not know how well she comprehended what she read. For his reading instruction, he conducted a reading workshop in which she chose what she wanted to read, completed a reading log, and gave book talks (see the section Independent Reading and Book Talks below). I support these activities, but I think that teachers also need to know how well their students comprehend what they read. Once students no longer participate in guided reading, I advise you to periodically conduct small reading groups to promote and evaluate their reading comprehension.

Authentic Student Discussion

Prior to the pandemic, when teachers implemented whole-class or small-group discussions, they tended to dominate teacher–student conversations;

that is, the teachers initiated (I) the questions, to which students responded (R), followed by the teachers' evaluation (E) of student answers, resulting in an interaction pattern called the I-R-E (initiate–respond–evaluate) or recitation (Cazden, 1988). This type of instruction does not promote the development of students' oral language, reading comprehension, or critical thinking.

Given the type of instruction provided during the pandemic, it is unlikely that students' computer interactions varied much from the I-R-E format. Therefore, to accelerate bilingual students' oral language development and learning during the post-pandemic era, it is important for them to participate in authentic discussions that do not involve the I-R-E or recitation.

You can begin to hold authentic discussions by having your students do think–pair–share during whole-class instruction. In think–pair–share, you assign students partners. Then, when you ask the class open-ended questions, you first ask the students to think about their individual answers. Next, you ask them to talk with their partners to decide on the pair's answer. Lastly, you ask one of them to share the pair's answer with the class.

Another way to promote bilingual students' oral language development and critical thinking is to organize and implement small-group student discussions about books or texts that bilingual students have read or are reading or about videos that they have watched. However, before implementing student-led discussion groups, you first need to model how you want your students to interact in small groups.

You can introduce your students to effective discussion practices during whole-class discussions. According to Stahl and García (2022), effective discussion practices involve open-ended questions without set answers (e.g., What did you think about Arnold's decision to ignore Carrie?); provide uptake by building on participants' answers or asking follow-up questions; require participants to pay attention to what is being said in the group; and emphasize that everyone in the group participates through self-selected turn taking. Posting the features of effective discussion practices and referring to them when you model and implement small-group discussions will help to facilitate quality discussions. Assigning specific students to serve as small-group captains or leaders, who make sure that the group stays on topic and that everyone gets a turn, is important.

Prior to holding student-led small-group discussion groups, it often is useful to ask bilingual students to read the same text or to watch the same video and to write responses to the text or video before discussing it. The written responses provide students with information they can reference during the discussion. Allowing bilingual students to choose the language that they want to use during the discussions and encouraging them to translanguage usually results in greater participation than when you assign them a language to use.

Independent Reading and Book Talks

Bilingual students should do independent reading, or reading on their own, on a daily basis. Stahl and I (2015, 2022) recommend that you give students an end goal for their independent reading. The end goal could be book talks, in which students orally share with the class or small groups what they liked or did not like about the books they read. Book talks are useful because your students get ideas from their peers about what to read. Another end goal is a group project in which students read and contribute specific information about a topic.

You may assign your students to do independent reading at home or when you meet with guided reading groups or groups for small-group reading instruction. My colleague and I (Stahl & García, 2015, 2022) recommend that students in kindergarten or first grade participate in independent reading for 10–15 minutes daily. Students who are in grades 2–6 should do independent reading for 20–40 minutes daily.

Additionally, I recommend that students keep a daily reading log, in which they write down the titles and authors of the books that they read independently, which pages they read on specific dates, and indicate how much they liked or did not like what they read and why. Students can use their reading logs to decide on which books to share during the book talks. I recommend that teachers periodically collect the reading logs to see if students are reading a variety of books at the appropriate independent levels. If they are not, then a student–teacher conference should be held so that you can redirect the student.

CONCLUDING REMARKS

Sometimes, when I visit bilingual classrooms, I note that there is very little instructional focus on bilingual students' oral language development. The comprehensible input, comprehensible output, and student–student interaction necessary for bilingual students' optimal oral language and literacy development in their L1 and L2 were missing. It is important to remember that oral language activities not only promote your students' oral language development and listening comprehension, but they also promote specific literacy skills, such as, phonology, syntax, vocabulary, and reading comprehension.

Scheduled use of the activities in this chapter should help your bilingual students to develop their L1 and L2 oral languages and literacies without creating large amounts of student stress. What you implement, how frequently, and in which languages depends on the ages of your students, the instructional context (e.g., early-exit TBE, late-exit TBE/maintenance TBE, one-way or two-way DL, ESL, all-English), and your students' L1 and L2 language proficiencies. For example, beginning L2 learners of all ages will benefit from rhymes and songs. Daily guided reading sessions are important for beginning L1 and/or L2 readers, but not as important for students who read at grade level in their L1 and L2.

Not all of the instructional activities that promote your bilingual students' literacy development in two languages were presented in this chapter. Some of the instructional activities important for your bilingual students' L1 and L2 literacy development (e.g., beginning L1 and L2 reading, reading comprehension, writing, vocabulary and academic language instruction, and disciplinary literacy) require their own chapters and appear later in this book.

CHAPTER 5

The Selection and Use of Texts with Bilingual Students

GUIDING QUESTIONS

- Why is it important for bilingual students to read expository texts?
- How do story maps help bilingual students comprehend what they read?
- What are inconsiderate texts?
- What are the most common expository text structures in English and Spanish?
- How do graphic organizers facilitate bilingual students' reading comprehension?
- What are the benefits of predictable books for beginning L2 learners?
- What are the advantages and disadvantages of decodable and leveled texts?
- Why is it important for bilingual and dual-language students to read and interact with multicultural texts?
- What role might dual-language texts play in the biliteracy development of bilingual students?

Ms. Saez is a 90–10, one-way, Spanish–English dual-language third-grade teacher. Her students receive 60% of their instruction in Spanish and 40% in English. The Fonsecas' 9-year-old, whom you met in Chapter 1, is in her class.

> When Ms. Saez met with one of her small reading-comprehension groups in Spanish, she realized that the students had not paid attention to the Spanish expository text on erosion that she had asked them to read because they shared ideas that were not in the text. So, she modeled how to use a cause-effect graphic organizer, and she asked them to reread the expository text, paying attention to the cause-effect text structure in the text. After they reread the text, she assigned them to work in heterogeneous (mixed reading level) groups to complete the cause-effect graphic organizer for the erosion text. Then, she met with the students to discuss their comprehension of the text. This time the students showed that they had read and understood the information in the text.

As teachers of bilingual students, you should select high-quality L1, L2, multicultural, and dual-language texts for your bilingual students to read, discuss, and learn from. Multicultural texts focus on the lives and experiences of people of color and/or those from diverse backgrounds (Clark, Flores, Smith, & González, 2016; Harris, 1993; Willis, García, Barrera, & Harris, 2002). The phrase "diverse backgrounds" refers to people who are not from the societal majority (i.e., they are *not* from the middle or upper class, native-English speakers, or Anglo). Multicultural texts also can include people with disabilities and those who differ in religion and gender from the majority. In this book, a dual-language text is defined as a text presented in two languages. Throughout the chapter, a plus before the title of a text (+) indicates that it is multicultural, and a (+) before the author's name indicates that the author is known to be of color or from a diverse background. When books in Spanish are discussed, the English translations of the titles are in parentheses.

To keep pace with the academic progress of monolingual native-English speakers in the United States, bilingual students need to read and comprehend texts that address state standards and those of professional associations, such as the National Council for the Social Studies (2013) and Next Generation Science Standards Lead States (2013). According to the Common Core State Standards (CCSS; National Governors Association [NGA] Center for Best Practices & Council of Chief State School Officers [CCSSO], 2010), all elementary students should comprehend, write, and use narrative and expository or informational texts.

The discussion in this chapter begins with narrative texts because they generally are easier for bilingual teachers to find in English, Spanish, and other languages than expository or informational texts. Multicultural texts and dual-language texts are discussed in more detail toward the end of the chapter.

NARRATIVE TEXTS

Fictitious Narrative Texts

Fiction, drama, and poetry are the three types of narrative texts that are fictitious or not true (Stahl & García, 2022). To write fiction, authors employ their imaginations, their senses, their experiences, and other people's experiences. Different genres or types of fiction include fables, fairytales, fantasies, folktales, historical fiction, mysteries, mythology, realistic fiction, and science fiction, among others. An example of English fantasy fiction is *The Hobbit* (Tolkien, 2002). +*¡Qué montón de tamales! (Too many tamales!)* (+Soto, 1996) is an example of Spanish realistic fiction and multicultural literature.

Authors who write dramas use dialogue and artistic performance to convey stories (Stahl & García, 2022). At least four genres characterize dramas in literature: comedy, tragedy, melodrama, and farce. Dramas in the performing arts are ballets, dances, mimes, operas, musicals, and plays. An example of a bilingual musical, in which Spanish and English are used, is +*In the Heights* (+Miranda, 2008).

To write poetry, authors employ words, rhymes, and rhythm to create images and emotions (Stahl & García, 2022). One of the more popular collections of published poems in English for children is *Where the Sidewalk Ends* (+Silverstein, 2014). A popular publication of Spanish poems for young children is +*Todo es canción: Antología poética* (*Everything is a song: Poetry anthology*) (+Ada, 2016). When poems are put to music, they become songs.

Narrative Nonfiction Texts

There also are narrative texts that are nonfiction. Popular forms of narrative nonfiction are autobiographies and biographies, which are based on real people but are written like narratives (Stahl & García, 2022). An autobiographical example is +*Pasando páginas: La historia de mi vida (Turning Pages: The Story of My Life)* by +Supreme Court Justice Sonia Sotomayor (2018), available in Spanish and English. Personal accounts in magazines or newspapers often are nonfiction narratives. Table 5.1 provides a list of narrative fiction and narrative nonfiction texts available in English, Spanish, and/or other languages for elementary students to read.

Narrative Text Structure

How an author organizes a text is called text structure. The text structure for narrative fiction and narrative nonfiction in English and Spanish is the

TABLE 5.1. Narrative Fiction and Narrative Nonfiction in English, Spanish, and Other Languages

English narrative fiction: Texts and recommended grade levels	Spanish (SP) and other languages (Other)	English narrative nonfiction: Texts and recommended grade levels	Spanish (SP) and other languages (Other)
Rosie Revere, the Engineer (Questioneering) (Beatty, 2013), PreK–3	SP	+*One Plastic Bag: Isatou Ceesay and the Recycling Women of the Gambia* (Paul, 2015), 1–3	SP
Mouse Soup (Lobel, 1983), K–3	No	*Bunny the Brave War Horse: Based on a True Story* (MacLeod, 2014), 1–3	Other
The Princess in Black (Hale & Hale, 2015), 1–3	SP	*Messi: A Boy Who Became a Star* (Herman, 2017), 1–3	SP
The Nocturnals: The Mysterious Abductions (Hecht, 2016), 3–5	No	*What If You Met a Cowboy?* (Adkins, 2013), 1–4	No
The Lightning Thief (Percy Jackson and the Olympians, Book 1) (Riordan, 2006), 2–6	SP and Other	*Sybil Ludington's Revolutionary War Story (Narrative Nonfiction: Kids in War)* (Marisco, 2018), 2–4	No
Where the Red Fern Grows (Rawls, 1996), 3–7	SP and Other	+*Bruce Lee: A Kid's Book about Pursuing Your Passions (Mini Movers and Shakers)* (Nhin, 2020), 2–4	No
Bridge to Terabithia (Paterson, 2008), 4–7	SP and Other	+*The Story of Ruth Bader Ginsburg: A Biography Book for New Readers* (+Katz, 2020), 2–4	No
Holes (Holes series) (Sachar, 2000), 5–6	SP and Other	*An Elephant in the Garden: Inspired by a True Story* (Morpurgo, 2013), 4–6	No

story grammar. Although story grammars vary somewhat according to the genre or type of narrative, narratives usually include a beginning, a middle, and an end; a narrator who tells the story; and the following components (Stahl & García, 2022):

- The setting (time and place that the story occurs).
- The characters (major and minor).

- The problem(s) that the major character(s) need to resolve or goal(s) that the major characters need to attain.
- Events during which the major character(s) attempt to resolve the problem or attain the goal.
- The ending: How the major character(s) resolve or do not resolve the problem or attain or do not attain the goal.

In addition, narrative fiction often has a message, moral/lesson, or theme.

Narrative Graphic Organizers: Story Maps

Graphic organizers are visual depictions of a text's organization. The graphic organizer for the story grammar is the story map. Story maps show how an author has structured or organized a narrative. They can vary in their complexity, with some just focusing on the beginning, middle, and end of a narrative, while others include all of the story's components (Stahl & García, 2022). The website *www.readingrockets.org* provides templates for story maps that you can download.

Completing a story map for a narrative helps students read the narrative carefully or closely, paying attention to the important details. When students can identify the features of a narrative according to its story map and the message or theme of the story, then they usually comprehend the narrative. Figure 5.1 shows a completed story map in English for the narrative fable *The Three Little Pigs*.

Setting: Countryside where the mother pig and three little pigs live.

Major Characters: Three pigs and the wolf

Minor Character: The pigs' mother

Initiating Events: The mother pig tells the three little pigs they are old enough to leave her house. The wolf is hungry.

Event 1: The first pig quickly builds a house of straw, which the wolf blows down. The pig runs to his brother's house.

Event 2: The second pig quickly builds a house of twigs, which the wolf blows down. The two pigs run to their brother's house.

Event 3: It takes the third pig a while to build a house of brick. However, the wolf cannot blow it down.

Ending: The wolf enters the brick house through the chimney, but the three pigs start a fire and scare the wolf. He never returns.

Moral or Lesson: Hard work takes time but is worth it.

FIGURE 5.1. Completed story map for "The Three Little Pigs."

You should explicitly teach bilingual students how to identify and use story maps to facilitate their text comprehension. This instruction can be in whole-class or small groups, and it begins in first grade. Throughout your instruction, you need to acknowledge students' correct answers and explain their incorrect answers. I recommend that you teach your students according to the GRR (gradual release of responsibility; see Pearson & Gallagher, 1983, Chapter 8). That is, as the teacher, you will define the task, model what you want your students to do; provide collaborative practice by working with them; give them guided practice so that they work on their own but with your help; and lastly, assign your students to do the task independently. The easiest way to teach narrative text structure is to model each story map component as you conduct an interactive teacher read-aloud of a narrative text. Before you begin, give each student a story map to complete for the book you are going to read and discuss. Then, before reading any of the text, you should post the definitions of the different story map components.

DEFINITIONS OF STORY MAP COMPONENTS

The setting: Time and place that the story occurs.

Major characters: The focus of the story. Those who have a goal or a problem. They attempt to meet the goal or solve the problem throughout the book.

Minor characters: A minor focus of the story. They appear in parts of the book but not throughout the book.

Problem/Goal: What the major character(s) want to solve or achieve or obtain.

Events: What the major character(s) do to attain the goal or solve the problem.

Ending: How the story concludes: What do the main characters do, not do, or attain?

Plot: The events in the story and the ending.

Moral/Lesson: A message or a lesson learned from the story.

Theme: What the story reveals about the human condition.

Then, as you read aloud a narrative text, you should conduct a think-aloud by explaining how you are determining each of the story map components. Next, give your students a story map to complete for a new text that you read aloud. Then, ask your students to work in pairs to identify the clues for each story map component. Once they give the correct answers for a component, go to the next component. If they give you an incorrect answer, be sure to explain why it is incorrect. You will need to repeat this work with story maps and texts until your students can do the story maps on their own.

EXPOSITORY TEXTS

Expository texts are nonfiction texts that provide facts and information. For this reason, they often are called informational texts. You can find these texts in the library, online, in the mail, in magazines, newspapers, and textbooks, or you can purchase them from bookstores or online vendors. According to the CCSS (NGA & CCSSO, 2010), half of the texts fourth graders in United States schools read should be expository texts, with the percentage increasing to 70% when students are seniors in high school (Collier, 2013). One reason for the high percentage of expository texts in high school is that these are the texts that teach students about the past and current world around them. They inform students.

Locating expository texts that elementary students enjoy reading is not easy. Sometimes, authors of expository texts use narrative features to make the texts appealing to elementary students. Two English examples are *Giant Squid* (Fleming, 2016) and *Feathers: Not Just for Flying* (Stewart, 2014). Stead (2014) recommends that you ask your school librarian for titles of expository texts that will interest your students. She also advises you to keep a log of expository texts that you use, to record your students' evaluation of the texts for future use, and to share your log and students' evaluations with other teachers.

Expository Text Structures

When authors of expository texts organize the main ideas and details according to text structures that match their purposes, then the texts usually are easier for students to comprehend than when they do not (Stahl & García, 2022). For example, if the author's purpose is to compare and contrast two animals, then it is helpful when the author compares and contrasts the characteristics of the two animals by employing signal or clue words. Signal words for the comparison–contrast text structure in English (or Spanish) include "different (*diferente*), similar (*similar*), same (*lo mismo*), however (*sin embargo*), and in contrast (*por el contrario*). Table 5.2 shows the most common text structures, signal words (Meyer, 1985), and short text examples in English.

Inconsiderate and Considerate Expository Texts

Armbruster and Anderson (1985) complained that many English expository texts were written so that they were inconsiderate; that is, the authors did not make it easy for readers to comprehend them. For example, not all authors write an expository text according to a single text structure. Sometimes they employ multiple text structures in one text, making it difficult

TABLE 5.2. Expository Text Structures

Text structure	Organizational purpose	Signal or clue words	Text example
Description	To identify features or characteristics of a person, place, event, or object.	*for example, such as, another type, for instance*	There are different types of annual plants. For example, impatiens, begonias, and marigolds are all annual plants.
Sequence	To list events, procedures, processes in order of occurrence.	*first, second, third, then, next, finally, last*	When you brush your teeth, you first have to put toothpaste on your toothbrush. Then you have to wet the toothbrush. Next, you put it in your mouth . . . .
Cause–effect	To explain what initiates something and the end result.	*cause, therefore, led to, resulted in, if–then*	Erosion caused the Grand Canyon. When it rained, water entered cracks in the rocks, resulting in their breaking up.
Comparison–contrast	To identify similarities and differences.	*different, same, similar, however, in contrast, like, whereas*	Both dogs and cats serve as pets. However, dogs are social animals, whereas cats are independent animals.
Problem–solution	To indicate a problem and its resolution.	*problem, caused, solved, response, so, because, as a result, therefore*	Scientists and doctors discovered that smoking caused cancer. Secondhand smoke also adversely affected people. However, many people did not stop smoking. So, some states and communities banned smoking in public indoor areas.

to identify a single text structure. When this occurs, you, the teacher, need to chunk the text by identifying the sections of text that logically fit certain text structures and provide students with this information. Other times, you may be able to figure out the author's purpose and superimpose a text structure on the text. Again, you should tell your students why you chose the text structure that you superimposed.

Several reading researchers have provided recommendations for selecting expository texts for students (Armbruster & Anderson, 1985). Walsh (2015) explains that texts

- should be well organized at the text level so that readers can easily identify the text structure, main ideas, and supporting details.
- should be well organized at the sentence level; that is, they should include transition words, conjunctions, and clear pronoun referents so that readers can make accurate connections or inferences across sentences and paragraphs.
- should have introductory paragraphs that tell the readers what they are going to read.
- should include headings and subheadings to guide the readers' comprehension.
- should define difficult vocabulary within the text.
- should include clear graphs, tables, and charts to help students understand the text. (Walsh, 2015)

Fewer expository texts are available in Spanish compared to English for children's use in the United States. Several publishing companies in the United States publish Spanish translations of English expository texts, such as the National Geographic Readers and Smithsonian: Informational Text. Spanish narrative and expository texts for children also can be purchased from publishers in other countries, such as, Argentina, Colombia, Mexico, Venezuela, and Spain. Increasingly, publishers in the United States are developing and selling dual-language informational books, written in English and Spanish, as well as a few other languages (Domke, 2020).

How to Use Expository Text Structures with Bilingual Students in Grades K-2

Teachers often introduce comparison–contrast, sequence, and description text structures to help students in grades K–2 understand and recall the information in expository texts. Young students find these text structures easier to understand when graphic organizers illustrate them because the graphic organizers show the relationships among the ideas in the texts. For example, you can use Venn diagrams to illustrate the comparison–contrast text structure. The shared area of the Venn diagram lists what the items or topics have in common, while the separate areas list the differences:

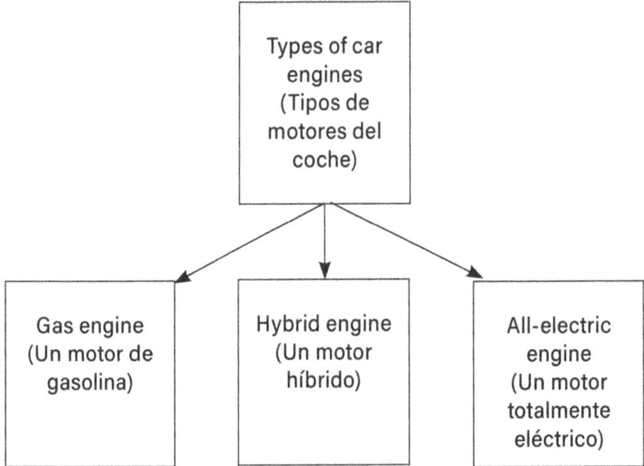

FIGURE 5.2. Example of a description graphic organizer (Spanish translation in parentheses).

Flowcharts illustrate the steps or procedures in a sequence text structure.

Figure 5.2 provides an example of a graphic organizer for the description text structure.

How to Teach Expository Text Structures to Bilingual Students in Grades 3-6

When students are in grades 3–6, you should use the GRR (Pearson & Gallagher, 1983; Chapter 8) to explicitly teach them how to identify and employ text structures when they read and write. You should teach and practice only one text structure at a time. To get started, you first need to find or write a short text that fits the text structure you are teaching (Akhondi, Malayeri, & Samad, 2011). Next, you should orally explain your thinking (i.e., do a think-aloud) about how you use the author's purpose and signal or clue words to identify the text structure. Then, you should give your students the opportunity to identify the text structures in several short texts that you provide. After they have successfully identified the text structures for about four texts, you should ask your students to write short texts following the specified text structure by using the appropriate signal words.

Use of Frames to Initiate Student Writing

You can give your students frames to get started on their text structure writing (Stahl & García, 2022). Frames are paragraphs in which key words have been deleted, which students have to provide. Figure 5.3 shows a frame for the sequence text structure in English. Because bilingual students may not always have the necessary language proficiency to identify the missing words, you may have to provide them with word options. There are two sets of word options for the sequence text structure in Figure 5.3: (1) first, second, third, and fourth or (2) first, next, then, and lastly or finally.

Student Use of Graphic Organizers

After completing the above instruction for each text structure, you should show your students how to use graphic organizers. Using graphic organizers should help your students to identify the main ideas and supporting details in expository texts (Akhondi et al., 2011; Stahl & García, 2022).

You can start by giving your students a completed graphic organizer for a text with a clear text structure. You can use a published text or write your own text. You should review the completed graphic organizer by showing your students how it matches the text structure in the text.

Next, you should give your students a blank graphic organizer along with a new text that follows the same text structure, and you should ask them to complete it in pairs. After your students complete the graphic organizer, be sure to review your students' work, sharing what they did well and what they need to improve. Continue this work until your students have a good command of how to use graphic organizers with each text structure. Figure 5.4 shows a graphic organizer for the problem–solution text structure.

SPECIFIC TYPES OF TEXTS

Texts for Beginning Readers

Beginning English readers often are given two types of texts to read: decodable texts and leveled texts. Because Spanish is fairly easy to decode, Spanish-speaking countries rarely use Spanish decodable texts. In the United States, beginning Spanish readers sometimes are given leveled texts to read.

To make a peanut butter and jelly sandwich, you ____________ need two slices of bread, a jar of peanut butter, a jar of jelly, and a knife. ____________ you need to put the bread on a plate. ____________ you open the jars of peanut butter and jelly. ____________ you use the knife to spread the peanut butter and jelly on the bread. Now, you are ready to eat the peanut butter and jelly sandwich.

FIGURE 5.3. Frame for sequence text structure.

Problem: People who live in subtropical and tropical parts of the world can get malaria when a mosquito infected by a parasite bites them. Malaria is a disease that can be fatal.

Action: Scientists developed vaccines and insecticides that killed infected mosquitoes. People began to wear protective clothing and sleep under protective nets. The United Nations provided funds to eradicate malaria in 15 African countries.

Results: Since 2006, the death rate from malaria has been reduced by 45.3%.

FIGURE 5.4. Example of a problem–solution graphic organizer.

Decodable Texts

Decodable texts include words with letter–sound patterns that already have been explicitly taught to students, along with "a few necessary high-frequency words, such as *the*, *is*, and *on*" (Cunningham, 2017, p. 250). Because decodable texts provide beginning readers with the opportunity to apply their phonics skills to the reading of simple texts, Stahl and I (2015) recommend that they be used during English word study/phonics instruction. However, they are too simple to be used during other reading activities.

Leveled Texts

Unlike decodable texts, the words in leveled texts do not necessarily follow taught letter–sound patterns. Leveled texts in English and Spanish are texts ordered according to their text complexities, which include their word patterns, themes, and number of words (Hiebert, 2024). Students are assigned to read texts at specific reading levels according to how well they read unrehearsed graded passages in terms of word recognition accuracy and comprehension (Stahl & García, 2015). For example, my colleague and I explain (Stahl & García, 2015) that when reading with their teacher's support, known as instructional reading, authors of leveled texts recommend that students read leveled texts with 90–98% of word accuracy and excellent or satisfactory comprehension. To read on their own, or for independent reading, authors of leveled programs recommend that students read leveled texts with 95–100% word accuracy and excellent or satisfactory comprehension. When students demonstrate limited comprehension of a leveled text, then the required word recognition rate increases.

Although leveled texts may include trade books, these texts are usually written specifically for a leveled-text program. Two of the more popular leveled-text reading programs are Guided Reading in English (grades K–8)

(Fountas & Pinnell, 2011) and Guided Reading in Spanish (grades K–2) (Fountas, 2012).

Criticisms of Decodable and Leveled Texts

Critics of decodable texts complain that they are overly simple with limited vocabulary, stilted language, and nonengaging content (Schwartz, 2020). Cunningham (2017) explains that good readers in grade 3 and above need to know not only how to decode words during reading but also how to spell big (i.e., multisyllabic) words "based on similar patterns from other big words" (p. 200). According to Hiebert (2024), neither decodable texts nor leveled texts provide beginning English readers with the opportunities to see and understand large numbers of English words in texts, which are necessary for them to become proficient readers.

Basal Reading Series

Sometimes, school districts provide bilingual teachers with basal reading series. A basal reading series typically includes three to four large texts for the teacher (i.e., the teacher's edition) and smaller texts for the students. The teacher's edition includes the same texts that are in the student text: original narrative texts (fiction, some poems, and a few plays) or narrative excerpts from famous writers or published works, along with short informational texts. In addition, the teacher's edition includes instructions on how to use the texts, on what skills to teach, and on how to assess students' literacy performance. The series also includes student assignments and worksheets. A set of instructional texts at various reading levels for guided reading instruction sometimes are included, as are narrative and expository texts for teacher read-alouds. I suspect that with the advent of the Science of Reading, some companies will provide decodable texts instead of leveled texts for beginning readers. Given the large number of texts and instructional items in basal reading series, they usually are expensive, making it difficult for school districts to purchase and provide other books.

Although several basal reading series are available in English and Spanish (often called bilingual editions), the Spanish texts usually are translations of English texts. Before adopting a bilingual edition of a basal reading series, school personnel need to evaluate the quality of the non-English version. Several years ago, I had Spanish–English bilingual teachers call me to complain about the poor translations in a Spanish version of a well-known basal reading series. Feminine articles were used for masculine nouns and vice versa. Also, the authors treated learning to read in Spanish as if the students were learning to read in English. The basal reading series in Spanish emphasized phonemic awareness and sight words, which teachers in

Spanish-speaking countries typically do not emphasize when they teach students how to read in Spanish (Goldenberg et al., 2014).

Trade Books for Interactive Teacher Read-Alouds and Independent Reading

Trade books are written for the commercial market. They include fiction and nonfiction, big books, picture books, predictable books, and chapter books.

Big Books, Picture Books, and Predictable Books

Big books and picture books include narrative and expository texts. Big books have large print and illustrations that teachers show their students when they read the books aloud. Picture books include illustrations or photographs that help to convey the story or information being shared. The illustrations or photographs in picture books help students who are not fluent readers comprehend what is being read and to participate in a shared read-aloud, especially when the teacher reads the books aloud several times. Multicultural picture books provide images that help readers from diverse backgrounds see themselves in the books and affirm messages of cultural inclusivity and social equity for all readers (Marcus, 2012).

Predictable books include a rhythmic pattern and/or repetition. They help students who do not know how to read or who do not know how to read all the words in a book so that they can comprehend the book. An example of a predictable book is *Brown Bear, Brown Bear, What Do You See?* (Martin & Carle, 1992), which is also available in Spanish (*Oso pardo, oso pardo, ¿que ves ahí?*) and other languages. When predictable books are repeatedly read aloud, students become familiar with them and develop their oral and sight vocabulary. Many times, students will join in the book reading with you, doing a partial choral reading or a shared reading.

Predictable books and picture books often are written for students in K–2, but you also can use them with older students who do not know how to read well or who do not know how to read well in an L2. Both types of books are excellent for interactive teacher read-alouds and for beginning readers to read independently, especially after the teacher repeatedly has read the books aloud.

Chapter Books

With students in grades 3–6, you should use chapter books for interactive teacher read-alouds and students' independent reading. *Charlotte's Web*

(White, 1952) is an example of a chapter book. When I was conducting research in a fourth-grade Spanish–English bilingual teacher's classroom, she conducted an interactive teacher read-aloud of *La Telarana de Carlota,* the Spanish version of *Charlotte's Web.* She and I both were surprised when some of her Latinx students asked her what *pajo* (straw) meant. Upon reflection, we realized that her students lived in the inner city and probably had not visited a farm or had any reason to know the word. The interactive teacher read-aloud gave her students the opportunity to identify key vocabulary that they did not know in Spanish, their L1.

Before doing a teacher read-aloud of a chapter book, you first need to read the book and chunk it into meaningful sections. Then, I recommend that you have your students participate in an interactive teacher read-aloud of the individual book sections. Chapter books that you already read aloud to your students also are good books for your bilingual students to read independently because they have the appropriate prior knowledge and know what to expect in the book. State standards usually provide a list of English chapter books appropriate for students in grades 3–6 in the United States.

Multicultural Literature

All students should be exposed to multicultural literature by reading it, hearing it read aloud, and discussing and working with it. Multicultural literature refers to texts written by authors of color or from diverse backgrounds and/or texts about topics or stories that authentically portray the lives and experiences of people of color or from diverse backgrounds (Clark et al., 2016; Willis et al., 2002). To become motivated and competent readers, students of color or from diverse backgrounds need to see themselves in texts. Anglo students need to learn about the experiences of students different from themselves so that they are comfortable with people of color and those from diverse backgrounds. Table 5.3 presents a list of multicultural texts for use with bilingual students.

Most narrative and expository texts published in the United States focus on the experiences of Anglo students (Clark et al., 2016). The Associated Press (2021) reported that in 2020, the percentage of children's books published by authors of color represented only 26.8% of all the children's books published. Children's books about people of color or diverse people or their experiences represented 30% of the total number of children's books published. These percentages were much lower than the percentage of students from diverse ethnic/national/racial groups in the United States. According to the United States Census Bureau, in 2020, over 42% of the United States population identified as non-Anglo or as members of diverse groups. It is important to note that this percentage is lower than it should

TABLE 5.3. Multicultural Texts

Title, author, publication date	Grade level	People of color and/or diverse group
A Long Walk to Water (Park, 2011)	5–6+	Sudanese
Bendy-Bendy Road (Poudyal, 2023)	PreK–2	Nepalese
Brown Girl Dreaming (Woodson, 2016)	5–6	African American
Eyes That Kiss with the Corners (Ho, 2021)	PreK–3	Vietnamese
Hello, Universe (Kelly, 2020)	3–6+	Filipino
Inside Out and Back Again (Lai, 2011)	3–6+	Vietnamese
One Crazy Summer (Williams-García, 2011)	3–6+	African American
The Sky of Afghanistan (Eulate, 2012)	K–2	Afghan
The Proudest Blue: A Story of Hijab and Family (Muhammad, 2019)	PreK–3	Muslim
Soft Rain: A Story of the Cherokee Trail of Tears (Cornelissen, 1999)	3–6+	Cherokee
Tofu Takes Time (Wu, 2020)	PreK–3	Chinese
We Are Water Protectors (Lindstrom, 2020)	PreK–1	Ojibwe
When My Name Was Keoke (Park, 2012)	4–6+	Korean
When You Trap a Tiger (Keller, 2020)	3–6+	Korean
Anna María Reyes Does not Live in a Castle (Burgos, 2018)	4–6+	Dominican American
The Crossroads (Diaz, 2018)	6+	Guatemalan American

be because it does not include people who identified themselves as bi- or multiracial or as members of more than one ethnic/national/racial group.

When bilingual students can see themselves in texts, their motivation to read often improves, as do their text comprehension and learning because they can make connections between their background knowledge and what they are reading and learning (Clark et al., 2016; Willis et al., 2002). Students who do not have the appropriate background knowledge often experience difficulty in learning how to connect what they are reading with their background knowledge.

López-Robertson (2012) reported that bilingual students' discussion of multicultural texts facilitated their understanding of social justice issues and aided their development of critical consciousness, which improved their sense of school belonging (DeNicolo et al., 2017). Lee (2021) reported that when Korean American third graders in her Korean heritage language classroom read multicultural literature that portrayed Korean culture, it fostered their positive self-esteem and identities.

Dual-Language Texts

Although the number of published texts originally written in Spanish and other minority languages in the United States is not large, the number of dual-language texts published in English, Spanish, and other languages in the United States appears to be increasing. In this book, a dual-language text is defined as a text presented in two languages, whereas a bilingual text is defined as a text that includes words in more than one language (Domke, 2020). An example of a Spanish–English dual-language text is +*Pepita Speaks Twice/Pepita habla dos veces* (+Lachtman, 1995). An example of a bilingual text written in English but with Spanish words and phrases is +*Abuela* (+Dorros, 1997).

The formats of dual-language texts vary considerably (Domke, 2020). Sometimes the lines of text in each language are arranged so that one line is above the other, and the meanings of the two lines of text are the same or similar. Other times, the first half of a page is in one language, while the second half is in another language, often with an illustration in between. The two halves may be translations of each other or may convey similar meanings. Sometimes, versions of the text in each language are on separate pages or in two halves of a book. Given that the written text is duplicated in two languages and that illustrations often accompany the text, dual-language books tend to be short.

If your purpose in using dual-language texts is to provide your bilingual students with texts to read in a language other than English, then I recommend that you use texts in which the text first was written in the partner language, not English. When texts are translated from English, the translations do not always reflect the rhetorical styles and vocabulary that authentically characterize other languages (Domke, 2020).

A number of publishers in the United States provide dual-language texts in a variety of languages. Among these publishers are EastWest Discovery Press, Lee & Low Books, Scholastic, and Vista (Santillana). For instance, languagelizards (*www.languagelizard.com*) publishes early-childhood bilingual texts in English and 50 other languages, including Arabic, Chinese (Cantonese and Mandarin), French, Haitian Creole, Hindi, Hmong, Korean, Polish, Portuguese, Russian, Tagalog, and Vietnamese. Table 5.4 provides a list of dual-language texts published in English and other languages. You will notice that many of these books are for young bilingual children (preschool through grade 3).

There still is little empirical research on how bilingual students approach, read, and learn from dual-language books (Domke, 2022).

TABLE 5.4. Dual-Language Texts in English and Partner Languages

Title, author, publication date	Grade level	Partner language
A Day with Grandpa (Rose, 2020)	K–6	Arabic, Polish, other languages
Augustus and His Smile (Rayner, 2007)	PreK–1	Arabic
Beautiful Short Stories in English and Korean: Bilingual/Dual Language Picture Book for Beginners (Choi, 2018)	Not listed	Korean
Dim Sum, Please! (Mandarin edition) (Choi & Choi, 2021)	Not listed	Mandarin
Fly Little Bird/Vole, petit oiseau (Blum, 2021)	Not listed	French
Maya's Blanket: La manta de Maya (Brown, 2015)	1–2	Spanish
Marisol McDonald Doesn't Match/Marisol McDonald No Combina (Brown, 2013)	PreK–3	Spanish
Mulan: The Story of the Legendary Warrior Told in English and Chinese (Li, 2020)	PreK–3	Chinese
Nelly's Box/La boîte de Nelly (Arkolaki, 2022)	1–3	French, Greek, other languages
Rainbow Weaver/Tejadora del arcoíris (Marshall, 2016)	K–2	Spanish with Mayan words

Several researchers have hypothesized that reading dual-language books will promote bilingual students' metalinguistic awareness, vocabulary knowledge, and biliteracy development (Beeman & Urow, 2012; Escamilla et al., 2014). In support of the metalinguistic hypothesis, researchers in Canada reported that students in first (Naqvi, Thorne, Pftischer, Nordstokke, & McKeough, 2013) and fifth grade (Zaidi, 2020) who heard dual-language books read aloud in English or French and the languages spoken at home (Urdu, Punjabi, Tagalog, or Spanish) demonstrated enhanced metalinguistic awareness.

Very little empirical research has been done on how bilingual teachers can use dual-language texts to promote the literacy development of bilingual students. Domke (2022) recommended that bilingual teachers use dual-language texts to promote students' biliteracy development by identifying the similarities and differences in their two languages.

CONCLUDING REMARKS

When selecting texts for bilingual students to hear read aloud, to read with their teacher's support, to read independently, or to advance their learning, it is important to provide them with expository and narrative texts in both English and the partner language. Expository texts are especially important because these texts teach students new information. One way to help improve bilingual students' comprehension of narrative and expository texts is to teach them about narrative and expository text structures. Chapter 8 provides more information on how to improve bilingual students' reading comprehension of both types of texts. Chapter 11 explains how to use the texts for disciplinary literacy instruction in the language arts, science, and social studies.

When possible, I encourage you to use partner-language texts that originally were written in the respective language. You may have noticed that all the dual-language books listed in Table 5.3 are for children in preschool to third grade. I suspect that these books initially were written for use in early-exit TBE or ESL programs, which often do not go beyond third grade. Fortunately, there are chapter books in Spanish for older students to read. Given the critical focus of some multicultural texts, it also makes sense that more of these books are recommended for students in the intermediate grades (3–6).

I wish you and your students good reading!

L1 Literacy Instruction and Early Reading Instruction in Spanish and Other Languages

GUIDING QUESTIONS

- Why should emergent bilingual students receive L1 literacy instruction?
- Why should emergent bilingual students' L1 instruction continue throughout elementary school?
- What are the features of a rich literacy classroom?
- What is the syllabic approach for teaching beginning reading in Spanish?
- Why should schools continue to develop bilingual students' oral language in Spanish throughout elementary school?
- What is the reason for teaching the Spanish alphabet after students learn to read in Spanish?
- What do teachers need to know about teaching literacy in Arabic or Chinese?

Ms. Balik, the Turkish language teacher for a Transitional Program of Instruction (TPI), could not understand why Yusef, one of her Turkish-speaking students, was having difficulty learning to read in Turkish. Unlike English, Turkish has a transparent orthography in which each sound is represented by a single letter. Yusef also spoke Turkish well and had appropriate Turkish vocabulary for a first grader. Once Ms. Balik's Turkish first graders learned the Turkish alphabet and sound–letter correspondence in Turkish, they usually were able to decode Turkish first-grade texts with relative ease. However, Yusef seemed confused.

Ms. Balik asked to see Yusef's school record. It was then that she realized that Yusef had spent six weeks in an all-English classroom before the Turkish class began. She asked Ms. Reynolds, his teacher in the all-English classroom, about Yusef's performance in her classroom and what she had taught the students during the first six weeks of school. Ms. Reynolds told her that she taught the students the names of the letters in the English alphabet and began phonics instruction. Ms. Balik wondered if learning the English alphabet and some phonics in English before the Turkish alphabet and Turkish phonics was what had confused Yusef.

This chapter focuses on the role of the L1 in students' literacy development. Given the large numbers of Spanish-speaking, emergent bilingual students and students enrolled in Spanish–English dual-language programs in the United States, the emphasis here is on early reading instruction in Spanish. In addition, brief descriptions of literacy instruction in Arabic and Chinese, respectively, the second and third most frequently spoken minority languages of emergent bilingual students in the United States (National Center for English Language Acquisition [NCELA], 2019–2020), are presented.

THE IMPORTANCE OF L1 LITERACY INSTRUCTION

To accelerate the reading development of bilingual students after the pandemic, this book recommends that emergent bilingual students receive literacy instruction in their L1 or home language before they receive it in English, their L2. This does not mean that teachers and parents should not read English books to emergent bilingual children or that the children should not speak or write English at the same time that they are learning to read in their L1, but it does mean that explicit reading and spelling instruction in English, such as English phonics instruction, should be delayed until the children have established their L1 literacy performance. The vignette about Yusef, which opens the chapter, shows the difficulties that some students have when they are taught to read in English, their L2, before they are taught to read in their L1. Also, students' L1 literacy instruction should be based on the L1 structure and L1 practices characteristic of the countries in which the L1 is the societal language. Too often, bilingual students receive L1 reading instruction based on or influenced by English reading practices.

The Advantages of Learning to Read First in Languages with Transparent Orthographies

When the L1 has a transparent orthography (consistent sound–symbol writing system), such as Turkish and Spanish, then it usually is an easier language for students to learn to decode than English. English has an opaque orthography; that is, there are many irregularities in the sound–symbol writing system. Several researchers reported that young emergent bilingual students translanguaged by independently applying the strategies they had learned to use when they read in one language to read in another language (Camlibel & García, 2012; López-Velásquez & García, 2017). When this translanguaging occurs, it should be easier for students to apply what they learned about reading in a transparent language to reading in an opaque language, than vice versa.

In a study that compared the literacy development of two Spanish-speaking first graders, my colleague and I (López-Velásquez & García, 2017) reported that Nina, the student who received Spanish literacy instruction first, was able to effectively apply what she had learned about decoding in Spanish to English decoding, whereas the student who learned English literacy first (Andrea) could not effectively apply what she knew about English decoding to Spanish decoding. For example, Nina effectively applied the syllabic approach that she had learned in Spanish to decode in English. In the syllabic approach, the student divides a word into syllables, says each syllable, and then blends the syllables to read the entire word.

However, Andrea, the student who learned to decode in English, could not effectively use the onset-rime approach that she had learned in English to decode in Spanish (López-Velásquez & García, 2017). In the onset-rime approach, the student reads the word by identifying the initial sound (the onset), followed by the rime. Thus, to read *cat*, the student reads *c*, then *at*, blending the sounds to get *cat*. However, the onset-rime approach does not work well with multisyllabic words. For example, Andrea tried to use this method to decode the Spanish word *familiares* (family members or relatives), but she could not figure out how to do it. Spanish has a lot of multisyllabic words, even in beginning reading texts, which makes the employment of the onset-rime approach problematic.

Continued L1 Instruction throughout Elementary School

Teachers should continue to provide emergent bilingual students with L1 instruction throughout elementary school, even when the students have learned to speak and read in English (Escamilla et al., 2014). Continued L1 instruction facilitates students' development of background knowledge, vocabulary, and academic learning, which they can utilize when learning in English. Continued L1 instruction also helps bilingual students to develop strong bilingual and academic identities, that is, positive attitudes about themselves as bilingual individuals and learners in school (Hamman-Ortiz & Palmer, 2020).

RICH LITERACY ACTIVITIES COMBINED WITH EXPLICIT READING INSTRUCTION

The pandemic's emphasis on remote instruction meant that many young emergent bilingual students did not receive the rich literacy exposure and environment needed to facilitate their reading. Therefore, to accelerate students' reading, this book recommends combining rich literacy activities with explicit instruction on L1 reading strategies.

So that your students understand that literacy conveys meaning and involves communication between the reader and the author, I strongly encourage you to create a rich literacy setting in your classroom. A rich literacy setting involves implementing many of the activities described in Chapter 4: rhymes and songs, morning messages, shared reading, interactive teacher read-alouds, the language experience approach, and student discussion. Escamilla et al. (2014) also recommend that you conduct Lotta Lara to develop students' oral language and reading fluency.

Lotta Lara

Lotta Lara (Escamilla et al., 2014) involves nine repeated readings of the same text over a period of three days, accompanied by instruction on vocabulary and linguistic structures in the text (e.g., how to express events that happened in the past and conditional language). Before beginning Lotta Lara, the teacher should select, read, and pre-plan the use of a text in terms of what the students are studying, as well as their reading levels, cultural backgrounds, and language proficiencies. When reading the text, the students need to see the text or have their own copies of it. On the first day of Lotta Lara, the teacher introduces linguistic structures and vocabulary in the text, provides background knowledge, reads the text aloud, and has the students participate in echo and choral readings (see Chapter 4). On the second day, the vocabulary and linguistic structures previously introduced are reviewed. The students also do echo and choral readings of the same text with the teacher. On the third day, they work in partners to read the text aloud. Comprehension (e.g., making inferences) and oral language extensions related to the text (e.g., how to express cause and effect orally and in writing) are provided and practiced throughout the three days.

Classroom Library

A rich literacy setting also involves a classroom library of books in students' L1 and L2 that students can look at freely. Books that you read aloud to your students should be in the classroom library along with big books, predictable books, picture books, informational books, and chapter books (see Chapter 5). There should be a time during the school day when your students are encouraged to select a book and look at it individually or with a partner. In partner reading, two students take turns softly reading the text aloud to each other.

Student Discussion

Lastly, emergent bilingual students need to continue to develop their oral language, which is a foundation for their reading and writing. Therefore, you should create opportunities for students to interact and discuss with you and each other what they are learning, hearing read, reading, and writing. In these discussions, students should be free to use their L1 and/or L2 and to translanguage.

EARLY READING INSTRUCTION IN SPANISH

If your state does not provide standards to guide your Spanish language and literacy instruction, then I suggest you refer to the Common Core Language Arts/Literacy Standards in Spanish (San Diego County Office of Education, December 2012). This publication includes linguistic areas specific to Spanish (e.g., decoding emphasis on vowels, teaching of accents) along with translations of the appropriate English CCSS (NGA for Center for Best Practices & CCSSO, 2010). Two other resources are the World-Class Instructional Design and Assessment's (WIDA) Spanish language standards (WIDA, 2013) and Spanish language arts standards (WIDA, 2023b).

Syllabic Approach

One of the most popular Spanish reading instructional approaches in Mexico, Latin America, and Spain is the syllabic approach (Escamilla et al., 2014). YouTube videos from Chile, Mexico, and Spain show how to use the syllabic approach. Texts that cover beginning reading in Spanish also review this approach, such as Freeman and Freeman (2009, 2023), as do commercial Spanish reading programs (*Estrellita: Accelerated beginning Spanish reading*, 2023).

When implementing the syllabic approach, teachers first instruct students about each of the five vowel sounds. After students learn the vowels, teachers instruct students on how to say and write the consonants. Then, they teach students how to read vowel–consonant combinations in the form of syllables and words. After students learn how to read words, teachers teach them the names of the letters in the Spanish alphabet.

Vowels

Table 6.1 shows the five Spanish vowels (*a, e, i, o,* and *u*), their sounds in Spanish, their phonemes, and their approximate pronunciations in English. Unlike English, there usually is only one sound for each Spanish vowel. However, sometimes a vowel sound changes depending on the consonants that surround it. For instance, in Spanish, the *u* is silent after *q*, as in the word *quieto* (still) (Ford & Palacios, 2015).

YouTube videos from Chile, Mexico, and Spain show how to use the syllabic approach to teach the five vowel sounds to beginning readers of Spanish. They warn that you should teach the vowel sounds, not the vowel names. You teach the vowel names when you teach the Spanish alphabet at the end of your syllabic instruction.

To make sure your students understand the relationship between your vowel instruction and reading, I recommend that you begin instruction of each vowel with a teacher read-aloud of a text that includes the vowel you are teaching. Before posting the text so that your students can see it, you should underline or highlight every appearance of the vowel that you are teaching. Then, explain to your class that they are going to learn how to say and read this vowel, as you point to the words with the vowel in it. In the following text example, the letter *o* is in bold, with the translation in parentheses.

> Ve**o** las h**o**rmigas en el pati**o**. Ah**o**ra, están en el c**o**med**o**r. Las ve**o** en la c**o**cina. ¡Esper**o** que n**o** se c**o**man t**o**da la c**o**mida!
>
> (I see the ants on the patio. Now, they're in the dining room. I see them in the kitchen. I hope they don't eat all the food!)

Then, when you begin your vowel instruction, show your students a chart with the vowel in printed capital letters and lower-case letters, along with illustrations of words that start with the vowel. For example, if you are teaching the vowel *a*, use a chart with the vowel printed in the

TABLE 6.1. Spanish Vowels

Vowel (capital)	Vowel (lower-case)	Spanish vowel sound	Phoneme	Approximate English sound
A	a	a = *paso* (*step)	/a/	ah as in *father*
E	e	e = *peso* (*weight)	/e/	eh as in *fed*
I	i	i = *piso* (*apartment)	/i/	ee as in *eel*
O	o	o = *poso* (*hole)	/o/	oh as in *oh no*
U	u	u = *puso* (*he/she put)	/u/	oo as in *moon*

Note. Asterisk (*) indicates English translation.

capital (*A*) and lower-case letter (*a*), along with cursive examples of the capital and lower-case letters. On the chart you should have illustrations of words that start with *a*, such as *abeja* (bee), *árbol* (tree), *ardilla* (squirrel), and *almohada* (pillow). Post the chart where everyone in the class can see it. When you point to the vowel, you say the vowel sound, and again before naming each of the illustrations, asking your students to repeat after you. Do this repeatedly until your students can say the vowel sound by themselves. Then, ask them to volunteer other words, items, and foods that begin with the vowel sound. For example, for the vowel *a*, they could volunteer *alfombra* (rug), *amario* (closet), *agua* (water), *araña* (spider), and *acera* (sidewalk). Be sure to write the words where the students can see them, underlining the vowel *a* in each of the words. If you have illustrations or drawings of the words, post these for each word. Have your students repeat the vowel sound and the words that begin with it multiple times. Once your students have learned the vowel sound, use the same process to teach the next vowel. When they have learned several vowel sounds, mix up the order of the vowels before asking them to tell you the vowel sounds.

Consonants

There are 22 consonants in the Spanish alphabet—the same 21 consonants in the English alphabet plus an additional consonant, *ñ*. In addition, there are three consonant combinations that do not occur in English: *ch*, *ll*, and *rr*. You should not teach the Spanish consonant names until after your students have learned all the vowel and consonant sounds and can read syllables and simple words.

I advise that you follow Ford and Palacios's (2015) recommendations for teaching Spanish consonants. They recommend that you first teach several of the most frequent consonants in Spanish: *m*, *l*, *s*, and *p*. Then, before teaching other consonants, you can combine the taught consonants with vowels to create frequent words (e.g., *mamá*), which should be motivating for your students. Then, you should teach the next most frequent consonants (*n*, *b*, *d*, *t*, and *f*), also combining them with vowels to create words. The last set of consonants you should teach are *c*, *g*, *h*, *j*, *k*, *q*, *r*, *v*, *w*, *x*, *y*, and *z*.

The teaching methods for the consonant sounds are similar to the vowel instruction. First, you post and read aloud a short story or poem that has words in it that include the consonant, which you have underlined. Then, you show your students a consonant chart similar to the vowel chart, with the consonant written in capital and lower-case letters and in cursive, along with illustrations of words that begin with the consonant. So, for the sound *m*, you could use the words *martillo* (hammer), *mariposa* (butterfly), *manzana* (apple), *mono* (monkey), and *maleta* (suitcase). When your students can identify the consonant sound by themselves, ask them to volunteer other words, items, and foods that begin with the consonant sound, which you post along with illustrations or drawings of the words. Have your students repeat the consonant sound and the words that begin with it multiple times. Once they know several consonant sounds, mix up the order of the consonants before asking them to name the sounds and words that begin with the sounds.

Consonant and Vowel Combinations

After your students have learned a consonant sound, you should show them how to combine it with a vowel to create a consonant–vowel (CV) pattern (Ford & Palacios, 2015). For example, for *m*, you should show your students how to combine the sound of *m* with the vowel *a* to say and write the syllable *ma*, followed by the word *mamá* (mother). Then, you should teach each of the following syllables (*me, mi, mo,* and *mu*) and how to combine two of the syllables to create words: *mesa* (table), *mima* (spoils), *moto* (motorcycle), and *mujer* (woman). Next, you should show them how to read simple sentences with the created words: *Mi mamá me ama.* (My mother loves me). *Amo a mi mama.* (I love my mother). *Mi mamá me mima.* (My mother spoils me.)

The next step is to teach your students how to combine consonants and vowels to read *el* and *la*. You should pair the articles with the respective words that already have been presented, and have your students practice reading them aloud in the class and to each other in partners.

Then, you need to teach your students how to read words with the CVC pattern, such as *sol* (sun), followed by words with consonant blends (in bold), such as ***bl**usa* (blouse) and diphthongs (underlined), such as *ciudad* (city) (Ford & Palacios, 2015, n.p.). When teaching dipthongs (e.g., *ai, ei, ie, io*), you need to explain that when there are two vowels in a single syllable, they blend to make one sound.

Ford and Palacio (2015, n.p.) indicate that the silent *h* in words like *hora* (hour) and the silent *u* after *g* or *q*, in words such as *guiso* (stew) and *quieto* (still), should be taught after students have learned most of the consonant sounds. Letters that vary in their sounds according to their placement in a word, such as *c* and *g*, usually are taught last, as are consonants that occur infrequently, such as *z, k, x,* and *w*.

A Spanish kindergarten teacher with whom I collaborated created large cards with the initial CV patterns for key words on them along with pictures or photos of the objects or animals. For instance, for the *mo* syllable, she had a picture of a monkey (*mono*), the word *mono*, and the syllable *mo* written in big letters. After the teacher introduced each of the cards and had her students repeat the syllables and words after her, she asked individual students to read the syllables and words on the cards.

You also can use this technique to teach other syllables, the three letter combinations—*ch, ll,* and *rr*—and dipthongs. Then, if you have a word center, you can place the cards in the center and assign pairs or small groups of students to the center to test each other on the vowel and consonant sounds, the syllables, and how to read words with the letter combinations or dipthongs.

Reading Simple Books

Once students can decode several words, you may ask them to read small books that use the words. The teacher I mentioned earlier created little books with short narratives based on the sounds, syllables, and words that she already had taught her students. The students read the books aloud with her, in partners, and by themselves. Several companies in the United States also publish beginning readers in Spanish, such as the American Reading Company (ARC) Press (*https://americanreading.com/arc-press*) and Estrellita (*www.estrellita.com*, 2023).

According to Ford and Palacios (2015), once children know the basic sound–symbol correspondences in Spanish, then they can easily decode most Spanish words. In fact, by the end of first grade, most Spanish-speaking children can read simple Spanish texts with a high level of accuracy. Sight words, frequent words that are difficult to decode, such as *the* and *said* in English, do not occur in Spanish as they do in English.

A major assumption is that the words that students decode are in their oral vocabulary, so they automatically know what the words mean. However, after receiving syllabic instruction, students also can decode unfamiliar words for which they do not know the meanings. To aid your students' comprehension, you should remember to facilitate their oral language development by implementing many of the activities introduced in Chapter 4: songs and rhymes, the morning message, choral and shared reading, and interactive teacher read-alouds, along with Lotta Lara (Escamilla et al., 2014). In addition, to make sure that your students understand the purpose of decoding, you need to provide them with opportunities to discuss and write responses to texts that you read aloud or that they read.

Of course, decoding is not all that beginning readers need to do to comprehend Spanish texts. Spanish reading comprehension instruction in both the whole-class setting and small groups will help bilingual students to advance their Spanish reading (see Chapters 5 and 8). Chapter 7 identifies the reading strategies that should be taught to bilingual students who are beginning readers in Spanish and English. Chapter 8 describes a dialogic strategy program that was successfully implemented with

Spanish-speaking second graders in an early-exit transitional bilingual education classroom.

Teaching the Spanish Alphabet

After students have begun to read simple books, they are ready to learn the Spanish alphabet. In 2010, the Real Academia de Español (Royal Spanish Academy) made several changes to the Spanish alphabet. They decided that the following letter combinations were not letters in the Spanish alphabet: *ch, ll, rr*. Also, they changed the names for the following letters: *r, v, w*, and *y*. The letter name for *r* is now *erre*. The letter name for *v* is *uve*; for *w*, it is *doble uve*; and for *y*, it is *ye*. One reason the Spanish alphabet should be taught after teaching the letter sounds is that some of the letter names do not match the letter sounds. For instance, students cannot use the letter name for *h*—*hache*—to decode words with "*h*" in them or *jota*, the letter name for *j* to decode words with *j* in them.

If students already know the vowel and consonant sounds, they should learn the alphabet easily. You can tell them that some of the vowel and consonant sounds are the same as the letter names, but others are different.

To teach the alphabet, use a chart with capital and lower-case letters and pictures or illustrations of words that begin with the letters. Use a pointer to point to each letter, say the letter names, and have students repeat each name after you several times. Then, point to different letters on the chart and have students tell you the names. You also can dictate the letters in the alphabet to your students. Then show the students cards with the capital and lower-case letters of the alphabet on them. Have them say and repeat the names after you. Put the cards in a word center, where students can practice identifying the letter names on the cards. Students also can learn to sing an alphabet song (many of them are on YouTube). In addition, you can conduct shared reading of Spanish alphabet books. A list of Spanish alphabet books is provided in the following box.

SPANISH ALPHABET BOOKS

Abecedario de los animales (Ada, 1990)

Abecedario escondido (Santamans, 2017)

Día a día, letra a letra, de la A a la Z (Oro, 2017)

El ABC de la comida Puertorriqueña (Juliá, & Montalvo, 2020)

El abecedario de Lucía (El mundo de Lucía) (Mariscal, 2017)

La casa de las letras (Punset & Serrano, 2014)

Puerto Rico en ABC (Orta, 2020)

LITERACY INSTRUCTION IN ARABIC AND CHINESE

This section briefly discusses a method for teaching literacy in Arabic or Chinese to elementary-age students in the United States. After Spanish, the two languages most frequently spoken by emergent bilingual students (K–12) in the United States are Arabic and Chinese (NCELA, 2019–2020). Brief comparisons with literacy instruction in English and Spanish are provided, along with recommended websites and readings for additional information.

The Arabic Language

Arabic is the second most frequently spoken minority language by emergent bilingual students in the United States. In 2019–2020, there were 124,410 speakers of Arabic in grades K–12 (NCELA, 2019–2020). Arabic is spoken in 24 countries. However, most speakers of Arabic speak a dialect of their particular region. The focus in this chapter is on the written version of Arabic, Modern Standard Arabic, henceforth called Arabic in this chapter.

There are several important differences among Arabic, English, and Spanish. English and Spanish are Romance languages; Arabic is a Semitic language. English and Spanish use the Roman or Latin script, whereas Arabic has its own script. Arabic is written from right to left in cursive (Lebanese Arabic Institute, 2023), whereas English and Spanish are written from left to right. English and Spanish have upper-case and lower-case letters, but Arabic makes no such distinction.

Like English and Spanish, however, Arabic is an alphabetic language; that is, it is a language in which letters represent sounds. As shown in Figure 6.1, Arabic has an alphabet of 28 letters—all consonants—plus three vowels and special characters (The Thinking Muslim, 2023).

Early Literacy Instruction in Arabic

Arabic experts explain that the first step in teaching students to read and write in Arabic is to teach the Arabic alphabet (The Thinking Muslim, 2023). Experts recommend that you teach each consonant individually over a one-week period. Teachers begin their instruction by saying the individual name of the consonant letter as they show it. Students repeat the letter name after their teachers. Then the sequence is repeated until students can say the letter correctly. It is advised that the teacher print or write the letters on paper, cut them out, and ask the students to color them. Experts also recommend that students create each letter with Play-Doh and/or trace it in sand. Once students learn several consonant letters, the teacher should test

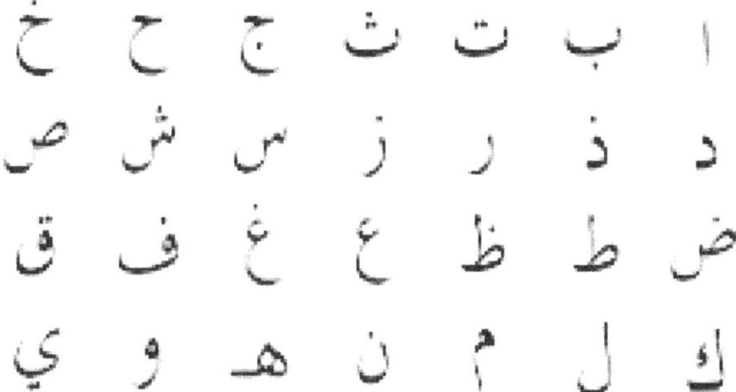

FIGURE 6.1. Arabic alphabet. From Flicker-Arabic Alphabet.jpg from Wikimedia Commons (September 12, 2023).

students' knowledge of them by showing them random letters and asking them to name them.

Teachers do not show the students Arabic words that use the consonants because the letters take different forms according to their positions in the words—initial, medial, or final (Lebanese Arabic Institute, 2023). Their forms also change according to whether they are connected to a letter in a previous word. Most letters connect to other letters on the right side. There are only six letters that do not connect.

Every word has a vowel (Lebanese Arabic Institute, 2023). According to the Lebanese Arabic Institute, there are three short vowel markers. A short diagonal mark above the letter, the *fatħah*, indicates a vowel (e.g., بَ). A short diagonal mark below a letter, called the *kasrah*, indicates another vowel (e.g., دِ). The third vowel, known as the *dammah*, involves placement of another mark above the letter (e.g., حُ). In addition, there are long vowel markers, which change the pronunciation of the short vowels.

For more information on how to teach literacy in Arabic, I recommend that you consult the following books: Awde and Samano (1986), Edutainment and Al Amani (2021), Lebanese Arabic Institute (2023), and The Thinking Muslim (2023). KiddiTube Arabic (2024) also has useful information.

The Chinese Language

Chinese is the third most frequent language spoken by emergent bilingual students in K–12 in the United States. In 2019–2020, a total of 87,256 emergent bilingual students in grades K–12 reported speaking Chinese (NCELA, 2019–2020). When students report speaking Chinese, they usually mean that they speak Mandarin, Cantonese, or a Chinese dialect. Mandarin is the official language of China and Taiwan, while Cantonese is spoken in Hong Kong and China's Guangdong (Canton) Province (Boland, 2021). Because Mandarin is spoken by more people than Cantonese, this book focuses on Mandarin.

Mandarin is not an alphabetic language like English or Spanish. Instead, it is a logographic language. In logographic languages, symbols or characters indicate word meanings or units of meaning (Saville-Troike, 2006). The basic unit in Mandarin is the character. Unlike English or Spanish letters, which have sounds but no meanings, Chinese characters do have sounds and meanings (Boland, 2021). The information on Mandarin characters and English meanings in Table 6.2 is from *Go Abroad China* (2019, n.p.).

The character is the smallest pronounced unit, or spoken syllable, and a lexical morpheme—the smallest language unit that carries meaning (Ho & Bryant, 1997). Every syllable in Mandarin maps onto a character (Cheung, McBride-Chang, & Wing, 2016). However, a Mandarin syllable can have four tones or pitch contours (high, rising, low, then rising, falling), all of which denote different meanings (Wu & Anderson, 2007). When two or more simple characters are combined, they are called compound/complex characters. The compound/complex characters include radicals, which carry phonetic or semantic information (Boland, 2021). Wu and Anderson point out that even second graders can use the phonetic radical to understand characters that are not "fully regular" (p. 52). Because characters often have more than one meaning, readers often have to observe the context to know the meaning of specific characters (Cheung et al., 2016).

The characters are created with brush strokes. For example, the character for "soil" or "earth" involves three brush strokes: 土 (Choi, 2023).

TABLE 6.2. Mandarin Characters and Their English Meanings

Mandarin character	English meaning
大	Big
子	Child/son
家庭	Family
家	Home
文	Language/literature
爱	Love
人	People
日	Sun

Remarkably, to read a newspaper in Mandarin, you need to know approximately 3,000 characters (Boland, 2021).

Early Literacy Instruction in Mandarin

The best method for teaching young children how to read in Mandarin has been a source of controversy (Lam, 2011; Wu & Anderson, 2007). Several experts contend that young children should memorize characters before being asked to read or write them. But other experts recommend that young children should be taught to learn characters as they read them. Still others think that the best way to teach young children is to employ Pinyin or Zhu-Yin-Fu Hao, two phonetic systems that transcribe the Mandarin pronunciation of Chinese characters into the Latin alphabet. Pinyin is the name of the system used in mainland China, while Zhu-Yin-Fu Hao is the name of the system used in Taiwan. Choi (2023) points out that to effectively use Pinyin, students should already know 600 characters. Also, because Pinyin has 35 vowels, 23 consonants, 4 tones, and a neutral tone, she warns that teaching Pinyin at the same time as the English alphabet may be confusing. Others report that if children already know a phonetic language like English, then Pinyin and Zhu-Yin-Fu Hao may be useful ways to teach them to read in Mandarin.

Regardless of the method, all the experts agree that when you teach students how to recognize or write characters, you should focus on concepts that students already know and can say in Mandarin. This means that you need to continue to develop students' oral Mandarin. To do this, I recommend that you use the rich literacy activities mentioned earlier in this chapter. For instance, you can conduct teacher read-alouds of Mandarin stories and books appropriate for the grade you are teaching. Posting the pages of the stories or books as you read them so that all your students can see them, together with pointing to the characters as you read them, should be helpful (Choi, 2023). Choi also recommends that you post labels in Mandarin of the items (clock, wall, window, door, bookshelves, etc.) in your classroom and periodically review them with your students by saying the individual words and pointing to the respective label and item. When you teach characters with one or two strokes, you can show the children how to write the characters.

To learn more about teaching young children how to read and write in Mandarin, I recommend that you refer to the following articles and chapters: Cheung et al. (2016); Ho and Bryant (1997); Hsiang, Graham, Wong, Wong, and Skar (2022); and Wu and Anderson (2007). Several blogs and websites also provide useful teaching information: Boland, R. (October 14, 2021) and Choi, B. (November 11, 2018).

CONCLUDING REMARKS

When students lose their L1 as they acquire English, they experience subtractive bilingualism. This often leads to weak academic student identities and low academic performance. This is one reason why it is important to continue to provide emergent bilingual students with academic instruction, including literacy instruction, in their L1.

During the pandemic, most emergent bilingual students did not participate in rich literacy activities. To accelerate their literacy development, I recommend that you provide them with rich literacy activities and explicit L1 reading instruction. You will need to show students how to employ an interactive approach to read in their L1, drawing from bottom-up skills explicitly taught—such as syllables in Spanish, consonants and vowels in Arabic, and Mandarin characters—along with top-down skills and knowledge, such as background knowledge related to the text and purpose for reading. I did not focus much on comprehension strategies in this chapter, because I cover comprehension in Chapters 5, 7, and 8. However, please do not forget to emphasize comprehension strategies, along with bilingual/translanguaging strategies, when you work with students on their L1 reading. The combination of rich literacy activities with in-person, explicit L1 reading instruction will help advance the literacy and academic performance of emergent bilingual students.

CHAPTER 7

Bilingual Students' Beginning Reading Instruction in English

GUIDING QUESTIONS

- What are the predictors of emergent bilingual students' English reading comprehension?
- Why is English phonemic awareness instruction unnecessary for all bilingual students?
- Why should the literacy development of bilingual students in both languages be assessed before implementing English phonics instruction?
- How should English phonics instruction be adapted for emergent bilingual students?
- Why is it important for bilingual students to learn English sight words?
- What are the limitations of emphasizing bilingual students' fluent oral English reading?
- What should be included in the beginning English reading comprehension instruction of emergent bilingual and dual-language students?

Ms. Olson is starting her first year of teaching third-grade, Spanish–English dual-language (DL) students. The DL program at Ms. Olson's school has been following the biliteracy squared instructional sequence (Escamilla et al., 2014) for teaching reading in Spanish and English: the DL students in K–2 receive daily Spanish reading instruction for 90 minutes, with 60 minutes of English oral and literacy activities, including writing. In grades 3–6, they receive 60 minutes of daily Spanish oral and literacy activities, and 90 minutes of English reading instruction.

> Bilingual school personnel have completed reading assessments for all the students in Ms. Olson's classroom. The students are strong Spanish readers who read at or above the third-grade level, but they are beginning English readers. Ms. Olson wonders if she needs to start her students' English reading instruction with phonemic awareness (the ability to hear, identify, and manipulate sounds in spoken words), or if she can assume that her students already have developed it. Ms. Rueda, the bilingual coordinator, tells her that her students have probably already developed their phonemic awareness. Ms. Olson still is unsure about where she should begin her students' English reading instruction.

In this chapter, reading research and theories related to bilingual students' English reading development, comprehension, and instruction briefly are discussed. Next, rich literacy activities that should be combined with explicit English reading instruction are reviewed. Then, beginning English reading instructional practices for bilingual students are identified and discussed.

RELEVANT READING RESEARCH AND THEORIES

In a review of research on emergent bilingual children's reading (G. García, 2000), I reported that L1 reading was a stronger predictor of L2 reading than L2 oral proficiency for emergent bilingual students in grades K–2, but L2 oral proficiency was a stronger predictor of L2 reading than L1 reading for emergent bilingual students older than grade 3. Research data support the predictions. For instance, researchers reported that knowing how to read in one language appeared to aid reading in the other language. Meta-analyses (studies that combine statistical findings on a single issue) of emergent bilingual students' reading showed that those students who received reading instruction in the L1 and English scored significantly higher on English reading measures than emergent bilingual students who only received English reading instruction (Francis, Lesaux, & August, 2006; Rolstad et al., 2005).

The predictors also make sense when you think about them. For instance, just because young children know how to speak or understand a language does not automatically result in their being able to read it. Also, some L2 learners learn how to read in their L2 without knowing how to read in their L1. What differentiates the L2 reading of emergent bilingual students after grade 2 is bilingual students' ability to comprehend complex L2 text, which requires knowledge of L2 vocabulary, syntax, and discourse structures, which comprise L2 proficiency.

A Model of Emergent Bilingual Students' English Reading Comprehension

According to the RAND Reading Study Group (2002), reading comprehension involves "the process of simultaneously extracting and constructing meaning through interaction and involvement with written language" (p. 11). The reader, the text, and the purpose for reading, or the activity, influence reading comprehension, which occurs within a larger sociocultural context (Snow & Sweet, 2003).

Informed by the RAND reading definition and drawing from research findings with L2 learners and emergent bilingual students (August & Shanahan, 2006; Bernhardt, 2011; G. García, 2000; Goldenberg, 2011; Helman, 2016; Proctor, Boardman, & Hiebert, 2016), a reading model has been developed. It predicts the English reading comprehension of elementary, emergent bilingual students, which includes their L1 reading performance, their L2 oral language proficiency, their effective use of general reading comprehension strategies (e.g., activating appropriate background knowledge and making purposeful predictions and appropriate inferences), their L2 vocabulary knowledge, their depth of background knowledge, and their use of translanguaging practices (e.g., direct translating, paraphrased translating, summary translating). Bernhardt (2011) would add linguistic distance to this model. Linguistic distance refers to how many language characteristics two languages share (e.g., alphabets, letters, sounds, syntactic features) (Lems et al., 2017, p. 35). You will notice that three variables often included in monolingual English reading models—phonemic awareness, phonological awareness, and decoding—are not included in the proposed English reading comprehension model. Although the variables are important for beginning reading in English, they are not strong predictors of emergent bilingual students' English reading comprehension.

In a study that compared the phonemic awareness and reading performance of young Spanish-speaking students in Mexico and the United States, Goldenberg et al. (2014) reported that the Mexican students had low Spanish phonemic awareness before learning to read compared to the Spanish-speaking students in the United States but outperformed the latter students on Spanish reading tests at the end of second grade. Goldenberg et al. hypothesized that phonemic awareness was not a prerequisite for learning to read in Spanish.

Durgunoğlu, Nagy, and Hancin-Bhatt (1993) found that the English word recognition of Spanish-speaking beginning readers was predicted by their Spanish phonological knowledge and Spanish word recognition, not their Spanish or English oral proficiencies. The authors concluded that cross-linguistic transfer, or what now is called translanguaging, accounted for the students' performance in English word recognition.

In a review of predominantly quantitative studies on L2 children and youths' English reading, Shanahan and Beck (2006) concluded that L2 students who received explicit English decoding instruction decoded as well as native-English speakers, but their English reading comprehension was much lower. One problem was that the L2 learners of English often did not know the meanings of the English words they decoded. In a qualitative think-aloud study with six Latinx fourth graders who were strong readers in Spanish but grade-level or below-grade level readers in English, my colleague and I (G. García & Godina, 2017) found that unknown English vocabulary, not decoding, adversely affected the students' English reading comprehension.

Godina and I (G. García & Godina, 2017) also reported that translanguaging was the best way to characterize Latinx fourth graders' utilization of reading strategies to comprehend texts in both languages. That is, they used all their linguistic resources to explain their reading, regardless of the text language. Similar to the findings in Jiménez, García, and Pearson's research with middle-school bilingual students (1995, 1996), five of the six fourth graders demonstrated a unitary view of reading across the two languages. They demonstrated using 66.8% of the same general strategies (e.g., drawing on appropriate background knowledge, effectively making inferences, summarizing what they read) when they read in Spanish and English. In addition, they translanguaged when they participated in think-alouds about what they were reading in each language. For instance, to explain what they read, they used translation strategies (direct, paraphrased, and summary) and paraphrased in one language what they had read in the other language. They also code-mixed (juxtaposed two or more words in the two languages) to figure out unfamiliar vocabulary.

Research on the English Reading Instruction of Bilingual Students

Unfortunately, only limited research has been conducted on the effective English reading instruction of emergent bilingual students in the United States (Mercuri & Musanti, 2021). The National Literacy Panel on Language Minority Children and Youth (August & Shanahan, 2006) expanded their review of findings on the English reading of bilingual children and youth in the United States to include the L2 and foreign language reading of adults, children, and youth in other countries because the United States findings were so limited.

Based on the expanded review, the authors in the August and Shanahan (2006) report concluded that the five instructional emphases identified by the National Reading Panel (National Institute of Child Health and Human Development [NICHD], 2000) for native-English-speaking students' English reading development also appeared to be relevant for L2 learners of English:

- *Phonemic awareness* (the ability to hear, identify, and manipulate sounds in words).
- *Phonics* (the use of spelling patterns and sound–letter correspondence in words to decode or figure out how to accurately pronounce and orally read words).
- *Fluency* (the rapid, accurate, and expressive oral reading of words and texts).
- *Vocabulary* (knowledge of word meanings).
- *Comprehension* (understanding and interpreting the meaning of texts).

However, the L2 review (August & Shanahan, 2006) stated that the National Reading Panel's (NICHD, 2000) focus did not include everything that was needed for L2 learners to become strong English readers. Two of the missing areas were L2 learners' oral language development and the home language. Another area that the National Reading Panel did not address was translanguaging.

In the next section, I present a discussion of beginning English reading instructional practices for bilingual students, which takes into account four of the five National Reading Panel's (NICHD, 2000) instructional emphases (phonemic awareness, phonics, fluency, and comprehension), plus L2 learners' oral language development, home language, and translanguaging. When planning English reading instruction for bilingual students, I encourage you to pay attention to your state's English language development standards for emergent bilingual students and literacy standards for all students. Although bilingual students' writing and vocabulary development influence their reading development, these topics are discussed separately in Chapters 9 and 10.

INSTRUCTIONAL PRACTICES FOR BILINGUAL STUDENTS LEARNING TO READ IN ENGLISH

Rich Literacy Activities

Many of the same oral language and literacy activities described in Chapter 4 should be used when teaching English reading to bilingual students: rhymes and songs, morning message, echo reading, choral reading, shared reading, interactive teacher read-alouds, shared writing, the language experience approach, independent reading, and student discussion. Interactive teacher read-alouds and whole-group and small-group discussion of English picture books, predictable books, big books, chapter books and informational books (described in Chapter 5) all help students to become engaged in reading, to develop their knowledge of the English language and beginning literacy skills in English, and to comprehend texts. However, please remember that if English is your students' L2, then you need to employ many of the techniques (e.g., sheltering, L1 use, and translanguaging) described in Chapter 3 to scaffold or support your students' understanding of English activities and texts.

English Reading Instructional Practices for Bilingual Students

The English Alphabet

Knowing the letter names in the English alphabet is important for beginning reading instruction in English (International Literacy Association, 2018). Accordingly, one of the first tasks for teachers of bilingual students is to find out if their students know the alphabets in English and their other language (their L1 if they are emergent bilingual and their L2 if they are English-dominant DL students). When discussing the two alphabets, you should have both alphabets posted so that the students can see them. Visual presentation of the alphabets should include words and illustrations or drawings of items that begin with the alphabet letters. If you know the alphabets, say the letters and the words as you point to the letters, the words, and illustrations.

Student Comparison of Two Alphabets. I recommend beginning your instruction by asking your students what they notice or know about the alphabets in the two languages. For example, if your students know the Spanish alphabet, then over the course of the discussion, it should be pointed out that the Spanish and English alphabets share the same 26 letters (Ford & Palacios, 2015). The one Spanish letter that does not exist in the English alphabet is the ñ.

If your students do not know the English alphabet, then you need to teach it to them. If most of your students do know the English alphabet, then work in small groups with those students who do not know it.

Teaching the English Alphabet. Two literacy activities that will help your students learn the English alphabet are the alphabet song and repeated readings of alphabet books. YouTube plays several versions of the song. Be sure to show your students the written version of the song as you repeatedly sing it with them. You also should repeatedly read alphabet books aloud to your students by utilizing echo reading, shared reading, and choral reading (see Chapter 4). After reading each alphabet book, be sure to place it in your classroom library for students to look at or to read. To encourage your students to focus on the alphabet letters and the words that begin with the letters, Cunningham (2000) cautions you to select alphabet books with familiar illustrations and a small amount of print on the pages.

ENGLISH AND BILINGUAL ALPHABET BOOKS

Z is for Moose (Bingham, 2012)

The Adventures of Paddington: My First Letters Book (HarperCollins Children's Books, 2024)

The Very Hungry Caterpillar's ABCs (The World of Eric Carle) (Carle, 2016)

The Alphabet Book (Bright and Early Board Books) (Eastman, 2000)

A Is for Airplane/A es para avión (Multilingual edition) (Howell, 2003)

I Spy Little Letters (Marzollo, 2012)

A Is for Apple (Smart Kids Trace and Flip) (Tales, 2011)

To teach the English alphabet, you should point to the letter and say the letter name and the word that begins with the letter. Make sure that your students know that the letter name in English sometimes is different from the letter sound. For instance, the letter *a* can have seven different sounds (underlined): the *a* in *apple, father, about, ball, ate, air,* and *climate.*

Then, you and your students should repeat the English letter name and the word that begins with the letter multiple times. Once your students show that they are learning the letter names, you can point to the letter and ask your students to tell you the letter's name. Student partners can test each other by using individual alphabet charts or flash cards with the letters printed on them. Whether as a class or in small groups, your students can work together to create their own alphabet book(s).

In addition, I recommend that you create a word center, where students can participate in activities that help them to recognize and learn the English letter names. Later, they can use the word center to practice letter–sound correspondence and to learn new vocabulary. In the center, they can create sandpaper letters, which help them to physically feel the letters, and they can complete alphabet letter puzzles. Give them memory games where they match cards with the letters on them. Let them play the game of "Fish," but with letter cards that they have to match. Have partners draw flash cards with individual English letters on them and have one partner ask the other to identify the letter. Once they recognize all the letters, they can dictate the letters to each other.

Assessment and Development of Phonemic Awareness

In the opening vignette of this chapter, Ms. Rueda said that the third graders had likely already developed their phonemic awareness (the ability to identify and manipulate sounds in spoken words). Remember, the third graders already know how to read in Spanish, and as beginning readers in English, they can read some words. They likely developed their phonemic awareness in Spanish when they learned how to use a syllabic approach for reading. They should be able to use this awareness when working in English without any further phonemic instruction. August, Calderón, and Carlo (2002) validated this assumption when they found that Spanish-speaking second graders' phonemic awareness in Spanish predicted their English phonemic awareness at the end of third and fourth grade. Nonetheless, because phonemic awareness plays an important role in students' early English reading instruction, if your students do not understand how to identify and manipulate sounds in spoken words in their L1 or L2, then you should help them develop this awareness.

However, please do not use phonemic awareness instruction developed for native-English speakers without adapting it for emergent bilingual students. A friend who was tutoring an Arabic-speaking, emergent bilingual first grader complained to me that the little boy could not complete the English workbook that the school had provided. The first grader was supposed to look at an English word in the workbook and tell the tutor another English word that rhymed with the word. Because his English proficiency was still developing, it was difficult for him to independently identify English words that rhymed.

I advised the tutor to choose three concrete English words (two that rhymed, one that did not) and show them to the student. Concrete words are words that can be demonstrated through the human senses (e.g., hear, see, smell, and touch), such as *ball, tall*, and *ran*. If the student does not know what the words mean in English, then the tutor should use sheltered English to teach the student what each word means. Then, I recommended that the tutor model and show the student what he was to do. For instance, the tutor should tell the student that he or she was going to read each word and that the student should say which words had similar sounds or rhyme. Here, I also suggest that the tutor teach the student what the word rhyme means by orally discussing and showing pictures of rhyming examples and nonexamples. As the tutor reads and points to each word, he or she should make sure that the student can see the printed word with the accompanying illustration.

Herrera, Perez, and Escamilla (2010) present several English phonemic awareness activities specifically designed for emergent bilingual students that you could use. Cunningham (2000) also recommends English phonemic awareness tasks that you can adapt for emergent bilingual students. Both sets of authors recommend that the phonemic awareness tasks include texts that teachers' read aloud. For example, Cunningham recommends that you conduct repeated teacher read-alouds of predictable books in English, such as *Hattie and the Fox* by Mem Fox (1992) and conduct rhyming activities using the words in the book. One of Cunningham's phonemic awareness activities, which I adapted, is described next.

After doing a shared reading of *Hattie and the Fox* (Fox, 1992) several times, I recommend that you demonstrate what you mean when you say rhyming by showing two items that have rhyming names, such as *can* and *fan*. These words are polysemous (i.e., they have more than one meaning), so you could show the items for both meanings (e.g., a can of food and a trash can; a Spanish-type fan and an electric fan). Say and write the rhyming words so that students can see them. Ask students what they notice about the words. They should point out that the beginning letters are different, but the rest of the words are the same. Then, after reading *Hattie and the Fox* again, Cunningham (2000) suggests that you write *hen* and *pig* on a whiteboard (p. 13). In addition, you should show illustrations for each word. Tell your students that you are going to say words that rhyme with one of the words, and their job is to tell you which words rhyme with the word. Then, show them printed labels and illustrations for the following words (*dig, pen, ten*, and *big*) and individually say the words. Have your students tell you which words rhyme with *hen*, then *pig*. Write the rhyming words under the respective word. Make sure that your students know the meanings of all the rhyming words you list.

Phonics Instruction

When students receive English phonics instruction, they learn how letters (graphemes) and sounds (phonemes) are organized to form written words. The aim of English phonics instruction is to teach students how to use letter–sound correspondence to decode (pronounce or orally read) and spell written English words. Unlike other alphabetic languages, such as Spanish, the relationship between written letters and spoken sounds in English is not always transparent or predictable. There are many irregularities in the letter–sound relationships, complicating students' efforts to decode English words.

Phonics Instructional Sequence

English phonics usually are taught to native-English speakers in the following order (Herrera et al., 2010; International Literacy Association, 2018):

- The consonants.
- The short vowels (e.g., *a* as in *cat*, *e* as in *net*, *i* as in *sit*, *o* as in *dot*, and *u* as in *up*).
- Often, the use of onset rime (*c-at*) to read word families (e.g., *s-at, f-at, m-at, r-at*).
- The consonant digraphs (e.g., *sh, th, wh*) and blends (e.g., *bl, st, tr*).
- The long vowels (e.g., *a* as in *made*; *e* as in *seed; i* as in *bike*; *o* as in *go*; and *u* as in use).
- The complex vowels (e. g., *ai, au, oi, ou, ow*).
- Homophones—words that sound the same but that have different meanings (*tale/tail*), and homographs—words that are spelled the same but with different meanings (*read/read*).
- Words with inflected endings (e.g., *ed* in *walked*).

I recommend that you follow this sequence when you teach English phonics to bilingual students, though you should skip extensive instruction on letter–sound correspondences that bilingual students already know. You will need additional time to teach the letter–sound correspondences for English sounds that do not exist in Spanish.

Phonics Instructional Methods

There are several methods for teaching English phonics. The International Literacy Association (2018) recommends systematic, explicit phonics instruction—"direct teaching of a set of letter-sound relationships in a clearly defined sequence" (Armbruster et al., 2006, p. 12). In addition, the International Literacy Association points out that English phonics instruction usually includes analytic instruction, which emphasizes student comparison of words "to identify patterns and apply this knowledge to new words (e.g., *ran/can*)" or to make analogies between segments of words (e.g., onset and rime, *r-an/c-an/f-an/m-an/p-an*), and synthetic instruction (p. 5). In synthetic instruction, "individual letter sounds" are blended to create words (e.g., *f-a-t/fat*) (p. 5).

However, I do not recommend or endorse any specific type of phonics program. In my experience, individual teachers do not choose a phonics program; district or school personnel choose the program. Instead, my purpose is to explain how teachers should adapt an English phonics program for emergent bilingual and dual-language students. One of the first steps is to find out what your bilingual students can do in their L1 and L2 related to English phonics.

Assessment of Bilingual Students' Literacy Knowledge and Performance

Before you begin to teach beginning English reading (and writing) to bilingual students, several researchers recommend that you find out what your students know and can do in terms of literacy in English and their other language (L1 for emergent bilingual students and L2 for English dominant DL students) (Bear & Smith, 2016; Helman, 2016). Then, you need to learn as much as possible about the similarities and differences in the linguistic structures of the other language (often known as the partner language in DL classrooms) and English.

You can get some of the above information by reviewing your students' school records and by talking with their previous teachers. You can probably find the linguistic structure information online. If you speak the other language, then you should use it to briefly interview each student, have each student orally read a short passage in the other language, and draw and write about a personal experience topic (e.g., what they want to learn in school). After the students have drawn and written, you should ask them to read what they wrote to you. If possible, you should record their oral reading. If you do not speak the other language, then you should ask an adult who speaks the other language to administer these tasks for you. On different days, you should conduct the same types of tasks in English. Analyses of these tasks will help you to estimate your students' oral proficiencies and literacy performances in the other language and English. For instance, analysis of emergent bilingual students' English writing tells you if they know to write from left to right, any alphabet letters, the alphabetic principle (i.e., a written letter or group of written letters represents sounds), the concept of word, any letter–sound correspondences or phonetic writing, and conventional writing (Helman, 2016).

Adaptation of English Phonics Instruction for Bilingual Students

The English phonics instruction that you provide to your bilingual students needs to be adapted according to what your students already know and can do in both languages. For instance, if the phonics program your school uses follows an explicit sequence for teaching letter–sound correspondences, I suggest that you follow the sequence but limit the amount of instruction on letter–sound correspondences that your bilingual students already know. You should remind your students of the correspondences that they already know but spend most of your instructional time on the correspondences they do not know.

For example, 10 consonants in Spanish and English have the same or nearly the same sounds: *b, c, d, f, l, m, n, p, q, s* (Peregoy & Boyle, 2000). When students know the equivalent consonant in Spanish, then you do not need to teach the English consonant according to an explicit instructional sequence. Instead, you should find out if the student knows the Spanish consonant sound and can use it to say the English consonant sound. If the student is not doing this, and does not know the English consonant sound, then you need to point out which consonants are similar in Spanish and English, remind the student to use the Spanish consonant sound to approximate the English consonant sound, and have them practice doing this. Table 7.1 provides a Spanish–English phonics chart, which shows some of the elements of phonics that are the same in Spanish and English. The chart is derived from Kole's (2003) work as cited in Herrera et al. (2010, p. 70).

There are sounds (phonemes) in English that do not exist in other languages, which you will have to explicitly teach emergent bilingual students. For example, Spanish has 27 letters and 22–24 phonemes, whereas English has 26 letters and 44 phonemes (Bear & Smith, 2016; Herrera et al., 2010). In Spanish, each vowel has only one sound, while in English, depending on the dialect, there are 11–19 different sounds for the vowels. Also, some English consonants have multiple sounds.

When implementing phonics instruction with emergent bilingual students, you need to make sure that your students understand that the point of English phonics instruction is to figure out what the words on the page mean or to comprehend what they read. Implementing the following recommendations will help you to keep the focus on students' reading comprehension:

1. Combine phonics instruction with teacher read-alouds of texts that include the taught phonemes in known words in the text. For instance, if you are teaching the short vowel "o," you should have it underlined in words in the text that you are reading aloud, as shown in the following excerpt: "Elizabeth decided to chase the dragon and get Ronald back" (Munsch, 2004, p. 5). Before reading the text aloud, you should tell your students why you underlined the phoneme. Also, when you read the text aloud, make sure your students can see the text. Be sure to point to the words as you read them aloud.

2. Teach your students how to decode already known English vocabulary words and skip infrequent words. Sometimes, English phonics instruction includes words that emergent bilingual students will not know. For instance, a phonics lesson on short vowel patterns had students examine

TABLE 7.1. Spanish/English Phonics Table

	Word examples	
Same phonics elements in Spanish and English	Spanish (translation in parentheses)	English
/b/ spelled b	*bicicleta* (bicycle)	*bicycle*
/c/ in ce, ci	*cero* (zero)	*ceiling*
	cine (film)	*cigar*
/d/ spelled d	*dieta* (diet)	*diet*
/f/ spelled f	*familia* (family)	*family*
/g/ spelled g in ga, go, gu	*gato* (cat)	*gave*
	gota (drop)	*goat*
	guiso (stew)	*gun*
/l/ spelled l	*liso* (smooth)	*lips*
/m/ spelled m	*mamá* (mother)	*mother*
/n/ spelled n	*no*	*no*
/p/ spelled p	*poso* (hole)	*people*
/s/ spelled s	*sopa* (soup)	*soup*
/t/ spelled t	*tigre* (tiger)	*tiger*
/q/ spelled q	*queso* (cheese)	*quiz*
/y/ spelled y	*yo* (I)	*yes*
/ch/ spelled ch	*chato* (flat)	*chicken*
/oo/ spelled u	*busca* (look for)	*moon*
/l/ blends (bl, cl, fl, pl)	*blusa* (blouse)	*blouse*
	clase (class)	*cloud*
	flores (flowers)	*flower*
	pluma (pen)	*plate*
Diphthong /oi/ spelled oi, oy	*oir* (to hear)	*noise*
	hoy (today)	*toy*

Note. Derived from Kole (2003) as cited in Herrera et al. (2010, p. 70).

net, vet, hen, den, peg, beg, and *keg* (Helman, 2016, p. 175). The only word that emergent bilingual students are likely to know is *hen.* I would skip *keg* and *peg* because they are not words that appear very often in elementary English texts. However, if you use the other words in your phonics instruction (i.e., *net, vet, hen, den,* or *beg*), be sure to teach their meanings (see Chapter 10).

3. Some phonics lessons may include English words that emergent bilingual students probably will not need to know. For instance, another phonics lesson on short vowels included the following words *bag, rag, wag, nag, tag,* and *sag* (Helman, 2016, p. 174). It is unlikely that beginning readers will know or need to know the meanings of *nag* and *sag,* so these words

should be skipped. You could teach the meanings of *bag* and *rag* by showing the students the actual objects or pictures of them. You could either skip *tag* and *wag* or teach them, depending on their importance to your instruction and comprehension of a text. Tag is a game children play in elementary school. To teach *tag,* you could show a short YouTube video of children playing tag. And you could teach *wag* by telling them "Dogs wag their tails" and show them a picture of dogs doing this.

Teaching Sight Vocabulary

Bilingual students need to know how to approach and write high-frequency words that are difficult to decode (e.g., *for, they, with, what, why, who*) (Cunningham, 2017, p. 90). Given that these words appear frequently in English texts, and do not always have explicit meanings, many reading educators think that it is best for native-English-speaking students to memorize the words, so that their attempts to decode the words do not slow down their text reading (Cunningham, 2000). Because educators want students to recognize the words by sight and not by decoding, they are called sight words.

Sometimes bilingual students independently learn words when teachers repeatedly read the same texts aloud. For instance, if the word *girl* is repeated in a text, along with an illustration of a girl, students may learn to recognize the meaning of this word. However, because English sight words will help your bilingual students to read in English, you should start teaching them as soon as you initiate beginning reading instruction in English. Ten sight words—*the, of, and, a, to, in, is, you, that,* and *it*—comprise one-fourth of all the words typically read and written in English (Cunningham, 2017, p. 88).

I suggest that you begin each week by teaching up to five sight words from texts that your bilingual students are reading. If students know the equivalent sight words in their L1, then you can teach them the L1 translations for the English sight words. However, if they do not know the words in the L1 or if the words do not exist in their L1, then, when possible, you should teach the meanings of the sight words. If that is difficult (for instance, how do you explain the meaning of *the* or *to*?), then you should teach them to associate the sight words with other English words.

Sight-Word Associations

Several of Cunningham's (2017) sight-word associations for native-English speakers are useful for bilingual students. For example, Cunningham suggests that you underline *of* and teach students how to recognize *of* by reading and showing them labeled photos of "a piece <u>of</u> cake, a box <u>of</u> cookies,

[and] a bowl <u>of</u> cereal" (p. 90). Once students know how to use *of* and *for*, you should teach them how to use *from* (p. 91). If some students in your class are from other locales in the United States or from other countries, Cunningham recommends that you say and show your students a frame for *from*: Miguel is <u>from</u> ___________. Lupita is <u>from</u> ___________. I am <u>from</u> ___________. To make their understanding of *from* more concrete, you can show them the locales or countries on a map as you read the frames.

Word Walls

Cunningham (2017) also recommends that you develop word walls to post the sight words in your classroom. She advises that the word wall should only include a maximum of five new words per week. Confusing words should be printed in different colors (i.e., *for* and *from*). Students should practice the words by locating them in texts and on the word wall. When the teacher reads the words aloud, students should chant them in unison and write them. (See Cunningham for other ways to use the word wall to promote bilingual students' English literacy development.)

English Oral Reading Fluency

Reading fluency refers to students' fast, accurate, expressive oral reading. When native-English-speaking students read English texts fluently and with prosody (e.g., with appropriate phrasing and intonation), reading experts think that they do not need to focus on decoding, and can pay attention to the meaning of the text (Armbruster, Lehr, & Osborne, 2006). Without fluency, native-English-speaking students' oral reading is halting, slow, and laborious (Cunningham, 2000). Native-English speakers who cannot read English text fluently usually have problems with text comprehension, do not like reading, and do not read as much as those who read fluently (Cunningham, 2000).

Given the relationship between native-English-speaking students' reading fluency and reading comprehension, educators recommend that teachers conduct timed reading fluency measures to estimate students' English reading comprehension (Herrera et al., 2010; Lems et al., 2017). In timed reading measures, teachers listen to students read aloud and count the number of errors that students make per 100 words.

Limitations of English Oral Reading Fluency for Bilingual Students

The importance of English reading fluency for bilingual students' English reading comprehension has not been well researched (Herrera et al., 2010; Montero & Kuhn, 2016). Fluent oral reading of English texts is not an easy task for many current and former emergent bilingual students (G. García, 2003; Lems et al., 2017). They often do not know the meanings of all the words they are asked to read and they do not know what the syntax signals. Because they are L2 learners of English, trying to read like they speak—a guideline teachers often give to native-English speakers—rarely works. Also, teachers often misinterpret students' accents as reading errors.

Sometimes, bilingual students know the meanings of English words, but they cannot pronounce them accurately. For instance, a Spanish-speaking fourth grader who read above grade level in Spanish and English reported in a think-aloud that she sometimes understood English words that she had difficulty decoding: "The atmosphere of Venus is another sci . . . science . . . sickness . . . significant. I know that word [*significant*] but I can't say it. I can't pronounce it" (G. García & Godina, 2017, p. 288).

Other times, emergent bilingual students can decode words but do not know what the words mean. Given the difficulties that emergent bilingual students experience when orally reading English, I do not recommend that teachers use timed reading fluency tests with current or former emergent bilingual students until more is known about the relationship between bilingual students' fluent oral reading of English and their English reading comprehension.

Instructional Practices to Improve Bilingual Students' Oral English Reading

Although the relationship between emergent bilingual students' fluent oral reading in English and their English reading comprehension is unknown, this does not mean that teachers should not help bilingual students to improve their oral English reading. The activities that teachers use to improve the oral reading fluency of native-English speakers should be helpful. These activities include teacher modeling of fluent English reading with prosody (i.e., expression) during teacher read-alouds; teachers' repeated readings of the same texts; student participation in readers' theater in which students read different parts according to the characters' descriptions (Escamilla et al., 2014); students' independent reading on a daily basis; and students' daily writing (Herrera et al., 2010; Lems et al., 2017).

An instructional activity specifically designed to improve the oral reading of bilingual students in English and/or Spanish is Lotta Lara, which was introduced in Chapter 6 (Escamilla et al., 2014). Lotta Lara involves repeated readings of the same text over a period of three days.

Cunningham's (2000) warning about not interrupting the oral reading of native-English-speaking students to point out or correct any errors also should apply to bilingual students. Cunningham advises teachers and students to not correct students' oral reading errors when the students read aloud because the corrections will disrupt the students' oral reading.

Instead, any corrections and explanations about the errors should be made respectfully after the students have completed reading aloud.

The Promotion of Text Comprehension

Usually, there is not a lot of comprehension instruction for native English-speaking students in grades K through midgrade 2 because the English texts that students read are fairly simple (Stahl & García, 2015). However, Stahl and I recommend three practices to improve the English reading comprehension of native-English speakers in these grades, which also are appropriate for bilingual students: interactive teacher read-alouds, shared reading and writing, and teacher-led small group reading instruction. (All three practices are described in Chapter 4.)

Researchers have determined that several comprehension strategies effective with native-English-speaking students in grades K–2 (Shanahan et al., 2010) also should be taught to bilingual students in these grades:

- Using story maps and simple informational text structures (e.g., sequence) to understand and recall texts (see Chapter 5).
- Visualizing (i.e., creating a picture of what is read in your mind) (see Chapter 8).
- Generating and "answering high-level questions" (Stahl & García, 2015, p. 80)—open-ended questions (see Chapters 4 and 8).
- "Summarizing/retelling . . . key elements of a text" (see Chapters 8 and 12, Stahl & García, 2015, p. 80).
- "Generating inferences" (Stahl & García, 2015, p. 80; see Chapter 8).
- "Monitoring and applying fix-up strategies" (Stahl & García, 2015, p. 80), such as "reread, read ahead, and talk with others" (Stahl & García, 2015, p. 81).

I recommend that you utilize the GRR (Pearson & Gallagher, 1983; see Chapter 8) to teach the above strategies when you conduct teacher read-alouds and shared reading.

CONCLUDING REMARKS

It is important to adapt beginning English reading instructional methods that were developed for native-English speakers according to what is known about the effective instruction of emergent bilingual students. There are three major differences between the two groups of students that affect the beginning English reading development and instruction of emergent bilingual students: their English language proficiencies, knowledge of another language, and ability to translanguage.

Although English-dominant DL students are English proficient, their beginning English reading development and instruction also may be affected by their knowledge of another language and ability to translanguage. Before providing them with beginning English reading instruction, it is helpful to find out what they already know about reading and writing in their L2 and English.

In terms of instruction, please remember to shelter bilingual students' L2 reading instruction. Also, remember that when you ask emergent bilingual and DL students to orally explain or write about what they comprehend, they are likely to provide a more complete view of their text comprehension when they are encouraged to translanguage. If you do not know the other language, then ask a bilingual adult to help you to interpret what they said or wrote. Similarly, there are times, when your or another class member's use of translanguaging can clarify your instruction (see Chapter 3).

Not everything that you need to know about working with beginning English readers is covered in this chapter. Chapter 8 examines how to improve bilingual students' reading comprehension in more detail; Chapter 9 provides information on how to teach writing to bilingual students; and Chapter 10 focuses on vocabulary instruction.

CHAPTER 8

Reading Comprehension Instruction for Bilingual Students

GUIDING QUESTIONS

- What is the bilingual advantage?
- What are three different ways to assess and activate bilingual students' background knowledge?
- How does thematic instruction build bilingual students' background knowledge?
- What types of inferences should bilingual students implement to comprehend texts?
- Why should bilingual students flexibly employ the five cognitive strategies in dialogic strategy instruction?
- How can participating in literature circles help bilingual students' reading?
- What bilingual/translanguaging strategies do bilingual students use to comprehend and discuss texts?

Ms. López is working with a small group of DL second graders who are having difficulty making accurate reading inferences. The Garcías' second grader introduced in Chapter 1 is in her class.

Ms. López read the following text aloud to the students in the small group: "Juan Carlos knew he was in trouble when he saw his dad's face. It had an angry frown on it."

She asked Julia, "Who has an angry face?"

Julia reread the text silently and asked, "Juan Carlos?"

Ms. López asked Julia, "How did Juan Carlos know he was in trouble?"

Julia replied, "He saw his dad's face."

Ms. López said, "Okay, that's correct. Whose face is angry?"

Julia, looking at the text, answered, "His dad's?"

Ms. López replied, "Yes, that's correct. How do you know that?"

Pointing to the last sentence in the text, Julia answered: "Because it says it here."

Ms. López exclaimed, "Excellent, Julia. You just made an inference!"

Ms. López explains to the reading group that to figure out "it" in the second sentence, Julia had to make an inference by combining information from the first and second sentences.

Beginning in second grade, students in the United States are confronted with texts that require them to do more than decode and recognize the decoded words to understand them. Among other skills, students have to know how to activate the appropriate background knowledge, make inferences, and employ metacognitive and cognitive strategies to monitor, repair, and facilitate their comprehension. Inferences are educated guesses about what the author suggested or implied but did not explicitly state in writing. Metacognitive strategies are the strategies that readers utilize to think about, monitor, or evaluate their comprehension. Cognitive strategies are the mental processes or tools that readers use to repair or facilitate their comprehension. You should refer to your state's English language arts standards to guide your bilingual students' reading comprehension instruction.

THE BILINGUAL ADVANTAGE

Once bilingual students know how to monitor and facilitate their text comprehension in one language, they do not have to relearn how to monitor and facilitate their text comprehension in another language. According to translanguaging theory (O. García, 2009) and Cummins's (1981) interdependence hypothesis and cognitive underlying proficiency theory, they should be able to use all their knowledge or concepts acquired in one language while working in the other language. For instance, students can utilize the metacognitive and cognitive strategies they learned in one language to approach reading in another language. The only exceptions are when there are structural linguistic differences (e.g., structural underlying proficiencies; Cummins, 1981), such as how to show possession in Spanish and English, and cultural differences, such as narrative text structures in Japanese and English (see Chapter 9).

However, not all bilingual students automatically use what they know in one language to approach and read in another language (see Jiménez et al., 1995, 1996). Several of the sixth- and seventh-grade bilingual Latinx students who were less successful readers in the Jiménez et al.'s studies thought they would become confused if they used what they knew about reading in Spanish to read in English and vice versa. Therefore, it is important for you to remind your bilingual students to use what they know about reading comprehension in all their languages to comprehend what they read.

Background Knowledge

To comprehend texts, bilingual students need to activate the appropriate background knowledge about the text author(s), topic, genre, and text structure. Sometimes, bilingual students do not have the appropriate background knowledge needed to comprehend English expository and narrative reading passages. In a study that compared the English reading test performance of Spanish-speaking, Latinx fifth and sixth graders to that of English-speaking, Anglo fifth and sixth graders (G. García, 1991), I found that the Latinx students knew significantly less than the Anglo students about three of the six topics on the test (Canada, chimpanzees, and water as an erosive force), which adversely affected their test performance. When they demonstrated the same amount of background knowledge for three other topics, however, their reading test performance did not differ.

You can assess and activate students' background knowledge by utilizing several methods: getting students to brainstorm about the topic of the reading selection, doing a brief interactive picture walk of the text, conducting a "know, want to know, what I learned" (KWL; Ogle, 1986) activity, and/or implementing thematic instruction, which are described below. Throughout your instruction, let your students translanguage or use all their linguistic resources (O. García, 2009). If you do not understand their translanguaging, ask a student or adult proficient in English and the students' home language(s) to interpret for you.

Brainstorming about a Topic

To brainstorm about a topic or to conduct a semantic map (Johnson et al., 1986), print the name of the topic in the center of a whiteboard or flip chart. Next, assign students to work as partners to think of words relating to the topic. Have them write the topic on a sheet of paper and the words they think of below the topic. Then, call on partners to share a word not already written on the white board or flip chart and to explain its relationship to the topic. When you ask students to orally explain their choice of words, you are introducing other students to background knowledge that some of them may not have. Be sure to carefully and politely correct any errors that students make so that you do not provide your students with incorrect background information.

PARTIALLY COMPLETED BRAINSTORMING CHART ON EARTHQUAKES

Measurements	*Physical Damage*	*Safety Recommendations*
Richter Scale	Cracks in ground	Retrofit buildings
Seismograph	Tsunamis	Stand in doorway
Magnitude	Landslides	Get under heavy table
Intensity		
Epicenter		

Interactive Picture Walk

An interactive picture walk works best with narrative texts that are well illustrated or expository texts with illustrations or photographs that match what is written. Before you or your students read any words in the text, you should go through the text page by page, asking students to look at the illustrations and to share what they think the text is about and what will happen next in the text. If you are introducing a long text, I recommend that you preview the book and choose the illustrations/photographs and pages that you want to discuss ahead of time. Then, just focus on these pages. At the end of the picture walk, you or your class should correct any erroneous predictions or summaries before reading the text.

KWL

In the KWL (Ogle, 1986), you ask students to complete a chart in pairs, individually, or as a class about what they think they know about the topic (the K) and what they want to learn about the topic (the W). Then, after they read the text, they complete the section on what they learned (the L). Because students sometimes enact the wrong knowledge about a topic, the KWL is a useful way to get them to adjust or change their erroneous background knowledge.

Thematic Instruction

An excellent way to build bilingual students' background knowledge is through thematic instruction (Brodeur, 1998). In thematic instruction, more than one subject or academic domain addresses the same theme. Teachers who implement thematic instruction usually work with other grade-level teachers to select a theme that is related to their state standards and included in their school district's required curriculum for their grade level, as well as to collect materials and resources for the theme. For example in a dual-language (50–50) school, the first-grade teachers chose to do thematic instruction in social studies (conducted in Spanish) and literacy (separate instruction every two weeks in Spanish and English) for four weeks per theme (G. García & Lang, 2023). One of the first-grade themes was explorers and explorations in the Americas.

Thematic instruction provides students with multiple opportunities to work with theme-related vocabulary, concepts, and information. Bilingual students' background and vocabulary knowledge related to a theme are increased as they repeatedly work with the theme in more than one academic domain and/or language.

Inferences

Authors do not explicitly state everything in their writing, and so readers need to make inferences or educated guesses about the authors' intent. Generally, to comprehend texts, readers have to make three types of inferences: "they have to combine information (1) within the text, (2) across the text, and (3) information from the text [with the reader's] background knowledge" (Stahl & García, 2022, p. 98). In a study that I conducted with Anglo and Latinx fifth and sixth graders (G. García, 1991), I used an adaptation of Pearson and Johnson's (1978) categorization of questions according to the types of inferences readers make to answer reading test questions. When the reader could answer the question by finding the question and answer in a single sentence, the inference was textually explicit. When the question and answer were in the reading passage, but not in the same sentence, then the inference was textually implicit. Textually implicit inferences can involve information either close to each other (e.g., in two adjacent sentences) or far from each other (e.g., on different pages in the text). When only some of the information needed to answer a question was in the passage and students had to use their background knowledge to answer the question, then the inference was scriptally implicit.

As a group, the Latinx students missed significantly more of the scriptally implicit questions than the Anglo students (G. García, 1991). The low- and average-performing Latinx students had an explicit approach to their text comprehension; that is, they thought that the answers to all the questions were stated in the passages. When they could not find the information in the passages to answer the scriptally implicit questions, then they selected incorrect answers that were in the passages. Their low performance on the scriptally implicit questions was one reason for their low reading test performance compared to the Anglo students. It appeared that none of their teachers had told the Latinx students that authors expect readers to combine what they know about a topic with what is written in the text to fill in missing information in the text. The answers often are not explicitly stated in the text.

Clearly, inferences are easier to make when you have the appropriate background knowledge for the text you are reading. Therefore, I recommend that you begin practicing each of the inferences with texts for which your bilingual students have high levels of background knowledge. Point out that they should activate their background knowledge for the text prior to reading it carefully. They can activate their background knowledge by thinking about or brainstorming what they know about the text topic, genre, and author or by initiating a KWL.

After they are successful in identifying inferences with texts for which they have background knowledge, then, have them practice each of the inferences with texts for which they have limited background knowledge. When they are able to determine each type of inference, give them a text to read silently and an assignment that requires them to identify the three types of inferences. As part of the assignment, ask them to work in pairs to write a brief explanation of how they determined each of the inferences. Collect their work and give them explicit feedback on what they did well and on what they need to improve.

In an effort to improve the reading comprehension instruction and performance of fourth graders in the United States (including bilingual students), the National Assessment of Educational Progress in reading (National Assessment Governing Board [NAGB], 2023) will include four types of inferential questions on its fourth-grade reading comprehension assessment in 2026. When you work with bilingual students on answering inferential questions, I encourage you to include practice on the following NAEP inferential questions:

- "Locate and recall questions," which are almost identical to textually explicit questions (NAGB, 2023, p. 7).
- "Integrate and interpret questions," which require students to not only integrate information in the text (like textually implicit questions), but also to combine the information with their background knowledge (NAGB, 2023, p. 7).

- "Critique and evaluate questions," which require students to "use what they know about 'text, language, and the ways that authors manipulate language and ideas to achieve their goals'" (NAGB, 2017, pp. 38–39 as cited in Stahl & García, 2022, p. 162).
- "Use and apply questions," which ask students to use information they read in a text or texts and to "apply it to something new, outside" of what they read," like "a product or project or to evaluate what is said in a different text" (Stahl & García, 2022, p. 162).

Use of the Gradual Release of Responsibility

I recommend that you employ the GRR (Pearson & Gallagher, 1983; Stahl & García, 2022) to teach your bilingual students how to make the different types of inferences and to employ metacognitive and cognitive strategies. When you implement the GRR, you need to provide your students with different types of knowledge about what you are teaching: declarative, procedural, and conditional knowledge. *Declarative knowledge* defines or explains the task you are teaching. So, for a textually implicit inference, you could say that this type of inference requires the reader to combine information in different places in a text. Also, I recommend stating that reading tests often require students to make textually implicit inferences. *Procedural knowledge* explains how to enact the task. So, for a textually implicit inference or test question, you could say that you need to look for information in different parts of the text and combine the information to make an inference or to answer a reading test question. *Conditional information* is knowing when and why it is appropriate to implement the task. For example, readers need to know when it is important to make a textually implicit inference or when a textually implicit reading test question has been asked. When the combination of information in the text improves your reading comprehension or allows you to answer a test question, then it is appropriate to make a textually implicit inference. Often, the reader has to combine information across the text to understand an assumption that the author has made but not stated.

The different steps for implementing the GRR are as follows. First, you, the teacher give *an explicit explanation* of the task, providing *declarative, procedural, and conditional knowledge.* Next, you *model* how to enact the task while reading. Then, you and your students *collaborate* to work on the task while reading. Next, your students participate in *guided practice* by working with each other on the task. You support them by providing feedback on what they are doing correctly or incorrectly. Finally, your students *independently apply* what they have learned about the task to their reading.

Cognitive Strategy Instruction

When cognitive and metacognitive strategies are taught to students, teacher educators often collapse them and call them cognitive strategies (Stahl & García, 2022). A number of researchers reported that bilingual Latinx students who implemented cognitive strategies (e.g., prediction, summarization, using context) while reading in English and/or Spanish comprehended texts better than bilingual Latinx students who did not (G. García et al., 2021; Jiménez et al., 1995, 1996; Klingner & Vaughn, 1996; Silverman et al., 2013). Native-English speakers who employed cognitive strategies while reading also comprehended texts better than students who did not (Stahl & García, 2015, 2022).

However, researchers do not understand the role of cognitive strategy instruction in students' improved reading comprehension. When researchers assessed native-English speaking students' specific knowledge of the taught cognitive strategies, this knowledge did not predict their improved reading comprehension (Kamil et al., 2008; Stahl & García, 2015, 2022). The researchers speculated that cognitive strategy instruction might have improved the students' reading comprehension because it resulted in their increased comprehension monitoring and thinking about text. At a school where I was collaborating with second- and fourth-grade bilingual teachers in transitional bilingual education classrooms to implement cognitive strategy instruction through teacher read-alouds, the principal asked me what I had done. She told me that she observed the bilingual fourth graders reading texts during lunch and on the stairs before school and during recess, something that had not happened before. It is possible that the cognitive strategy instruction gave the fourth graders increased confidence and agency, which motivated them to read more.

Dialogic Strategy Instruction

In a study that my colleagues and I conducted with bilingual Latinx second and fourth graders in high-poverty schools (G. García et al., 2021), we found that those students whose teachers had them participate in dialogic strategy instruction for seven months (three times/week for 30 minutes each) significantly improved their performance on standardized reading tests compared to other bilingual Latinx second and fourth graders who participated in an experimental treatment that focused on high-level discussions of texts or a treated vocabulary control group for the same amount of time. According to Wilkinson and Son (2011), what makes dialogic strategy instruction effective is the dialogic part of the instruction, or students' agency in independently selecting and discussing cognitive strategies as they interpret texts.

In the García et al. (2021) study, all the second graders received literacy instruction in Spanish and were tested in Spanish, while all the fourth graders received literacy instruction in English and were tested in English. We also encouraged the fourth-grade teachers to shelter their English instruction and to let students translanguage when they employed strategies and discussed texts. To implement dialogic strategy instruction, the teachers taught their students how to flexibly implement five cognitive strategies while reading: summarization, prediction, clarification, questioning, and visualization (G. García et al., 2021). Table 8.1 presents more information about each of the strategies. Our goals were for the students to flexibly identify and use the five strategies as needed when they read and discussed expository and narrative texts in student-led, heterogeneous (mixed reading level), small groups of four to five students.

TABLE 8.1. Cognitive Strategies Emphasized in Dialogic Strategy Instruction

Cognitive strategies	Definition	Narrative text	Expository text
Summarization	Briefly explain what the text is about. If the text is 250 words, use about 50 words to describe the text.	Identify the main character, the problem, and the plot.	Use the text structure to explain the main ideas and supporting details.
Prediction	Based on the cover, illustrations, or what is already known about the text or read in the text, anticipate what will happen next.	According to your knowledge of story maps and what has been read, anticipate what will happen next.	According to your knowledge of the text structure employed in the text and what has been read, anticipate what will happen next.
Clarification	Indicate where you need help to understand the text.	Indicate where you need help to understand the text.	Indicate where you need help to understand the text.
Question and answering	Ask questions about what you do not understand in the text; find the answers to your questions.	Ask questions about what you do not understand in the narrative; find the answers to your questions.	Ask questions about what you do not understand in the expository text; find the answers to your questions.
Visualization	Make a picture in your mind of what you are reading.	Make a picture in your mind of what you are reading.	Make a picture in your mind of what you are reading.

Note. From G. García et al. (2021).

We asked the teachers to use the GRR to teach the five cognitive strategies (G. García et al., 2021). They began their strategy instruction by explaining and modeling each strategy with a text during teacher read-alouds, following the sequence of strategies in Table 8.1. For example, after explaining and modeling how to use prediction when reading, and assigning their students to work in pairs, the teachers read texts aloud, stopping at predetermined places in the texts. They asked pairs of students to write brief summaries of what had already happened in the respective texts. Then, based on the summaries, they asked the students to write on stickies what they predicted would happen next in the texts. Then, they had several students share their summaries and predictions with the whole class before reading more of the texts aloud to see if the predictions were correct. Next, the teachers and their students reflected on whether the predictions had helped them comprehend the texts. After providing their students with guided practice and independent practice on the prediction strategy, the teachers introduced the next strategy, clarification.

After the teachers introduced each of the strategies and had students practice using each of them, we asked them to place their students in heterogeneous (mixed reading levels) small groups of four to five students to discuss use of the strategies while reading (G. García et al., 2021). Figure 8.1 shows a simulated example of the bilingual Latinx fourth graders' use of dialogic strategy instruction while discussing a text.

The second-grade teacher adjusted her dialogic strategy instruction to address the needs of her second graders (G. García et al., 2021). She used teacher read-alouds for her dialogic strategy instruction in the fall semester because the texts that the second graders read were too simple to merit the use of cognitive strategies. During the spring semester, she had her students

Luís: I have a question. Why did all the dwarves go to Mr. Baggins's house?

Violeta: Good question.

Hector: Let's reread the pages just before that happens.

Angelica: Maybe, this is the answer. [Reads aloud part of page 7.] "With the spike on his staff he scratched a queer sign on the hobbit's beautiful green door."

Violeta: I think that is the answer. The dwarves saw the sign that Gandolf drew and thought that was the correct house.

Luís: But I don't see where it says this.

Hector: I think we have to make an inference.

FIGURE 8.1. Small group of bilingual fourth graders' use of Dialogic Strategy Instruction to comprehend *The Hobbit* (Tolkien, 2013). Adapted with permission from Stahl and García (2022, p. 107).

employ dialogic strategy instruction with their guided reading texts. She assigned a capitán (captain) for each small group who orally read the text as the other students read along silently or softly and directed the use of strategies and text discussion.

Other Strategies

You also can use the GRR and the methods in the García et al. study (2021) to teach other strategies. For example, several researchers reported that, in addition to the strategies in dialogic strategy instruction, the following strategies were effective with monolingual, native-English speakers (Kamil et al., 2008; Shanahan et al., 2010): making inferences; using fix-up strategies to repair miscomprehension, such as "rereading, reading ahead, and reading more slowly"; identifying text structures; activating background knowledge; employing context; and using graphic organizers (Stahl & García, 2022, pp. 98–99). You also should use the GRR (Pearson & Gallagher, 1983) to explain, model, and teach bilingual students how to use graphic organizers (i.e., story maps and expository text structures) to improve their L1 and L2 text comprehension (see Chapter 5).

Instructional Strategy Programs

Several instructional strategy programs have been implemented successfully with bilingual students. Two of these programs are reciprocal teaching and collaborative strategic reading (CSR).

Reciprocal Teaching. Palincsar and Brown (1984) initially created reciprocal teaching to help native-English speakers who were below average readers in middle school. Since then, reciprocal teaching has been used with all kinds of students in grades 1–8, including emergent bilingual students. It also has been implemented with expository and narrative texts.

In reciprocal teaching, the teacher posts and introduces definitions of four cognitive strategies (summarization, clarification, prediction, and questioning). Then, the teacher models how to use each cognitive strategy while reading a text. Next, the teacher supports the students' use of each strategy while reading a text. Then, the teacher places the students into heterogeneous small groups, and individual students take turns acting as the teacher during the strategy discussions of a text. Figure 8.2 shows how a small group of native-English-speaking first graders implemented reciprocal teaching.

Padrón (1992) compared the English reading performance of third-, fourth-, and fifth-grade bilingual Latinx students who participated in

STUDENT 1: My question is, what does the aquanaut need when he goes under the water?

STUDENT 2: A watch.

STUDENT 3: Flippers.

STUDENT 4: A belt.

. . . .

STUDENT 1: For my summary. . . . This paragraph was about what the aquanauts need to take when they go under the water.

STUDENT 5: And also why they need those things. . . .

FIGURE 8.2. Excerpt showing how first graders implemented reciprocal teaching. From Palincsar and Brown (1986, p. 771).

reciprocal teaching in English compared to third-, fourth-, and fifth-grade bilingual Latinx students who participated in an English inferencing program, Question-Answer Relationships (QAR) (Raphael, 1982). In QAR, teachers instruct students on how to answer questions by determining the source of the answers: in the text, in the students' heads, or a combination of the two. Padrón concluded that the students who participated in reciprocal teaching improved their English reading comprehension more than the students in the inferencing program.

Collaborative Strategic Reading. Klingner and Vaughn (1996) initially developed collaborative strategic reading (CSR) to improve the English expository reading comprehension of students with learning disabilities (emergent bilingual students and native-English-speaking students) in grades 6–8. Since then, it has been effectively employed with grades 4–6, emergent bilingual students with and without learning disabilities (Boardman & Lasser, 2016; Klingner & Vaughn, 1999, 2000).

Klingner and Vaughn (1999) explained that CSR combines cognitive strategy instruction similar to reciprocal teaching (Palincsar & Brown, 1984), with cooperative learning (Johnson & Johnson, 1989), so that students work in heterogeneous small groups to improve their comprehension of expository texts. CSR teaches students how to implement four strategies while reading and discussing expository texts. The strategies include the following:

- *Preview the Text:* Before reading the text, students initiate their background knowledge about the topic and predict what the text might be about.
- *Click and Clunk Comprehension:* As they read, the students monitor

their comprehension by saying "clunk" when they encounter comprehension problems, such as unknown vocabulary, and by saying "click" when they comprehend parts of the text. When they say "clunk," they are supposed to use specific fix-up strategies to resolve the problem. The fix-up strategies for unknown words include "reread the sentence and look for key ideas to help you understand the word; reread the sentences before and after looking for clues; look for a prefix or suffix in the word; break the word apart and look for smaller words" (Klingner & Vaughn, 1999, p. 740).

- *Get the Gist:* While reading, the students state the most important ideas.
- *Wrap-Up:* After completing the reading, the students summarize what they learned from the reading and ask and answer questions that teachers might ask about the reading.

After introducing the students to CSR and its purpose, the teachers use think-alouds, in which they verbalize their thinking, to introduce each of the CSR strategies to the whole class. Then they show the students how to implement each of the four strategies. Before students combine the four strategies to read and discuss expository texts, they practice each strategy in teacher-designed activities. The teachers also have the students role-play the different roles that they will enact in the small groups (i.e., group leader, clunk expert, gist expert, announcer to call on students, and encourager) (Klingner & Vaughn, 1999). Like dialogic strategy instruction, CSR takes a while for elementary age students to effectively implement.

CSR encourages bilingual students to use all their linguistic resources to participate in small-group discussions. For example, the following transcript shows how two bilingual fifth graders utilized English and Spanish to implement CSR during ESL content instruction:

> MARIO: Does anybody have any click and clunks? . . . Okay, do you know what voluntary means?
>
> FRANK: Voluntario? (Voluntary)
>
> MARIO: Si, que quiere decir? (Yes, what does it mean?)
>
> FRANK: Que ellos se mueven cuando ellos quieren. (That they move when they want.) (Klingner & Vaughn, 2000, p. 69)

High-Level Student Discussions and Engagement with Texts

Several researchers reported that emergent bilingual students improved their reading comprehension and engagement with texts when they participated in high-level discussions of texts. In this section, instructional conversations and literature circles are discussed.

Instructional Conversations

Saunders and Goldenberg (1999) developed instructional conversations for bilingual Latinx fourth and fifth graders with varied levels of English proficiency (emergent bilingual and English-proficient). Their aim was to improve the students' English story comprehension.

In instructional conversations, teachers instructed students on how to participate in high-level discussions of narrative texts by asking them to discuss open-ended themes from the texts (e.g., honesty, fairness, friendship) and to respond to open-ended questions (with no set answers) related to the themes and to the texts read (Goldenberg, 1992–1993). They also encouraged students to refer back to the texts to support the points they made in the discussions. Similar to a real conversation, they encouraged the students to participate in self-selected turn taking when discussing the texts. In addition, prior to the conversations, they had some of the students complete literature logs in which the students wrote responses to the themes and made personal connections to the texts.

After teachers implemented instructional conversations with and without literature logs, Saunders and Goldenberg (1999) compared the reading comprehension performance (on author-created factual and interpretive tests) of emergent bilingual students and English-proficient bilingual students who had been assigned to three different groups: (1) students who only participated in instructional conversations, (2) students who only participated in instructional conversations plus literature logs, and (3) a control group who did not receive any special instruction. They found that students in the instructional conversation plus literature log group scored highest on factual comprehension compared to the students in the instructional conversation and control groups. In terms of interpretive comprehension, the students who participated in instructional conversations and instructional conversations plus literature logs scored higher than the students in the control group. When they compared the performance of the emergent bilingual students with the English-proficient students, they found that the English-proficient students always scored higher on the interpretive measure (i.e., theme identification), suggesting that a key factor in the lower interpretive performance of the emergent bilingual students was their lower English proficiency.

Literature Circles

Literature circles are small, student-discussion groups that focus on literature that bilingual students choose to read and discuss (DeNicolo & Fránquiz, 2006; Martínez-Roldán, 2005). Teachers who use literature circles often provide their students with the choice of three to four books. Prior to the discussion, each member of the group reads and takes notes on the selected text. Then, the students bring their notes to the literature circle for discussion. Literature circles have been implemented with bilingual students as young as first grade. With students this young, adults at home sometimes read the texts to the students.

Literature circles are conducted like conversations in that students do not raise their hands to speak. The students in the circle direct and maintain the discussion, although some teachers assign student roles for the discussion (Daniels, 2002). The maximum time for a circle usually is 30 minutes. Literature circles often supplement the other reading instruction students receive.

Although proponents of literature circles do not provide data on improvements in bilingual students' reading comprehension, they do provide qualitative data to illustrate bilingual students' high engagement with the discussions and their demonstration of critical thinking (DeNicolo & Fránquiz; 2006; Martínez-Roldán & López-Robertson, 1999–2000). Daniels (2002) reported that literature circles provide students with opportunities for independent reading and writing and extensive talk about what they read. Martínez-Roldán (2005) pointed out that literature circles give students the opportunity to participate in discussions about books regardless of their reading or language proficiencies. When bilingual students read and discuss multicultural texts that focus on the experiences of characters similar to themselves, then literature circles provide them with opportunities to develop a sense of school belonging (DeNicolo et al., 2017).

Bilingual/Translanguaging Strategies

Several researchers showed how bilingual Latinx students employed strategies unique to their bilingual status to comprehend texts in English and Spanish (G. García & Godina, 2017; Jiménez et al., 1995, 1996). For example, Jiménez et al. reported that sixth- and seventh-grade bilingual Latinx students who were good English readers had a unitary view of reading across their two languages. They employed bilingual strategies (now called translanguaging strategies) to explain their reading: translation, code-switching—moving between two languages within sentences and across sentences or larger chunks of texts, and the use of cognates—words in English and Spanish with ancestral roots that look similar and have similar meanings. The good readers also made use of information acquired in one language while reading in another language, or what Jimenez et al. called the transfer of information across languages.

My colleague and I (G. García & Godina, 2017) reported similar findings for five of six fourth-grade bilingual Latinx students who were excellent readers in Spanish but grade-level or below grade-level readers in English. When they read and discussed expository and narrative texts in Spanish and English, they demonstrated three types of translating (direct, summary, and paraphrased translating), code-switched, and code-mixed (juxtaposed Spanish and English in a sentence). The five students also referred to information acquired in one language while reading in the other language. However, only the top two readers occasionally employed cognates.

Although none of the students in these studies (G. García & Godina, 2017; Jiménez et al., 1995, 1996) reported receiving instruction on translanguaging strategies, there is some evidence that bilingual students will benefit from translanguaging instruction. López-Velásquez and I (2017) found that two first graders, who predominantly received reading instruction in only one language, could apply what they had learned about reading in one language to read in the uninstructed language when my colleague, López-Velásquez, provided them with instructional support that aided their translanguaging. Other colleagues and I (G. García et al., 2020) found that third- and fourth-grade bilingual Latinx students benefited from explicit cognate instruction (for more on cognates, see Chapter 10). Jiménez et al. (2015) taught middle-school students how to translate sections of English texts to Spanish, which resulted in improvements in the students' comprehension of the English texts. Given these findings, explicit instruction on how to use translanguaging strategies to improve reading comprehension looks promising for bilingual students.

Addressing Standards to Advance Students' Reading Comprehension and Performance

Your reading comprehension instruction should not cease once students independently apply cognitive and translanguaging strategies while reading. The CCSS (NGA Center for Best Practices & CCSSO, 2010) provide information on other literacy tasks that advanced readers should know and perform. Sometimes, the CCSS, which were written for native-English speakers in the United States, are inappropriate for bilingual students (G. García, 2012). However, a CCSS publication by the San Diego County of Education (2012) identifies English and Spanish language arts/literacy standards appropriate for Spanish–English bilingual students. I suggest that you refer to this document and your state standards to plan and implement instruction that will further accelerate the literacy performance of bilingual students in grades 3–6.

CONCLUDING REMARKS

I encourage all teachers of bilingual students (emergent bilingual students, dual-language students, former emergent bilingual students, and bilingual students in all-English classrooms) to plan and implement purposeful reading comprehension instruction with their students. It is especially important for teachers of bilingual students to make sure that their students develop their background knowledge and know how to activate the appropriate background knowledge when they read. In addition, teachers should instruct and provide bilingual students with guided and independent practice on how to make different types of inferences and flexibly enact cognitive strategies as they read and discuss texts.

The findings in this chapter reinforce the importance of providing bilingual students with opportunities to discuss their use of strategies and what they learned from texts with other students in student-led small groups. You can improve your bilingual students' reading comprehension by having them participate in dialogic strategy instruction, reciprocal teaching, or CSR, along with opportunities to read and discuss engaging texts through instructional conversations and/or literature circles.

Lastly, it is important to remember that bilingual students can be taught to improve their reading comprehension in either or both languages. They also can use translanguaging strategies to interact with and display their reading comprehension. Given the monolingual instructional emphasis that many bilingual students receive, you may have to remind your students of the unique capabilities that they, as bilinguals, have to comprehend texts.

Bilingual Students' Writing Instruction

GUIDING QUESTIONS

- What is the relationship between reading and writing?
- When should teachers ask bilingual students to write in their L1 and L2?
- Are bilingual students' English writing errors more like those of native-English speakers or L2 speakers?
- What is the most effective instructional approach for teaching bilingual students how to write?
- What problems do some bilingual students face when participating in writing workshops in English?
- What can students' invented spelling tell you about their reading and writing development?
- How does modeled writing instruction aid bilingual students' writing?
- Why do bilingual students sometimes translanguage when writing?
- Why is it important to compare dual-language students' writing in their two languages?
- What cultural and linguistic differences may affect bilingual students' writing?

Ms. Aaron was teaching English writing to emergent bilingual fourth and fifth graders in her ESL class, which was part of a transitional program of instruction. The students were Chinese, Somalian, and Vietnamese. The Phams' 10-year-old, who was introduced in Chapter 1, was in Ms. Aaron's class.

To help her more advanced students develop their oral English and English writing, she sometimes had them view recorded videos of English sitcoms that included physical action and humor, such as *I Love Lucy*. She thought that the students comprehended the videos, especially when English captions were printed at the bottom of the frames. They also appeared to enjoy them. Some of her students even borrowed the videos to view at home.

During the 90 minutes that Ms. Aaron had for ESL instruction, she sometimes asked her more advanced students to work in pairs to write explanations of what they liked best in the videos. After they finished their writing, she reviewed what they wrote, putting any grammatical and spelling corrections in boxes above the writing errors. After she met in brief conferences with individual students about their writing and errors, the students were supposed to write and submit final versions of their writing with the errors corrected.

A university professor who was an expert in English writing for native-English-speaking students had been observing the ESL teacher's instruction over the past semester. She was concerned about the teacher's instruction because she thought the students should be engaged in free writing—writing about their own topics—and that the teacher should not correct the students' writing. She was an advocate of process writing and the writer's workshop. She did not understand why the ESL students did not work in peer groups to discuss whether their writing made sense. Once the students revised their writing for content, she also thought that other ESL classmates should edit it.

When the university professor approached the ESL teacher about her concerns, the teacher politely told her that she only had 90 minutes to work with the students. She had to help them improve their oral English, English reading, and English writing. Although she had her students do free writing in their diaries, she did not implement a writer's workshop with them.

Chapter 9 focuses on the writing instruction of current and former emergent bilingual students and dual-language students in grades K–6. A short review of writing theories, insights, and research begins the chapter. The chapter ends with a discussion of the cultural and language differences that may affect bilingual students' L1 and L2 writing.

WRITING THEORIES, INSIGHTS, AND RESEARCH

The amount of research published on the writing development and instruction of bilingual students in the United States is even less than that published on bilingual students' reading development and instruction (August

& Shanahan, 2006; Escamilla et al., 2014; Herrera et al., 2010). Until the advent of the CCSS (NGA Center for Best Practices & CCSSO, 2010), writing was not a curricular priority in United States elementary schools (Brisk, Kaveh, Scialoia, & Timothy, 2016).

Reading and Writing Relationship

A major theoretical insight from the English writing research is the strong relationship between reading and writing. Of necessity, writers are readers because they have to read, edit, and proof their writing (Raimes, 1998). Several researchers interpreted the reciprocal relationship between reading and writing to mean that the development of reading precedes the development of writing (Lems et al., 2017). According to Lems et al., writing in any language takes longer to develop compared to reading.

However, in Mexico, "oracy, reading, writing, and metalanguage"—talk about language—are interconnected and included in its national literacy curriculum (Escamilla et al., 2014, p. 52). Escamilla et al. explain that, in Mexico, students' writing is used to teach students how to read. Writing activities in Mexico include literature responses, "text summaries, writing . . . different genres . . . (e.g., biographies, poems), writing for different audiences, learning to take notes, and writing for different mediums (e.g., for newspapers, radio or television)" (p. 52).

Appropriate Age for Bilingual Students' Writing Instruction to Begin

Although bilingual students may take longer to master L2 writing than L2 reading (Lems et al., 2017), this does not mean that teachers should wait to ask young bilingual learners to write in their L1 or L2. Several researchers observed that kindergarten and first-grade bilingual Latinx children were able to write in English, their L2, before attaining oral English proficiency (Edelsky, 1986; Moll, Saez, & Dworin, 2001). Lang and I (G. García & Lang, 2018) reported that after receiving explicit syllabic instruction in Spanish and reading little books with words that included the taught syllables, several bilingual (Spanish–English) kindergartners in a 90–10 DL program employed invented and conventional spelling to write short narratives in Spanish.

Source of Bilingual Students' Writing Errors

A controversial L2 finding, informed by contrastive analysis (Lems et al., 2017), was that the English writing errors of L2 learners of English were not related to their L1 but were developmental errors similar to the writing errors of native-English speakers (Lightblown & Spada, 2011). However, analyses of Spanish–English DL students' writing by researchers who knew Spanish and English showed that the students' English writing was more influenced by their Spanish writing than the developmental writing of native-English speakers their age (Escamilla et al., 2014).

The one writing area in which the influence of Spanish writing did not apply was bilingual Latinx students' English spelling. Escamilla, Geisler, Hopewell, and Ruiz (2007) conducted a five-year study that compared the Spanish and English writing samples of Spanish–English, bilingual first, second, third, and fourth graders who participated in paired bilingual education (i.e., biliteracy squared; Escamilla et al., 2014). Although they found high and positive correlations for the students' content and punctuation when they wrote in Spanish and English, the correlation for spelling in the two languages was weaker.

Effectiveness of Different Types of Writing Instruction

In a review of research on the reading and writing instruction of emergent bilingual students, Genesee and Riches (2006) reported that the type of instruction that students received fell on a continuum with direct approaches at one end, interactive approaches in the middle, and process approaches at the other end. They defined direct instruction as a focus on explicit skill and subskill instruction. In an interactive approach, "students learned from others, initially by observation and subsequently by internalizing more mature literate behaviors exhibited by others" (Genesee & Riches, 2006, p. 11). Genesee and Riches defined process approaches as "engagement in authentic reading and writing for communicative purposes" (p. 5).

Genesee and Riches (2006) reported that few researchers studied the use of direct instruction when teaching writing to emergent bilingual students, while more of them studied the use of interactive approaches for teaching writing to emergent bilingual students. Interactive writing approaches include the use of the GRR (Pearson & Gallagher, 1983, see Chapter 8), cooperative learning, and shared writing (Hellman, 2016). Almost every interactive writing study that they reviewed had positive results. One reason why Genesee and Riches thought that interactive learning might be effective with emergent bilingual students was that it mapped onto cultural practices emphasized in some students' homes, such as, collaborative learning versus competitive learning and observing versus telling.

Another teaching approach that Genesee and Riches (2006) examined was process writing. Examples of literacy process approaches are the use of the reading workshop and writing workshop. In a writer's workshop (Calkins, 1987), students participate in the writing process by brainstorming topics, prewriting, drafting, sharing what they wrote with their peers to see if the writing makes sense, peer editing, and publishing their writing.

Genesee and Riches (2006) questioned the effectiveness of process writing approaches with emergent bilingual students. They cited de la Luz Reyes's (1991) finding that "overall, mere exposure to standardized writing conventions did not improve the students' use of them" (p. 291). Genesee and Riches concluded that evidence for the "effectiveness of [process] approaches was mixed" (p. 19).

Other researchers voiced concerns about implementing the writing workshop with L2 learners of English. First, they warned that L2 learners of English need more help with grammar, spelling, punctuation, word choice, and the selection of topics than the workshop format provides (Lems et al., 2017). Second, L2 learners of English frequently need a threshold level of English proficiency before they can provide or benefit from peer editing (G. García, 2003). As L2 learners, they do not always hear the L2 errors when they read aloud what others wrote or what they wrote. Third, the predominant narrative focus in the writing workshop does not provide L2 learners of English with instruction and practice on how to compose, that is, how to use information from a range of sources to create a new text (Lems et al., 2017). Lastly, explicit instruction on how to write coherently, that is, to use "signal words, connectors, and transition words," usually is not included in writing workshops (Lems et al., 2017, p. 237). To offset some of the problems, Kucer and Silva (1999) recommended that teachers who implement process writing approaches with emergent bilingual students explicitly teach areas in which students have difficulty and show the students what to do and how to accomplish it (p. 366).

Aims of Writing Instruction and Types of English Writing

The aims of writing instruction in the United States appear to be the same for L2 or bilingual students and native-English speakers: to enjoy writing and to become skillful and confident writers (Lems et al., 2017). To attain these aims, bilingual students typically are asked to do the same types of English writing as native-English speakers: expressive writing, responsive writing, and expository writing. According to Lems et al., expository writing is the most difficult type of writing for emergent bilingual students because it requires academic and vocabulary knowledge of English.

Lems et al. (2017) consider expressive writing to be the easiest type of English writing because it involves writing about personal experiences. Gibbons (2015) contends that the best way to begin writing instruction with emergent bilingual students is "to start with their own expressive language," to emphasize "meaning is more important than form," and to provide them with a "real" audience for their writing (p. 57).

Lems et al. (2017) contend that responsive writing is more difficult than expressive writing because it involves writing in response to topics introduced or learned at school. However, this may depend on the writing tasks and the age of the L2 learners. L1 and L2 writing research with elementary, emergent bilingual students showed that they were able to write text summaries and responses to texts that their teachers read aloud or to videos that they saw without much difficulty (Lee & García, 2021; McCarthey & García, 2005). The teacher read-alouds and videos appeared to provide the students with the necessary vocabulary and topical knowledge.

WRITING INSTRUCTIONAL PRACTICES

Student Names

Most young students learn to write their first names when they enter preschool or kindergarten. If your students do not know how to print their names, you and other adult volunteers should help each child learn how to write their first name by saying the name aloud and following the linguistic structure of the name to write it. For example, if the name is in Spanish, you should sound out and write each syllable. If the name is in English, you should sound out and write each letter. If the name involves unusual spelling (e.g., Joie pronounced Joy), then I recommend that you teach the student how to write the name as a sight word by memorizing it (see Chapter 7).

Names are part of students' identities and should not be changed. There is an engaging picture book, *The Name Jar* (Choi, 2003), which describes the ordeal that a Korean immigrant child had to endure when the native-English-speaking students in her class suggested she change her Korean name, which was difficult for them to pronounce and remember, to an American name.

Invented Spelling

You should encourage young bilingual students to write as they hear the words in their L1 or L2. This type of emergent writing is called invented spelling. An easy way to begin invented spelling is to ask students to draw a picture of one thing that they did that morning before school and to write a title or caption for the drawing. Be sure to give the students a limited amount of time to do the drawing, so that they have time to write the title or caption. Then, you should have them show you the drawing and orally read to you what they wrote. You or another adult should write what they said beneath their writing.

When evaluating young students' invented spelling, however, you need to understand the structure of the language in which the student is writing. For instance, in Spanish, young students often write the vowels before the consonants because they hear the vowels better than the consonants, whereas, in English, they often write the consonants first because they hear them better than the vowels (Mercuri & Musanti, 2021).

Toward the end of the school year, a first grader in a Spanish–English DL classroom (90–10) used invented spelling in Spanish to describe a picture of a man washing a window in a house. He wrote: "avia una ves el papá lava las ventanas y despues se canso mucho y se fue a dormir?" (Once upon a time the father washes the windows and afterward he was really tired and went to sleep.) The correct Spanish writing is as follows (corrections are in bold): "**Había** una ve**z** un papá **quien** lava**ba** las ventanas y despu**é**s se cans**ó** mucho y se fue a dormir" (Once upon a time there was a father who washed the windows and afterward he was really tired and went to sleep).

You can analyze your students' invented spelling to estimate where they are in their writing development and to plan your writing instruction accordingly. For instance, the Spanish example showed that the child had employed storybook language when he used "avía una vez" (once upon a time), which is a bit unusual for a narrative description. It is likely that in second grade he would benefit from lessons showing the difference between writing fiction and writing a narrative (see Chapter 5). He also should be taught or reminded to use a capital letter to begin the sentence and a period to end it. Sometime in the future, he needs to learn how to use the present progressive verb tense in Spanish to describe an ongoing event.

Escamilla et al. (2014) provide an example of a bilingual first grader's invented spelling in English: "De girls layk to plei wet dols" (p. 58). The correct writing is: "The girls like to play with dolls." They point out that the student knew to start the sentence with a capital letter but forgot to include a period at the end of the sentence. She also appeared to use her knowledge of Spanish to spell in English.

Sometimes, students do not want to make any mistakes and will not use invented spelling. When this happens, continue to ask the students to write about their drawings according to what they hear and know but do not insist on invented spelling. If you have word walls in your classroom (see Chapter 7) in which you display the sight words that your students have been taught, be sure to add words that students frequently misspell when writing. Then, ask your students to use the words on the word wall to write.

"El Dictado" or Dictation

An instructional activity that teachers in Mexico and Latin America frequently employ to promote Spanish literacy is "el dictado" or dictation

(Escamilla et al., 2014). Escamilla et al. also recommend that teachers utilize dictation to promote English literacy. Dictations in Spanish and English are a key instructional activity in biliteracy squared, a biliteracy curriculum designed for dual-language students (Escamilla et al., 2014).

In "el dictado," the teacher dictates specific words, phrases, and sentences for the students to write in their journals or on paper. Sometimes, teachers have their students do all their dictations in a bound journal and label each entry with the date so that they can keep track of the students' writing progress.

Through dictation, students are taught how to spell and punctuate their writing, specific vocabulary, and ways to comprehend what they read (Beeman & Urow, 2012). For instance, in PreK–2, when some teachers dictate in Spanish, they tell the students when to use a capital letter (la mayúscula), a lower-case letter (la minúscula), a comma (la coma), a semicolon (el punto y coma), and the accent (el acento).

According to Escamilla et al. (2014), the dictation should be a familiar topic and include words already known to the students. Before conducting the dictation, the teacher should read aloud to the students what will be dictated several times so that students know what to expect. Beeman and Urow (2012) explain that in kindergarten, teachers should dictate key words known to the students or a simple sentence with known words. In first grade, teachers can dictate a simple or complex sentence. In second grade, a two-sentence dictation is appropriate, while in third grade, three sentences or a simple paragraph is appropriate.

For the dictation, Urow and Beeman (n.d.) recommend that you give your students graph paper or paper divided into squares. You instruct your students to write each letter and punctuation mark in a separate square, leaving an empty square between words, which should help your students to learn word boundaries.

Escamilla et al. (2014) also recommend that you have your students write on one line but leave the other line empty. Any corrections that you or your students make should be written above the students' initial writing. Figure 9.1 provides a simulated example of a student's dictation in Spanish.

Usually, teachers spend three to five days for 15–20 minutes each day on one dictation (Escamilla et al., 2014; Urow & Beeman, n.d.). On day 1, the teacher reads what is to be dictated to the students. Then, the teacher dictates to the students, and the students write the dictation. Next, the teacher writes what was dictated on a whiteboard so that everyone in the class can see it. As the teacher writes, she explains any special features of the text. For instance, the teacher might explain how to use "rayas" (long dashes —) to show when a person speaks in Spanish or double quotations marks (" ") to show when a person speaks in English. Students are told not to erase their work, but to write the corrections above their dictated writing.

		E	l		h	i	j	o	
	c	o	r	r	i	ó		a	
	s	u		m	a	m	á	.	
	É	l		e	s	t	a	b	a
	c	a	n	s	a	d	o	.	

FIGURE 9.1. Example of Spanish dictation (Translation: The boy ran to his mother. He was tired.).

On day 2, the teacher explains additional punctuation, grammatical, or stylistic features. On day 3, the students work in pairs to dictate to each other, or if this is the last day of the dictation, the teacher re-dictates what was read on day 1 for evaluation purposes. If the teacher continues to use the dictation on day 4, the students sometimes add more text to the dictation. On day 5, they participate in another dictation of the expanded or original text for evaluation purposes. Escamilla et al. (2014) provide detailed information on how to conduct dictations in Spanish and English in grades K–5.

Modeled Writing

Teachers can use modeled writing in the L1 and/or L2 to demonstrate to bilingual students in grades K–6 "the process of writing a text," how to use specific writing features, and how to write different types of texts (Escamilla et al., 2014, p. 54). For instance, teachers can model how to begin a story by using "Había una vez" in Spanish, or its translation "Once upon a time" in English. They also can model how to use a story map (see Chapter 5) to draft a story or how to use the sequence text structure (see Chapter 5) to write instructions to make something or to walk somewhere. In addition, they can model how to write a summary of what was read or how to write responses to a reading.

Escamilla and her colleagues (2014) recommend that teachers model writing in a whole-class setting before asking their students to practice or enact the writing. They suggest that teachers write on a whiteboard so that everyone in the class can see the writing and participate in think-alouds to describe what they are doing and why.

In addition, Escamilla et al. (2014) advise teachers to use modeled writing to teach their students specific sentence structures and vocabulary to include in their writing. I observed a 90–10 Spanish–English DL teacher teach her first graders how to use descriptive language in Spanish to write about themselves. For example, in a whole-class setting, she drew a face with eyes and wrote a sentence frame on the whiteboard: "Mis ojos son ____________." (My eyes are ____________.) Then, she pointed to the drawing and to her eyes, and modeled how to complete the frame by including information about herself. Next, she asked her students to look at each other's eyes and provide words to complete the frames (e.g., negros—black, azules—blue, verdes—green, cafes—brown). She posted the words on the whiteboard with illustrations. Next, the students used the information on the board to write descriptive sentences about themselves in their notebooks.

Escamilla et al. also recommend that teachers provide examples of "connected discourse" for what they are modeling (p. 54). For instance, if you are working with fourth graders on how to state opinions with examples to justify the opinions, you should provide a writing example to demonstrate what you are teaching.

After teachers use modeled writing to create texts, they should model how to revise and edit texts and have their students do the revision and editing with them. If students already have learned how to write in one language and are beginning to write in the L2, Escamilla et al. (2014) recommend that teachers use modeled writing to explain writing features specific to the L2 and for making cross-language connections.

Shared Writing

One of the more popular shared writing approaches, the language experience approach, was introduced in Chapter 4. Shared writing can occur in the L1 or L2 and be used with students in grades K–6. When teachers and students participate in shared writing, they "construct a text together" (Escamilla et al., 2014, p. 55); that is, both the teacher and students are actively involved in creating and revising what is written. While teachers write by using a whiteboard or projecting the writing on a computer so all their students can see it, students add to the teacher's writing and edit and revise it. Escamilla and her colleagues recommend that teachers also use shared writing to compare writing differences in the bilingual students' two languages.

Shared writing provides students with the opportunity to try out different types of writing with their teacher's support (Escamilla et al., 2014). It can be used to teach students how to write for different audiences and in different genres, such as, descriptive writing, informational or expository writing, persuasive writing, and narrative writing.

Collaborative Writing

When students work with others to create texts, they are participating in collaborative writing. A simple form of collaborative writing is the dialogue journal. In a dialogue journal, the teacher sometimes begins the writing by asking her students several questions. Students then write their answers to the teacher's questions and turn in their journals for the teacher to read and respond to their answers. Teachers do not correct the students' writing, but may recast it by using the corrected writing in their responses.

In dialogue journals, teachers need to extend their students' writing by establishing a conversation with their students in which they ask them authentic questions to which they do not know the answers. The biggest problem that teachers typically have when employing dialogue journals is providing timely responses to their students' writing. Depending on the size of your class, you can collect half of your students' journals one week and respond to them the next week when you collect the other half of your students' journals.

A more complex form of collaborative writing is when students write a paper or develop a written project together. Throughout these endeavors, the teacher should monitor the students' writing and provide assistance as needed (Escamilla et al., 2014). Escamilla et al. recommend that you let students translanguage when they participate in collaborative writing, but that the "final product be in the target languages" (p. 57). When students have completed their writing, they should share it with the class.

Independent Writing

Students should be given time to write independently, that is, on their own. Sometimes, teachers assign independent writing after introducing modeled writing and shared writing. When teachers assign independent writing, they often work with students to brainstorm possible topics.

Writing Conferences

When students do independent writing, their teachers sometimes meet with them during individual writing conferences to provide feedback on their work. In a study that my colleague and I (G. García & Lang, 2018) conducted in a 90–10 Spanish–English DL school, one of the third-grade DL teachers decided to have her students participate in writing conferences. She had the students select one of their writing pieces in Spanish, complete a self-evaluation sheet about it, and turn in the writing and self-evaluation sheet before the conference so that she could prepare for the conference.

The self-evaluation sheet asked the students to identify their teacher's writing goals for them, their personal writing goals, and what the teacher and student needed to do to attain both goals. One of her students surprised her when he told her that to obtain both of their goals, she should use a red pen to help him improve his punctuation. She had never told her students that one of her writing goals was for them to improve their punctuation. However, she often used a red pen to correct their punctuation. She realized that she needed to emphasize larger writing goals for her students and stop using a red pen to correct their punctuation. Form 9.1, at the end of the chapter, provides a writing conference form that you can use during writing conferences.

Adapted Writing Workshop

If you want to use the writing workshop with your bilingual students, then I recommend that you adapt your writing instruction and the writing workshop so that it addresses the concerns researchers identified. For instance, you can use modeled writing to show your students how to use sources to compose, how to write coherently, and how to edit each others' writing. You can use dictation to show how to spell certain words and how to use specific grammatical structures. However, you still may need to provide your students with explicit instruction on how to expand their writing and make better word choices (Kucer & Silva, 1999).

When you explicitly show students how to accomplish these tasks outside of the workshop, you probably will need to implement a mini-lesson on these tasks during the workshop so that students apply what they learned outside the workshop while writing in the workshop. Providing bilingual students with an editing or proofing chart that covers writing errors reviewed during modeled writing or dictation should help the students to improve their peer editing.

Bilingual Students' Use of Translanguaging to Write

When writing in their L1 or L2, bilingual students may translanguage. Often their ideas "surpass [their] ability to write them in" a single language (Herrera et al., 2010, p. 213). One of my former PhD students and I discovered that Korean first graders sometimes translanguaged when they wrote in Korean, their L1, which was their weaker written language (Lee & García, 2021). The students attended public schools in English during the school week and a Korean heritage language classroom on Saturdays. We concluded that the first graders' writing would have been limited if they had not been able to translanguage when writing in Korean. When you do not understand your bilingual students' translanguaging in their writing, you should ask them to read aloud to you what they wrote or to tell you what they wanted to say in their writing.

Biliteracy Development

Because a major goal of DL education is biliteracy, Mercuri and Musanti (2021) recommend that DL teachers examine students' independent writing about the same or similar topics in their two languages. For instance, when they compared a second-grade student's expository writing about celebrations in Spanish and English, they pointed out that the student included an appropriate title in Spanish but did not include a title in English. They suggest that teachers compare students' writing in each language according to the students' appropriate use of vocabulary, grammar, and discourse structures (p. 175), and focus their writing instruction accordingly.

Advanced Writing Instruction

The English language arts CCSS (NGA Center for Best Practices & CCSSO, 2010) includes a focus on writing for elementary native-English speakers. I recommend that you refer to your English and partner-language state standards to provide your more advanced bilingual literacy learners with instruction that will accelerate their writing progress in their L1 and L2. If your state standards do not indicate what teachers should emphasize in Spanish and English, then I refer you to the CCSS English/Spanish language publication by the San Diego County of Education (2012). Chapter 11 on disciplinary literacy instruction also includes writing instruction for more advanced literacy learners.

CULTURAL AND LINGUISTIC WRITING DIFFERENCES

Teachers of bilingual students need to be aware of any cultural and linguistic differences that may affect bilingual students' writing and reading in each language. Learning about the different ways that writing occurs in each culture is one way to become aware of cultural differences in writing and reading. Studying the grammatical structures of each language allows you to identify the linguistic differences in the two languages. When you teach students to write in English and another language, you should make sure that bilingual students know how to write appropriately in each language. In addition, they need to know how to take into account any cultural and linguistic differences when they read in each language.

Cultural Differences

Discourse Patterns

English often has a different discourse pattern compared to other languages. Discourse patterns are how people in a culture express themselves (Herrera et al., 2010). Although there may be a variety of discourse patterns in a culture and language, a dominant pattern usually characterizes expository writing. For example, the dominant expository discourse pattern in English is linear (Herrera et al., 2010). Mercuri and Musanti (2021) observe that in English the topic usually is introduced first, with subsequent sentences presenting additional information about the topic. Expository academic writing usually has an introduction, a body, and a conclusion.

In contrast, the dominant discourse patterns in other languages are not as linear as English. Spanish expository writing usually begins with a topic, but the writing digresses in different directions, with the main idea at the end (Montaño-Harmon, 2001). As Spencer's (1990) discourse analysis of Spanish indicated, "the reader will be eased into the subject gently, . . . and some [sentences] will be of a more distant nature from the topic and will have only indirect reference to the subject at hand" (p. 72). Spencer also noted that in Spanish "language will be chosen carefully . . . for its artistic effect" (Kaplan, 1972, p. 64, as cited in Spencer, p. 72).

Montaño-Harmon (2001) pointed out that Asian languages, such as Chinese and Korean, tend to have an indirect or circular discourse pattern. To directly address an idea or thought is considered rude.

When bilingual students in the United States read narrative texts that are not translations of English texts, but texts originally written in another language, they may have problems comprehending the original texts. When I conducted research with Latinx fourth graders who were strong readers in Spanish, I discovered that not all of them could comprehend narratives originally written in Spanish (G. García, 1998; G. García & Godina, 2017). The students who were the strongest readers in Spanish and English comprehended the narrative texts originally written in Spanish, but the other students experienced difficulties. The latter's comprehension was adversely affected not only by the metaphorical language and symbolism in the original Spanish texts, but also by the long sentences and paragraphs. They were accustomed to reading Spanish texts that had been translated from English and that were written according to English norms.

Text Structures

Sometimes the text structure in nontranslated texts is different from what characterizes English narratives. For example, Matsuyama (1983) reported that narratives in Japanese tend to focus on character development, character motives, and character relationships in contrast to the English focus on character goal attainment. Similarly, Korean folktales frequently reflect Confucianism, emphasizing conformity to Confucian morals. Heroes are rewarded not for attaining a goal, as in English folktales, but for implementing Confucian ideals (Song, 2017). When you read narratives originally written in languages other than English to your bilingual students, you will need to point out the differences in text structures between English and the other languages.

Rhetorical Styles

Some languages have different rhetorical styles from those of English. For instance, students who write in Arabic often are taught to appeal to emotions, not to facts (Connor, 2002).

Instructional Methods and Writing Genres

Some immigrant bilingual children who began their schooling in their home countries may be uncomfortable with how literacy is taught in the United States. For example, Dien (2004) cautions that Vietnamese children may consider the writing process approach strange because they think they should write correctly the first time. They are not accustomed to writing drafts and revising their writing. Herrera and her colleagues (2010) observed that it often was difficult for Latinx students to write in English about events that occurred in Spanish, the students' L1. They reported that it usually is easier for bilingual students to write in their L2 about something that they have done or seen in the L2, such as when they went on a fieldtrip or watched a favorite television show in their L2.

Several of the genres common to writing instruction in the United States also may be difficult for some immigrant bilingual students to employ. For example, Dien (2004) points out that writing personal narratives, an assignment that is commonly given during writing instruction in the United States, is uncomfortable for some immigrant students and their parents because they believe that sharing personal matters outside of the home is inappropriate.

Linguistic Differences

Certain grammatical differences characterize writing in English compared to writing in other languages. For example, Mercuri and Musanti (2021) point out that in English writing, the adjective usually comes before the noun, whereas in Spanish and Arabic, the adjective typically follows the noun. Also, the subject for each sentence is always stated in English writing, whereas in Spanish the subject is indicated by the verb conjugation and is not always stated. In contrast, Chinese does not have any verb conjugations.

Languages also exhibit differences in capitalization. Arabic and Chinese do not have upper- and lower-case letters. In English, the initial letters of each major word in a book title are capitalized, as are the initial letters in the names of the month and names of the day. However, in Spanish, only the initial letter in the first word of the book title is capitalized (Mercuri & Musanti, 2021). The initial letters in the names of the month and days of the week are not capitalized in Spanish.

Bilingual students will also need to learn punctuation differences between English and Spanish. For example, in English, quotation marks at the beginning and end of a speaker's oral comments or dialogue are used. In contrast, in Spanish dashes are used to indicate dialogue. In English, exclamation points and question marks are placed at the end of statements, whereas in Spanish, they begin and end such statements. According to Mercuri and Musanti (2021), commas are used to separate items in a list in English, but they are not used for this purpose in Spanish.

Mercuri and Musanti (2021) recommend that teachers first present bilingual students with two paragraphs written about the same topic in their two languages, and then let the students identify the similarities and differences in the languages before explicitly teaching the differences. They believe that this type of instruction will improve bilingual students' metalinguistic awareness or knowledge about the two languages. However, after giving students the opportunity to compare the passages in the two languages, I recommend that you explicitly review the differences and help students to employ the appropriate structures, rhetorical styles, and punctuation when writing in each language.

CONCLUDING REMARKS

Several findings about bilingual students' writing might have surprised you. First, you might have been surprised to learn that bilingual students should be given the opportunity to write in both languages as soon as they enter school. Second, although Lems et al. (2017) said that reading instruction precedes writing instruction, that does not appear to be the case in Mexico, where students learn to read through writing. Third, sometimes bilingual students' L1 influences their L2 writing development. These findings are good examples of how theories and theoretical insights change as more research is conducted.

Although the writer's workshop is a popular instructional method employed with native-English speakers, it needs to be carefully used with

L2 writers. Dictation, modeled writing, and shared writing probably should be used with beginning L2 writers before the writer's workshop is initiated. I observed first-grade DL teachers complain about their students' inability to participate in the writer's workshop. They said that some students still did not understand the concept of a word, while others did not know how to write a complete thought (G. García & Lang, 2023). The instructions they received to encourage their students to use three fingers to think about the beginning, middle, and end of what they wanted to write, were unsuccessful with the DL first graders.

When you teach students to write and read in two languages, you should learn about the writing differences in terms of discourse patterns, text structures, rhetorical styles, instructional methods and genres, and linguistic structures. You also need to make sure that your students learn how to write appropriately in each language.

I hope that this chapter provided you with useful ideas about how to support your bilingual students' writing development. More information on writing in the content areas is presented in Chapter 11.

FORM 9.1. Writing Conference Evaluation

Student Name: Date:

Discussion Points:

Student Goal:

Teacher Goal:

Revisit Discussion:

Note. Adapted with permission from Stahl and García (2022). Copyright © 2022 The Guilford Press.

CHAPTER 10

Increasing Bilingual Students' Vocabulary and Academic Language Knowledge and Use

GUIDING QUESTIONS

- What are the two types of academic vocabulary?
- Why is continued L1 vocabulary instruction important for bilingual students?
- What does explicit vocabulary instruction involve?
- How can teachers figure out which academic words to explicitly teach?
- Why and how should affixes be taught to bilingual students?
- How should Spanish cognates be taught so that students use them when reading and writing in English?
- Why is it difficult for bilingual students to expand their L2 reading vocabulary through incidental word reading?
- What are the different ways that teachers can teach bilingual students to know and use unfamiliar vocabulary?
- What types of academic language should be taught to bilingual students?

Mr. Hernández teaches fifth grade in a Spanish–English one-way DL program. He is supposed to use grade-level texts in English and Spanish with his fifth graders, but the English vocabulary in the English texts usually is too difficult for most of his students to comprehend. He has an English basal reader, which lists 10–20 difficult vocabulary items for him to preteach before asking his students to read a selection. He follows the basal's recommendations for teaching the vocabulary, but his students rarely remember what the vocabulary items mean after his instruction has ended.

Mr. Hernández spoke with another DL teacher, Ms. Ramírez, about his problem. She asked him if any of the students already knew what some of the words meant in Spanish. Mr. Hernández replied that he didn't think he was supposed to use Spanish during his English literacy instruction. She suggested that he go ahead and find out if any of the students knew what the words meant in Spanish.

Mr. Hernández translated the English words into Spanish and gave the Spanish list to his students. He was surprised to discover that the majority of his students knew the Spanish meanings for over half the English words. He posted the English and Spanish words in parallel columns in his classroom and told his students to use the Spanish meanings to help them comprehend the English text. Mr. Hernández still was worried about using Spanish during English reading, but he was relieved that more of his students understood the English text.

This chapter focuses on how to improve the L1 and L2 vocabulary knowledge and academic language of current and former emergent bilingual and DL students. Academic language encompasses academic vocabulary and "formal language skills" that students need to succeed in United States schools—English grammar, "discipline-specific terminology [and] rhetorical conventions" (Great Schools Partnership, 2013). Baker et al. (2014) explain that academic vocabulary consists of "general academic words" [e.g., correspond, emphasis], which often are abstract and appear more often in academic writing than in social settings or conversations and "domain-specific words," which are "unique to a particular academic discipline" [e.g., photosynthesis in biology, atom in physics, and archive in history] (p. 14).

As the chapter vignette indicates, bilingual students can use all their linguistic resources to comprehend text. Therefore, it is important for teachers to continue to develop emergent bilingual students' L1 vocabulary and academic language so that students can employ them when they work in their L2.

INSTRUCTION ACCORDING TO DIFFERENT STAGES OF L2 LANGUAGE ACQUISITION

Several researchers recommend that teachers of emergent bilingual students take into account the different stages of L2 language acquisition when they teach academic vocabulary and academic language (Herrera et al., 2010). WIDA also provides guidelines for teaching bilingual students' according to their developing language proficiencies and grade levels (WIDA, 2013, 2020). In the following text, I edited Herrera et al.'s recommendations so that they are appropriate for all L2 learners, including English-dominant dual-language learners.

For beginning L2 learners (preproduction)—students who only know a few L2 words, Herrera et al. (2010) recommend that teachers pair them with more L2-proficient bilingual students from the same L1 to increase their motivation. In addition, they recommend that teachers "introduce new vocabulary in context, [and] provide visual cues . . . that . . . students can use to identify/understand the meaning of the new vocabulary terms" (p. 110). I assume that Herrera and her colleagues are talking about "concrete" vocabulary—words that can be taught by referring to one of the five senses: hearing, seeing, smelling, tasting, and touching. The sheltered L2 techniques described in Chapter 3 can help you to teach concrete L2 words. Herrera et al. also recommend that teachers help students connect new L2 vocabulary to known L1 words.

For early-production L2 learners—students who provide "one-word [L2] responses"—Herrera et al. (2010) recommend lots of teacher modeling and "peer work" to give L2 learners many opportunities to "talk using the vocabulary [related to] the topic or story" (p. 110). Teachers should also do the following:

- Implement hands-on activities that enable [bilingual] students to talk about, illustrate, and engage in meaningful practice of new vocabulary terms;
- Us[e] peer discussions (in the native language if possible) to articulate and define vocabulary terms;
- [Get] students [to] act out vocabulary terms while peers try to guess the words (Herrera et al., p. 110).

During the speech-emergence stage—when students begin to respond to L2 questions with L2 sentences (Herrera et al., 2010)—teachers should not correct students' use of the L2. They should "revoice" student responses, "modeling correct [L2] during instruction" (p. 110). Teachers also should use "small-group activities to support [students'] practice of vocabulary terms in meaningful contexts" (p. 110). With their teachers' monitoring, students should work with peers to develop their own definitions of words and to "write short paragraphs using key vocabulary words" (p. 110).

When students demonstrate intermediate fluency (i.e., they "begin to mirror language use that approximates that of their [native-speaking] peers"; Herrera et al., 2010, p. 110), their teachers should look for "fossilization of grammar errors" (i.e., the habitual use of incorrect L2 grammatical forms and structures) and try to offset them (Herrera et al., 2010,

p. 111). Herrera and her colleagues recommend that teachers use "whole-group activities" to model "correct grammar, get their bilingual students to participate in reader's theater to correctly speak the L2, and assign bilingual students to retell "critical content-area concepts" and stories in their L2 (p. 111). In reader's theater, students orally read a text aloud, acting it out.

According to Herrera et al. (2010), when students are at the advanced fluency level, they demonstrate "a level of oral language . . . similar to that of grade-level [native-speaking] peers" (p. 111). However, their teachers still need to provide culturally and linguistically responsive instruction (see Chapter 2); "provide explicit instruction and modeling of [new] academic vocabulary"; and "offer linguistic support via the native language when possible" (p. 111). How to teach cognates (L1 and L2 words with ancestral roots that look similar and have similar meanings) is explained later in this chapter.

EXPLICIT ACADEMIC VOCABULARY INSTRUCTION WITH MULTIPLE MODALITIES

The United States Department of Education convened a panel of researchers to determine the best research-based academic content and literacy instruction for elementary and middle-school emergent bilingual students. Based on a review of experimental and quasi-experimental intervention findings with emergent bilingual students in grades K–8, along with the panel's collective expertise, members of the panel (Baker et al., 2014) concluded that explicit vocabulary instruction combined with multiple modalities was the most effective way to develop emergent bilingual students' academic vocabulary and use.

Explicit vocabulary instruction involves telling students what the word means (declarative knowledge), how to use the word (procedural knowledge), and when to use it (conditional knowledge). In addition, teachers who provide explicit vocabulary instruction typically do some, if not all, of the following:

- Provide child-friendly definitions of words—definitions using words that children understand,
- Give examples and nonexamples (i.e., negative or incorrect examples) of words,
- Show how specific words relate to other words,
- Model how words are used in different contexts,
- Give students extensive collaborative and independent practice using the words.

Multiple modalities is a sheltered L2 technique that makes L2 instruction comprehensible (see Chapter 3). When it is used with vocabulary instruction, it usually means that L2 students see the word, hear it, write it, read it, say it, and act it out or see it demonstrated.

English Vocabulary and Emergent Bilingual Students' English Reading Comprehension

English vocabulary knowledge plays an important role in emergent bilingual students' English reading comprehension. Research with fourth- and fifth-grade Spanish speakers showed that the students' oral English vocabulary affected their English reading comprehension significantly more than their English decoding or word-level reading skills (Lesaux et al., 2010a). Additionally, my colleagues and I, along with other researchers (Goldenberg, 2011), reported that unknown English vocabulary was the most important obstacle that adversely affected the English reading comprehension of Spanish-speaking, bilingual students (G. García, 1991; G. García & Godina, 2017).

At least three sets of researchers reported that emergent bilingual sixth graders benefited from instructional interventions that provided them with explicit vocabulary instruction on words that they read in texts (Gallagher, Barber, Beck, & Buehl, 2019; Lesaux et al., 2010b; Snow, Lawrence, & White, 2009). For example, Lesaux and her colleagues designed and tested an 18-week program—the Academic Language Instruction for All Students—with sixth graders in all-English classrooms at seven middle schools. The English target words were from informational articles in *Time for Kids*. Among other activities, the intervention involved students working together to develop word definitions and to analyze the morphology of words—that is, separating words into word parts (the word roots and affixes—prefixes and suffixes). Lesaux et al. reported that the explicit vocabulary instruction significantly improved the emergent bilingual and native-English-speaking students' knowledge of the targeted words.

The Selection of Academic Words for Explicit Vocabulary Instruction

To implement explicit vocabulary instruction with multiple modalities, Baker et al. (2014) from the federal What Works Clearinghouse recommend that teachers select no more than five to eight academic words from an engaging text. They explain that teaching these words so that emergent bilingual students know and can use them requires multiple exposures to the words and students' active use of them over a three- to five-day period. This means that you will not be able to use explicit instruction to teach all the unknown words that L2 learners will encounter in L2 texts. Below are the recommendations that researchers made for selecting academic vocabulary for bilingual students' explicit vocabulary instruction.

What Works Clearinghouse Recommendations

Baker et al. (2014) recommend that words should be selected for explicit vocabulary instruction when they:

- Are central to understanding the text.
- Appear frequently in texts.
- Appear in other content areas.
- Have multiple meanings.
- Include affixes (prefixes or suffixes).
- Have cross-language potential or are cognates. (pp. 16–17)

To implement the panel's recommendations, I recommend that you use the following procedures. To determine how central a word is to a narrative text's meaning, use a story map to figure out the importance of words in the narrative text. If the text is expository or informational, then you should identify and use the explicit or implicit text structure in the text to figure out which words to teach (see Chapter 5 for information on story maps and expository text structures). The words you identify should occur not just once in an occasional text, but frequently in the text and in more than one text. You also should choose words that appear in more than one content area. Coxhead's (2000) Academic Word List is a resource that school personnel can use to identify frequent English academic vocabulary.

Beck et al.'s (2013) Three-Tier Categorization

Several researchers recommend that teachers of bilingual students implement Beck, McKeown, and Kucan's (2013) three-tier categorization of vocabulary items to identify English reading vocabulary for explicit instruction (Carlo, August, & Snow, 2005). Calderón et al. (2005) point out that although the Beck et al. system was developed for native-English-speaking students, with some adjustments it can be employed with emergent bilingual students.

Beck et al. (2013) explain that Tier-One words are basic words that already should be part of the oral and reading vocabulary of native-English-speaking students. These words typically have just one meaning; and they usually do not need explicit instruction. Tier-One examples include car, eat, father, friends, house, and mother.

Calderón et al. (2005) point out that, as L2 learners, emergent bilingual students do not always know the English Tier-One words, so teachers should assess their knowledge of these words. If emergent bilingual students participated in or are participating in L1 instruction, then they may know the equivalent L1 Tier-One words or concepts. Showing or telling these students the L1 translations may be all that is needed. For instance, Spanish-speaking, third graders who participated in bilingual education will likely know the Spanish word (mariposa) for the English Tier-One word "butterfly." When bilingual students do not know the L1 words, then their teachers should teach the English words by providing child-friendly definitions, photographs or drawings, acting out the words, and providing concrete examples. Extensive explicit vocabulary instruction usually is not needed.

Tier-Two words are general academic words that frequently are abstract and appear in more than one text (Beck et al., 2013). These are the words that teachers usually need to explicitly teach. Tier-Two words in English include frightened, human, increase, influence, navigate, and prioritize.

Calderón et al. (2005) point out that if Tier-Two words are L1 cognates, then you should tell your students the L1 cognate. Many Spanish–English cognates are high-frequency and well-known words in Spanish, but are less frequent and less-known words in English (Lubliner & Hiebert, 2011). If your students do not know the L1 cognate, then you will need to explicitly teach the L2 word. Cognate instruction is discussed later in this chapter.

Tier-Three words are domain-specific words that characterize specific content areas (Beck et al., 2013). According to Beck et al., content-area teachers should teach these words when they teach the related discipline and topic. Tier-Three examples in mathematics include angle and geometry; examples in social studies include economics and geography; and examples in biology include ecosystem and habitat. However, Calderón et al. (2005) recommend that classroom teachers of emergent bilingual students not ignore Tier-Three words when they appear in texts, but briefly translate or explain the L1 meanings of Tier Three words without elaborating on their English meanings.

The Implementation of Explicit Vocabulary Instruction with Bilingual Students

Over three to five days of instruction, teachers can use a variety of techniques to explicitly teach unfamiliar L2 reading vocabulary to students. For example, to get students to think about related words they already know, you can have them do a KWL (see Chapter 8) or a "word splash" (Herrera et al., 2010). In a word splash, the teacher writes the target word on the whiteboard and asks students to copy it on their own paper. Then, in pairs or small groups, students brainstorm words related to the target word, printing them in the L2 or L1 or drawing illustrations of the related words on their own paper. After completing the word splash, the students and teacher discuss the meanings of the words included in the word splash.

For narrative fiction, such as stories and fables, students can complete a Vocab-O-Gram (Blachowicz, 1986; Stahl & García, 2022). To prepare a Vocab-O-Gram, the teacher reads the text and identifies words from the story that fit the text's story grammar or map and lists them at the top of the Vocab-O-Gram. For example, for the text *Jumanji* (Van Allsburg, 1981), the listed words could be: bored, game, Judy, Peter, mother, father, guests, adventure, jungle, restless, horror, upset, rhinoceros, asleep, python, guide, and Jumanji. Then, before reading the text, students work in pairs to use the words to predict what they think will happen in the text in terms of the story grammar (e.g., setting, characters, events/actions, resolution or ending). When students do not know the meaning of a listed word, they write it under mystery words. After hearing the text read aloud, or after they read the text, they correct their predictions on the Vocab-O-Gram, marking out words in the mystery list that they now know.

For expository text, teachers can use a semantic features analysis to compare and contrast features of important concepts. Table 10.1 shows a semantic features analysis that compares earthquakes and volcanoes.

Five-Days of Explicit Vocabulary Instruction

Baker et al. (2014) present recommendations for five days of explicit academic vocabulary instruction. On day 1, they recommend that you activate students' background knowledge for the text selected. Then, you conduct an interactive teacher read-aloud of the text, asking your students to answer open-ended questions about the text. Next, you introduce each of the target words by posting them, reading each word in the text, getting your students to repeat the word after you, and locating the words in their own copies of the text. On day 2, before sharing child-friendly definitions of the words, you should find out what your students now know about the words. Then, let them look at the words in the text, and tell you what they think the words mean. As a class, help them write their own child-friendly definitions of the words, recording them in their own personal dictionaries. For day 3, Baker et al. (2014) recommend that you, the teacher, write three questions that tap into the meanings of the target words. The students then work in pairs to discuss their answers to the questions, using the text to justify their answers. Before day 4, you write sentences that use the words. If the words have multiple meanings, make sure you write sentences to illustrate each of the meanings. Then, on day 4, review the sentences with the students, and when practical, have them sketch pictures to illustrate the sentences. On day 5, you teach any affixes in the words. Alternatively, on

TABLE 10.1. Semantic Features Analysis of Earthquakes and Volcanoes

	Geological origin	Destructive	Seismic waves	After-shocks	Lava and ash	Magma
Earthquakes	x	x	x	x		
Volcanoes	x	x			x	x

day 5, you can give your students a graphic organizer and ask them to use the words to write a text that matches the graphic organizer.

Affix Instruction

Kieffer and Lesaux (2007) explain that affix instruction involves analyzing the "structure of words" or morphology (p. 134). Morphology focuses on morphemes, the smallest units of word meaning. In English, there are unbound morphemes—independent words or roots/base words that have their own meanings (e.g., man, house) and affixes or bound morphemes, which cannot stand alone (e.g., the "er" in dreamer and the "est" in easiest). When bound morphemes are added to the beginning of root words, they are prefixes (e.g., "pre" as in "preview"). When they are added to the end of root words, they are suffixes. There are two types of suffixes: inflectional suffixes, such as plural markers and tense markers, and derivational suffixes, which change a word's part of speech (e.g., when you add "er" to the root/base "run," which is a verb, the word becomes "runner," a noun).

Plural Markers and Tense Markers

Several researchers have reported that native-English speakers typically are taught how to use plural markers and tense markers in first and second grade (Manyak, Baumann, & Manyak, 2018). If your bilingual students are in first grade and above and do not know how to recognize and employ inflectional morphemes in English, then you need to teach them. For your instruction, Manyak et al. recommend that you select English words that have concrete meanings and that your students already know. Then, you should use the GRR (see Chapter 8) to teach your students how to recognize and use plural markers and tense markers.

More Advanced Affix Instruction

For students in grades 3–6, Baumann in Manyak et al. (2018) also recommends that you begin your affix instruction by using root words that students already know. In addition, he advises that you only teach affixes that can be attached to root or base words. You should avoid words in which prefixes have been "absorbed or assimilated . . . (e.g., accept, erase)" (p. 294).

To begin your affix instruction, Manyak et al. (2018) recommend that you group prefixes and suffixes into word families. For instance, the following prefixes are part of the "not" prefix word family "dis," "un," and "in" (Manyak et al., 294). When you add them to root or base words, such as honest, happy, and correct, the words become dishonest, unhappy, and incorrect, respectively, and mean not honest, not happy, and not correct. Some other prefix word families are location or place (i.e., "over" and "under") and bad ("mis") (Manyak et al., p. 294). Prefix word examples are "overeat," "underwater," and "misbehave" (p. 294). Examples of suffix word families are the "more and most suffix family" (e.g., "-er and -est") and the "person who suffix family" (e.g., "er, -or, and ist" (p. 249). Manyak et al. suggest that you teach these affixes first because they have "clear primary meanings" and are easy for elementary students to use (p. 294). For a list of commonly taught affixes for students in grades 3–5, see the Manyak et al. article (2018).

You also should teach students how to use morphology to figure out what affixed words mean. Manyak et al. (2018) recommend that you provide students with a list of affixed words and teach them how to find the root or base word by telling them that it is the principal part of the word. "It comes after a prefix and before a suffix." (p. 297). Then, have students define the root or base word in the list of affixes. Next, have students find the prefixes and/or suffixes and tell you what meanings they add to the root words. Please refer to Manyak et al. for other ideas on how to teach affixes to elementary students.

Kieffer and Lesaux (2007) focused on teaching affixes to fourth- and fifth-grade bilingual students. They recommend asking students to find prefixes and suffixes in the texts they read and to group them by the types of prefixes and suffixes. Afterward, you should hold a whole-class discussion in which the students discuss what makes the words similar or different (i.e., their meanings and parts of speech). Kieffer and Lesaux also advise you to create a word wall with the prefixes and suffixes grouped by meaning.

COGNATE INSTRUCTION

Many researchers recommend that teachers of bilingual students encourage their students to use cognates to figure out the meanings of unknown L2 words (Baker et al., 2014; Herrera et al., 2010; Lubliner & Grisham, 2017). As was mentioned previously, cognates are words in two languages with ancestral roots that look similar and have similar meanings (G. García,

Sacco, & Guerrero-Aria, 2020). Due to the history of English, cognates characterize many words in English and the Romance languages (French, Portuguese, Romanian, and Spanish), and fewer words in English and the Germanic languages (Danish, Dutch, German, Norwegian, and Swedish) (Lems et al., 2017).

Bilingual students potentially can make use of cognates to figure out the meanings of unknown words in one language when they know the meanings of cognate words in the other language. Cognates are especially useful for Spanish speakers because Spanish cognates occur frequently in Spanish but less so in English. Also, a large number of Spanish–English cognates characterize informational texts in English (Lubliner & Hiebert, 2011). In the cognate example that follows, note that there are 11 cognates in the 27-word passage.

> <u>During</u> the <u>past</u> few years, <u>scientists</u> have <u>investigated</u> <u>animals</u> that live <u>in</u> the <u>oceans</u>. Several researchers <u>focused</u> on whales. Whales are <u>intelligent</u> and <u>communicate</u> with each <u>other</u>. (G. García et al., 2020, p. 7)

However, if you are working with bilingual students in grades 3–4, your students will very likely need explicit instruction and guided practice to use cognates. My colleagues and I discovered that many Spanish-speaking students in grade 4 did not recognize or use cognates to figure out unknown English words in informational texts even when they were given cognate examples and a brief cognate definition (G. García & Nagy, 1993; Nagy, García, Durgunoğlu, & Hancin, 1993). In contrast, after receiving the same brief cognate definition and cognate examples, Spanish-speaking students in grades 5 and 6 identified cognates in English informational texts. We wondered if cognate recognition and use might be developmental.

Instruction that Helped Third Graders Use Cognates to Spell and Write

My colleague and I worked with a third-grade teacher and her third graders in a 90–10 Spanish–English DL program to improve their use of cognates (G. García et al., 2020). At the beginning of the school year, the DL teacher taught the third graders how to recognize Spanish–English cognates by presenting them with a cognate definition and examples. Then, throughout the school year, she had them spontaneously identify cognates when they recognized them in their mathematics, science, and social studies instruction or in their English and Spanish reading instruction. When students identified cognates, she posted the Spanish–English cognate pairs on posters on the walls of her classroom, and she and her students read them aloud.

During the spring semester, the DL students received science instruction on electricity from another third-grade teacher who only spoke English. To help the students, we prepared a list of Spanish–English cognates from books on electricity and gave the students the list (G. García et al., 2020). Table 10.2 shows a sample of the cognates that we gave them. The third-grade teacher asked the students to work in pairs to define the Spanish words and then had them share their definitions with the class. When their definitions were incorrect, she told them the correct definitions. Then, she printed the English cognates from the list on green index cards and the Spanish cognates on yellow index cards. She gave sets of cards to the students and asked them to work in pairs to match the cognates. Next, she asked the students to print the 15 cognate pairs on sheets of paper, to use a red pen to underline the word parts of the 15 cognate pairs that were different, and to use a blue pen to underline the word parts that were the same.

In addition, the third-grade teacher gave her students small notebooks to record the cognate pairs that they identified during their mathematics, science, and reading instruction (G. García et al., 2020). She again told them to utilize a red pen to underline the word parts that were the same and a blue pen to circle the parts that were different. In addition, when students wrote in English and misspelled a word that was a Spanish cognate, she circled the word in red, drew an arrow from the word to the margin, and wrote "cognate" with a question mark. After seeing her cognate comments on their writing, most students independently corrected the misspellings.

At the end of the school year, 14 of the 16 students in the DL classroom

TABLE 10.2. Sample of English-Spanish Electricity Cognates

English cognate	Spanish cognate
atom	*átomo*
battery	*batería*
charge	*carga*
circuit	*circuito*
conductor	*conductor*
electron	*electrón*
energy	*energía*
movement	*movimiento*
negative	*negativa/o*
transfer	*transferencia*

Note. Based on G. García et al. (2020).

participated in interviews with the teacher about their cognate use (G. García et al., 2020). Nine of the 14 said that they used Spanish cognates to spell or write in English. However, only three of them reported using Spanish cognates when they read in English. We concluded that asking the students to identify similar and different word parts of the written cognate pairs probably helped them to use cognates when they wrote and spelled in English. However, we thought that it was likely that very few of the third graders reported using cognates while reading in English because the teacher had not specifically taught them how to use cognates while reading English texts.

INSTRUCTION THAT IMPROVED FOURTH GRADERS' USE OF COGNATES WHILE READING

The cognate instruction that 13 Spanish-speaking, Latinx fourth graders from three different classrooms received was explicitly designed to teach them how to use cognates while reading informational texts in English (G. García et al., 2020). Over six months, they participated in four small-group or individual sessions (45–60 minutes each) on how to identify and use Spanish–English cognates while reading informational texts in English. The informational texts were about dinosaurs, elephants, llamas, and the planet Venus.

The fourth graders first participated in two training sessions on think-alouds (G. García et al., 2020). Next, to find out if the students knew the Spanish and English words that comprised Spanish–English cognates in the passages that they later were asked to read, they completed a yes–no vocabulary test first in Spanish and then in English (Anderson & Freebody, 1981; Nagy et al., 1993). Afterward, they completed a think-aloud while they read an English passage, which included cognates. Only 3 of the 13 students demonstrated using any Spanish cognates to figure out unknown English words in the passage.

Next, they were given a cognate definition and Spanish–English cognate examples (G. García et al., 2020). Then, they were asked to circle all the cognates that they saw in another passage. The students severely underestimated the number of cognates in the passage. I reviewed what they did and explained how Spanish cognates could help them when reading in English. Next, I gave them the same passage with all the cognates circled on it, and I asked them to do a think-aloud while reading it. Throughout the study, I counseled the students on how to use cognates to figure out unknown English words as they read. The following example shows how a student reacted to my reminder (Georgia) to think about Spanish when he did not know an English word (photographs) while reading:

GEORGIA: Me decías que tenías problemas con photographs, ¿verdad? (You told me that you had problems with photographs, right?)

JAIME: Uh-huh.

GEORGIA: ¿No pensaste en la palabra en español cuando estabas leyendo ayer? (You didn't think about the word in Spanish when you were reading this yesterday?)

JAIME: Eran fotografías. (They were photographs.) (G. García et al., 2020, p. 8)

By the end of the six-month study, 12 of the 13 students substantially increased their recognition of Spanish–English cognates (G. García et al., 2020). They also significantly improved their use of Spanish–English cognates to figure out previously unknown English cognates.

Cognate Instructional Recommendations

To teach bilingual students how to use cognates, I recommend that you combine the cognate instructional strategies that my colleagues and I employed with the DL and bilingual third and fourth graders (G. García et al., 2020). First, teachers should post and review a cognate definition and examples with their students. As part of the definition, I recommend that teachers share some of the information that we shared with the students in the García et al. (2020) study (p. 8):

- Spanish/English cognates are Spanish and English words that look alike (e.g., animal and animal) or similar (ficción and fiction) and that have the same or similar meanings.
- "They are two separate words in Spanish and English" (García et al., 2020, p. 8).
- "They aren't every word you know in Spanish and English" (García et al., 2020, p. 8).
- You can use the Spanish cognate (e.g., instituto in Spanish; institute in English) to help figure out an unknown English word, when it is a form of the English cognate (e.g., institutional), and vice versa (G. García et al., 2020).

Then, you should ask your students to volunteer cognates that they find in different content areas. Give them cognate notebooks to keep track of the cognates they and other students find. Have them differentiate the written parts of cognates that are the same and different. When students misspell an English cognate in their writing, encourage them to use their knowledge of the Spanish–English cognate relationship to correct the spelling. Have students circle all the cognates in an informational passage in English, before asking them to use Spanish cognates to figure out the unknown English words. Tell students that they have to make sure that the cognate they use "fits the meaning of a sentence or text" (G. García et al., 2020, p. 9). Periodically, model and scaffold students' use of cognates while reading. Remind your students to "read for meaning!" If their use of a cognate does not make sense, they should not use it! (G. García et al., 2020, p. 9). Lubliner and Grisham (2017) present other ideas for how to teach cognates.

Be sure to introduce your students to false cognates—Spanish/English words that look alike or similar but that have different meanings. Our students laughed at the false cognates that we showed them: embarazada (pregnant) and embarrassed; ropa (clothing) and rope; pie (feet) and pie. Purposefully, show your students how false cognates do not fit the meaning in a text.

Cognate and Affix Instruction

Once bilingual students know how to use Spanish–English cognates, you can teach them how to recognize cognates with affixes. For instance, the following Spanish–English cognates have similar affix patterns: electric-eléctrico, information-información, tranquil-tranquilo. If you have an affix wall posted in your classroom, Kieffer and Lesaux (2007) recommend that you include cognates with affixes on a section of the wall.

OTHER TYPES OF VOCABULARY INSTRUCTION WITH ELEMENTARY BILINGUAL STUDENTS

In addition to explicitly taught reading vocabulary, bilingual students need to develop L2 conversational and academic oral vocabulary and other reading vocabulary. This section presents key instructional research findings and recommendations for teaching these types of vocabulary.

Use of Picture Cards with Young Simultaneous Bilingual Students

Lems et al. (2017) observed that young bilingual children who hear two languages in the home often acquire vocabulary in both languages. Accordingly, Lems and her colleagues recommended that teachers instruct simultaneous bilingual students by using picture cards to teach concrete words in both languages. The picture cards include a picture and a word in each language on each side of the card. After teachers introduce the cards and show how they want children to use the cards, I recommend that teachers ask the children to work with partners in a word center to identify the words in each language on the cards.

Scaffolding to Promote DL First Graders' Oral Academic Language

Lucero (2014) showed how three first-grade Spanish–English DL teachers employed linguistic scaffolding to promote their DL first graders' knowledge and use of oral academic language in English and Spanish. Lucero explained that the teachers' scaffolded linguistic support should be comprehensible, promote student use of "new and potentially more sophisticated language," and facilitate student production of "more complete and complex sentences" than they could produce without the teacher's support (p. 538). She analyzed teachers' employment of micro-level linguistic scaffolding, which happens within "a single interaction or instructional episode," and macro-level linguistic scaffolding, which happens "across lessons in a unit" (p. 539).

When teachers implemented micro-level scaffolding, they gave students the opportunity to talk, "orally repeat[ed] key terms, [and] restate[ed] or rephras[ed]" what students said (Lucero, 2014, p. 545). Sometimes, teachers switched between academic oral language and everyday oral language to clarify a point, as shown below:

> MR. RILEY: Tell me about one of the properties you noticed of the ping-pong ball. Oscar?
>
> OSCAR: It's hard.
>
> MR. RILEY: It's hard. Is that a color, or a size, or shape or texture? What do you think? Hard. That's how it looks, or how it feels?
>
> OSCAR: How it feels.
>
> MR. RILEY: How it feels. So, when you're talking about how something feels, you're talking about the . . . texture. You're talking about the texture (Lucero, 2014, p. 545).

Lucero (2014) points out that the teacher "rephrased new academic language into conversational language" when the teacher asked the student if he was referring to how the ping-pong ball "looks or how it feels" (p. 545). The teacher ended the discourse by utilizing academic language to restate that he and the student had been talking about the "texture" of the ping-pong ball.

Paired Videos with Teacher Read-Alouds for Students in PreK-2

Silverman and Hines (2009) reported that pairing videos with teacher read-alouds about the same topics (e.g., habitats, such as the rain forest and savannah) helped emergent bilingual students in PreK through second grade learn new English vocabulary from the teacher read-alouds. In contrast, use of the videos with native-English speakers in the same classes as the emergent bilingual students did not increase the former students' vocabulary knowledge (p. 241). Silverman and Hines concluded that the multimedia nature of the videos provided additional scaffolding that aided the emergent bilingual students' oral vocabulary acquisition.

Teaching Word Families

Lems et al. (2017) recommend that word families or lexemes be taught rather than a single word or lemma. They recommend using a spider graphic organizer in which you write the lemma or focal word in the center and other members of the word family on spokes around it. For example, if you are teaching the word "human," it would be in the center; on the spokes, you would print humane, humanity, humanitarian, and inhumane. I once observed fourth graders, who had just been taught the word family "propose—proposition, proposal, proposing," enthusiastically use different versions of propose throughout the school day to earn points in a class competition.

Polysemous Words

Crosson (2016) explains that academic words often are polysemous; that is, they have multiple meanings. Some polysemous words have closely related meanings, such as "foundation of a building" and "foundation of a friendship" (Crosson, p. 87). Other polysemous words are homonyms; that is, they are spelled the same but have unrelated meanings, such as slices of toast and "a champagne toast" (Crosson, p. 87).

To improve emergent bilingual students' understanding of polysemous academic words in English, Crosson and McKeown (2016) recommend the following:

1. Teach a "core meaning" of the word applicable across contexts by using "friendly" definitions. Friendly definitions "use accessible language and convey" the word's meaning "and how it is used" (p. 92).
2. Teach the multiple meanings of polysemous words at the beginning of instruction.
3. "Engage students in interactions with the word that lead them to explicitly compare and contrast" the word meanings (p. 92).

Crosson (2016) gives the example of how to teach the word "sustain" at the outset of instruction so that students understand that it can mean to sustain weight in the physical sense and to sustain friendships in the mental sense (p. 93). She points out that in a polysemous instructional program,

Robust Academic Vocabulary Encounters (RAVE), she and McKeown (2016) used two questions to help emergent bilingual students remember the meanings or senses of polysemous words:

"WHAT'S THE SENSE OF IT?"

If your zoo membership is *valid*, what does that mean?
If your point about why zoos are good for animals is *valid*, what does that mean?

"WHAT'S THE DIFFERENCE?"

How might you *confine* a dozen jumping beetles? (physical sense)
How might parents *confine* their children's choices of what to order at a restaurant? (mental sense) (Crosson, 2016, p 93).

INCIDENTAL VOCABULARY ACQUISITION

Incidental vocabulary acquisition occurs when students learn the meanings of new words by hearing them repeatedly in conversations and encountering them in texts that are read to them or that they read and comprehend. Although monolingual English-speaking students increase their incidental vocabulary acquisition through wide or extensive independent reading, emergent bilingual students generally do not benefit as much from incidental vocabulary acquisition (Gallagher et al., 2019). Due to their developing English proficiency, emergent bilingual students frequently do not have the requisite English vocabulary knowledge and academic language to figure out the meanings of new English words while reading. Also, they do not read English texts as frequently as monolingual English speakers.

A possible way to help bilingual students develop incidental vocabulary knowledge from English reading is to teach them how to use context clues. The context clue recommendations are from Baumann, Edwards, Boland, Olejnik, and Kame'enui's (2003) vocabulary research with monolingual English speakers. Baumann et al. explain that students should be taught to do the following:

1. Read the sentences around the word to see if there are clues to its meaning.
2. See if they can break the word into a root word, prefix or suffix to help figure out its meaning.
3. Read the sentences around the word again to see if they can figure out its meaning.

ACADEMIC LANGUAGE INSTRUCTION

In addition to learning academic vocabulary, bilingual students also need to know the academic structures (grammar/syntax, punctuation, text structures), disciplinary language, and rhetorical styles that characterize English academic instruction in United States schools (Great Schools Partnership, 2013; Uccelli & Galloway, 2017). Sometimes, emergent bilingual students receive academic language instruction during the explicit English language development (ELD) instruction that they receive in DL or bilingual education programs (see Chapter 3); other times, they participate in academic language instruction during disciplinary literacy instruction (see Chapter 11). Through dictation, modeled writing, and Lotta Lara (Escamilla et al., 2014), teachers also can teach bilingual students how to employ academic language in their L1 and L2.

In their review of best practices, Gersten et al. (2007) argue that all emergent bilingual students, including students in the primary grades, should receive intensive, interactive academic language instruction. By interactive, they mean that emergent bilingual students should spend 90 minutes each week practicing and working on extensions of already taught academic tasks with "students at different ability levels or different English proficiencies" (p. 6).

Uccelli and Galloway (2017) explain that their academic language instructional program—Core Academic Language Skills (CALS)—instructed emergent bilingual students and monolingual English speakers, ages 9–14, to do the following:

- "Unpack . . . dense information," such as "understanding complex words and complex sentences (e.g., embedded clauses)."
- Understand and use connectives to logically link ideas or "to signal relationships (e.g., use words like 'consequently, as a result of')."
- How to "track . . . participants and themes (e.g., use of anaphora or 'expressions . . . to refer to prior participants or ideas')."
- How "analytic texts" are organized (e.g., text structures in paragraphs and texts).
- How to "understand metalinguistic vocabulary" (e.g., "hypothesize, generalize").
- How to "interpret . . . writers' viewpoints."
- How to recognize . . . the differences in academic registers compared to colloquial registers (p. 396).

When the students who participated in CAL were interviewed, however, they did not mention that the academic language instruction helped them to improve their text comprehension or learning (Uccelli & Galloway,

2017). Instead, they said that their use of academic language made them seem smart.

Several researchers and educators voiced concerns that language-minority bilingual students may not be motivated to learn and use academic language because they view it as representing a discourse that denigrates their language and excludes them (Flores, 2020; Great Schools Partnership, 2013). The Great Schools Partnership explains this point of view:

> . . . students of color, ethnic minorities, and English-language learners may feel that they are being 'forced' to learn a style of language that they associate with a cultural group they may feel excluded from (e.g., white, middle-class America or highly educated groups). Underlying racial, ethnic, or socioeconomic tensions can exacerbate these feelings, and students and their families may consequently feel conflicted about academic language. For example, correcting the use of urban slang in a writing assignment may be interpreted as a personal criticism by the student rather than an academic judgment, or parents may be uncomfortable when their children begin using unfamiliar words and expressions at home (n.p.).

To offset any racist or negative messages about academic language, I recommend that school personnel include students' cultural funds of knowledge (Gonzalez et al., 2005) in their instruction, work to create a school climate that fosters a sense of school belonging for their language minority students (DeNicolo et al., 2017), and develop and implement cultural and linguistically responsive instruction that helps minority students, including emergent bilingual students, to succeed in United States schools.

CONCLUDING REMARKS

Hopefully, implementing the recommendations in this chapter will enable you to substantially improve the L1 and L2 oral, reading, writing, and academic vocabulary and academic language performance of bilingual students. Two common-sense instructional techniques should not be used. Although bilingual students need to know how to use dictionaries, they should not be asked to look up words in dictionaries that you have not reviewed. Often, the words in dictionary definitions are more difficult than the words students are looking up. Similarly, you should not ask students to write sentences to demonstrate the meanings of newly taught words unless they already have received extensive instruction on the words. Writing sentences with newly taught words requires deep knowledge of the words' meanings.

To succeed in schools in the United States, bilingual students not only need to know and use academic vocabulary and language, but also how to use them. As educators, it is our responsibility to provide bilingual students with the tools and knowledge they need to succeed in schools, at the same time that we push for schools to become more culturally and linguistically responsive. I hope that this chapter has given you useful ideas that you can implement to improve your bilingual students' vocabulary and academic language development and use in academic settings.

CHAPTER 11

Disciplinary Literacy Instruction for Bilingual Students

GUIDING QUESTIONS

- What is disciplinary literacy instruction?
- Why should bilingual students participate in disciplinary literacy instruction?
- How does the Seeds of Science/Roots of Reading program integrate science with literacy instruction?
- How does CCDD: WordGen Elementary integrate social studies/history with literacy for students in grades 4–5?
- What types of support does CCDD WordGen Weekly provide for teachers of emergent bilingual students?
- Why is it important to teach disciplinary literacy according to the English and Spanish language proficiency levels of emergent bilingual and dual-language students?

As part of his science instruction on the life cycle, Mr. Thompson has decided to raise chicks in his third-grade, Spanish–English dual-language class during the fall semester. He has already purchased an incubator, a heat lamp, and a thermometer. The Fonsecas' 9-year-old from Chapter 1 is in his class.

When the district's curriculum director, Ms. Earnest, heard what Mr. Thompson was planning to do for his science instruction in the fall, she asked him to combine some of his literacy instruction with his science instruction. She explained that when he assigns his students to read and write about science, and provides them with opportunities to discuss what they are reading, writing, and observing about the life cycle and chicks, he will be helping his dual-language students to think, read, write, and talk like scientists. Because he will be integrating some of his reading instruction with his science instruction, he can spend 70 minutes on the integrated instruction rather than the typical 40 minutes allotted to science.

Ms. Earnest called the type of instruction that Mr. Thompson will implement disciplinary literacy instruction. She explained that it is a curricular innovation that she hopes the school's grade 3–6 teachers will implement during the next school year. During the summer, the district will offer the teachers professional staff development on it. Meanwhile, she promises to help Mr. Thompson select and obtain texts for his life cycle unit and figure out how to combine his instruction on expository reading comprehension and writing with his science instruction.

Disciplinary literacy instruction involves teaching reading comprehension instruction and writing within disciplines, such as language arts, science, and social studies, so that literacy skills specific to the disciplinary fields are taught according to the disciplinary standards (Stahl & García, 2022; Wright & Domke, 2019). Several researchers reported that when students were taught how to read and write like experts in the respective discipline, then their learning in the discipline, along with their literacy performance, often improved more than when they received separate disciplinary and literacy instruction (Cervetti, Barber, Dorph, Pearson, & Goldschmidt, 2012; Romance & Vitale, 2001). Although some states only provide standards for disciplinary literacy instruction in grades 6 and above (e.g., California), many teacher educators recommend that it be introduced in the elementary grades, so that students are prepared for it in grades 6 and above (Shanahan & Shanahan, 2014; Wright & Domke, 2019). Recently, researchers experimented with disciplinary literacy instruction in science and engineering with first graders (Palincsar, Fitzgerald, DellaVecchia, & Easley, 2020).

Bilingual students should participate in disciplinary literacy instruction for two reasons: First, disciplinary literacy instruction is an excellent method for developing bilingual students' academic language and vocabulary (Bravo, 2016). A disciplinary literacy approach provides students with multiple opportunities and contexts for developing background knowledge and conceptual vocabulary. For instance, disciplinary literacy instruction can facilitate students' expansion of everyday vocabulary to scientific vocabulary, teaching them to use words like "soil" in addition to "dirt," "predict" in addition to "guess," and "observe" in addition to "see" (Bravo, 2016, p. 185). Second, if native-English-speaking students are participating in disciplinary literacy instruction before grade 6, waiting to introduce it to bilingual students until they are in grade 6 or later guarantees that they will be behind in their academic and disciplinary literacy performance.

One of the easiest ways for teachers of bilingual students to implement disciplinary literacy instruction is to participate in already established programs implemented and tested with bilingual students. At least two programs exist: Seeds of Science/Roots of Reading (Cervetti et al., 2012), an integrated literacy and science curriculum for students in grades 2–5, and the elementary version of Catalyzing Comprehension through Discussion and Debate (CCDD: WordGen Elementary, 2023). CCDD: WordGen Elementary integrates literacy with language arts, mathematics, science, and/or social studies for students in grades 4–5 (*www.serpinstitute.org*).

CCDD: Word Generation also has a middle-school program that integrates literacy with English language arts, mathematics, science, and/or social studies for students in grades 6–8 (*www.ccdd.serpmedia.org*). The original version of CCDD: Word Generation in history/social studies (called Word Generation SoGen—Social Studies Generation) for middle school is reviewed briefly for those of you who teach grade 6 in elementary school. The original CCDD middle-school program did not work well because the CCDD lessons were too long for middle-school teachers to implement in the 45–50 minutes that they had for individual classes.

If you do not have access to any of the established programs, then I recommend that after reading about them, you and your school colleagues work together to develop and implement your own version of disciplinary literacy instruction. At the end of the program descriptions, I present examples of disciplinary literacy in bilingual classrooms along with guidelines and tips for the development of disciplinary literacy instruction with bilingual students in elementary school (K–6).

ESTABLISHED DISCIPLINARY LITERACY PROGRAMS

Seeds of Science/Roots of Reading

The Seeds of Science/Roots of Reading curriculum was a federally funded program developed for United States elementary students in grades 2–5 (Cervetti et al., 2012). It includes curriculum units and instructional practices that address disciplinary standards for students' expository reading comprehension, expository writing (see NGA Center for Best Practices and CCSSO, 2010), scientific discourse, and science inquiry learning (see Next Generation Science Standards Lead States, 2013). Cervetti and her colleagues explain that Seeds of Science/Roots of Reading involves "student reading, writing, investigating, and discussing to acquire knowledge about important science concepts, inquiry skills, and literacy skills that students need to be successful in science" (p. 634).

A Fourth-Grade Curriculum Example

The fourth-grade curriculum emphasizes an inquiry focus on light and light as a source of energy (Cervetti et al., 2012). Teachers implement four inquiry units of 10 sessions each (45–60 minutes each), for a total of 40 sessions. Within each unit, there are four sessions that include hands-on science activities. In addition, two sessions focus on reading, two on writing, and two on discussion, review, and assessment. Although Cervetti and her colleagues wanted the fourth graders to read trade books on light and energy, they could not find enough informational books, so they wrote some of the books. They had teachers use the GRR (Pearson & Gallagher, 1983; see Chapter 8) to explicitly teach the students how to discuss, read, and write like scientists and to use cognitive strategies (e.g., prediction and summarization) during science and reading.

For example, in the first unit on light, the students volunteer "what they know and wonder about light" (Cervetti et al., 2012, p. 638). Before reading a book about light in the dark, they predict whether people can see without light. Next, they use flashlights to gather their own evidence. Then, they revise their predictions based on their observations. Afterward, they create light tubes and employ them to investigate whether "light travels in a straight line" (p. 638). They list their observations on a large, posted concept map, which they continue to develop throughout the unit. Before they read a book on the speed of light, they predict how fast light travels compared to other items. Cervetti et al. (2012) explains that "by reflecting on the data, the students are better able to understand how fast light travels—a characteristic that is impossible for them to observe firsthand" (p. 638).

In terms of literacy, the students read nine books and employ two cognitive strategies: prediction and summarization. They use "key words . . . [to] construct main idea statements about passages in the book. They summarize what they have learned about the characteristics of light by writing details to support a topic sentence" (Cervetti et al., 2012, p. 638).

Program Results with Emergent Bilingual Students

Researchers have tested Seeds of Science/Roots of Reading with emergent bilingual students in grades 2–5 (see Cervetti et al., 2015). For example, Wang and Herman (2005) conducted a study of Seeds of Science/Roots of Reading with students in grades 2–3. About a third of the students were emergent bilingual students. They reported that the emergent bilingual students made similar gains as their native-English-speaking classmates on science measures and many of the literacy measures.

Duesbury, Werblow, and Twyman (2011) compared the performance of emergent bilingual fourth and fifth graders who received Seeds of Science/Roots of Reading instruction with a comparison group of emergent bilingual students who received their normal science instruction. The emergent bilingual students who participated in Seeds of Science/Roots of Reading outperformed the other students on measures of science understanding, the nature of science, and science vocabulary.

Catalyzing Comprehension through Discussion and Debate (CCDD: WordGen Elementary)

CCDD: WordGen Elementary is a federally funded research program that is still being modified and implemented based on evaluations (*www.serpinstitute.org*). The WordGen Elementary program for grades 4 and 5 includes a one-week introductory unit and 12 two-week units. The program integrates literacy with English language arts, social studies, mathematics, and science. Each daily lesson is 40–50 minutes.

Implementation of CCDD: WordGen Elementary

The example of CCDD: WordGen Elementary presented here focuses on the integration of literacy with social studies/history (*www.serpinstitute.org*). A social studies/historical aim is for the students to take and support a perspective. Each unit begins with a debatable question related to government and students' lives. For example, in grade 4, one of the questions is: "Should students be required to wear uniforms?," whereas, in grade 5, a debatable question is: "Do we need laws to regulate our behavior?" (*www.serpinstitute.org*). Students view a video newscast that introduces the question. Then, they read transcripts of interviews that two students conducted with an expert on the issue. Next, they participate in a reader's theater on the issue by reading a reader's theater script and discussing how the characters in the reader's theater might view answers to the debatable question. Then, they read short expository articles related to the question. Throughout, they focus on 5–10 vocabulary items, which are repeated throughout the unit and in the readings. They also have to take a stand on the debatable question, and write about it in a journal, a paragraph, or an essay. In addition, they read and discuss historical journal entries related to the question. Sometimes they participate in a mathematics and/or science activity related to the question.

Evaluation of CCDD: WordGen Elementary

Overall evaluations of the elementary CCDD: WordGen Elementary program after two years of implementation showed significant increases in fourth and fifth graders' taught vocabulary, perspective positioning (a key element of historian's work), and deep reading comprehension (*www.serpinstitute.org*). Although the CCDD: Word Generation developers designed the fourth- and fifth-grade programs for students in all-English, general education classrooms, when there were emergent bilingual students in the classrooms, whom they called English learners, they kept track of their performance. The program evaluations showed that on average the English learners made larger gains on the language-performance measures than the non-English learners who participated in the same CCDD program.

Catalyzing Comprehension through Discussion and Debate (CCDD: WordGen SoGen)

The original CCDD: WordGen SoGen program (2024; *www.ccdd.sermedia.org*) for middle-school students (grades 6–8) is reviewed here because it may help you and your colleagues to develop your own disciplinary social studies/history program for sixth graders in elementary school. The initial program consisted of three six-week units for 40–50 minutes each day on social studies topics covered in middle school (*www.ccdd.sermedia.org*).

Implementation of CCDD: WordGen SoGen

To begin each unit, a debatable question was raised. For example, one of the sixth-grade units focused on ancient civilizations. The students were asked the following question related to ancient Greece: "Was it better to be an Athenian or a Spartan?" (Goldman, Snow, & Vaughn, 2016, p. 261; *www.ccdd.sermedia.org*). Goldman et al. explained that the purpose of the unit was to help students think about an important issue: "How do schools [or other units, such as city states in Greece] organize themselves around different priorities with consequences for people's lives?" (p. 261).

Before focusing on the debatable question, the SoGen program had the students participate in a reader's theater to get them engaged (Goldman et al., 2016; *www.ccdd.sermedia.org*). The reader's theater translated the debatable question into a question related to the students' current lives: Which school is better: an academic high school or a sports-oriented high school? In pairs, the students decided on the positives and negatives of attending each type of high school. They also decided which participants in the reader's theater (e.g., cheerleaders, members of the debate team, football coaches, academic teachers, football players) were likely to hold specific positions about the high school question.

For literacy, the sixth graders worked in pairs to define 5–10 academic words related to the unit's focus. For example, the unit on Athens versus

Sparta included six vocabulary words: "democratic, elitist, competitive, ostracize, individualism, and conformity" (Goldman et al., 2016, p. 261). These were words that the students frequently saw in their readings and that they had multiple opportunities to use orally. After the reader's theater, they read short texts about Greece, Athens, and Sparta, and took "notes on 'the advantages of living in one city' (Goldman et al., p. 261) versus the other, and from the points of view of various stakeholders such as soldiers, women, and slaves" (Stahl & García, 2022, p. 151). They sometimes were given sentence starters for their notes, such as, "I support claim ___________. My reason is ___________" (*https://irp-cdn-multiscreensite.com*). They were also given additional evidence for each of the debate positions.

To prepare for the oral debate, the sixth graders were told how to organize their notes, claims for each city, "evidence that supported [the claims], . . . anticipated counterarguments, and possible responses" (Goldman et al., p. 261). When the debate ended, they employed a flowchart to organize their writing, identifying which city (Athens or Sparta) they preferred to live in and why. Then, they wrote an essay based on the flowchart.

Evaluation of CCDD: WordGen SoGen

After two years of implementing the initial CCDD: Word Generation for social studies/history, evaluators reported that the sixth- and seventh-grade participants significantly improved their taught vocabulary, perspective positioning, and academic language skills (*www.serpinstitute.org*). However, they did not perform as well as the fourth and fifth graders who participated in CCDD: WordGen Elementary. Two of the problems were that the middle-school teachers did not always implement the program as designed because it required collaboration across separate classes (e.g., English language arts and science or social studies), and the middle-school teachers had other required instruction that they had to complete.

In response to the middle-school implementation issues, the developers shortened CCDD: Word Generation Weekly to a 72 one-week program (*www.serpinstitute.org*). Now each lesson lasts only 15 to 20 minutes, making it easier for middle-school teachers to implement. The program is presently described as providing "supplementary curricular resources" for English language arts, mathematics, science, or social studies.

Supplemental Activities for Teachers of Bilingual Students

To make sure that emergent bilingual students benefit from CCDD, the developers of CCDD: WordGen Weekly provide supplemental activities (entitled Advancing Academic Language for All, 2024) for teachers and families to support English learners in the program (*www. access.serpinstitute.org*). The teacher activities show how to scaffold the academic language development of the English learners and to facilitate their participation in small-group and class discussions.

CLASSROOM EXAMPLES OF DISCIPLINARY LITERACY

Mercuri and Ebe (2011) provided several examples of disciplinary literacy instruction in science and mathematics for emergent bilingual and dual-language students. For example, a disciplinary literacy unit on plants for the primary grades focused on the following:

- The reading of "fiction and nonfiction books about plants."
- The singing of "songs about the topic to learn and practice new vocabulary."
- "Hands-on projects including drawings and writ[ing] about them, fostering literacy development."
- "Do[ing] math by measuring root and stem growth using millimeters and centimeters as . . . measurement units" (p. 84).

In addition to the above, I suggest adding student discussion of the texts, the planting and care of a garden (indoor or outdoor), and the observation and recording of plant growth under different conditions.

Mercuri and Ebe (2011) also showed how a Spanish–English dual-language teacher taught a disciplinary literacy unit in science to her third graders. The dual-language class was in a 90–10 program, which meant that the third graders received 70% of their instruction in Spanish and 30% in English. There were 21 students in the class. About one-third were from English-speaking families, while two-thirds were from Spanish-speaking families.

The teacher began her inquiry instruction by posting the following question in English and Spanish on a brightly colored poster where all her students could see it: "How Does Water Affect Our Earth, ¿Cómo afecta el agua a nuestra tierra/nuestro planeta?" (Mercuri & Ebe, 2011, p. 80). Then, she showed "a video on evaporation." Next, students were placed in small groups around tables to conduct an experiment on "water vapor." The teacher "pour[ed] hot water into individual plastic bins [on each table] and ask[ed] the students to cover them with the lids [on their tables]" (p. 80). She then asked them to make predictions about what would happen when they lifted the lids (Mercuri & Ebe, p. 80). The following is one group's discussion:

S1: I think water vapor will go up, will rise.
S2: It will evaporate.
S3: I predict that when we take the lid off it will have water on it.
S2: Why?
S1: Water vapor will condense and stick to the lid.
S3: Yes, it will be liquid again.
S2: Okay, let's write this on the graphic organizer for Miss M. (Mercuri & Ebe, p. 80).

Mercuri and Ebe (2011) pointed out that the third-grade DL teachers' water unit included language and content standards and involved inquiry learning. Throughout the unit, the teacher integrated science, language, and mathematics. For example, she introduced cognates such as "evaporation, precipitation, condensation, and accumulation" (p. 91). She also presented students with texts to read in English and Spanish. The teacher did not repeat content or language instruction in each language but expanded them in each language. Toward the end of the unit, she had students summarize what they had learned by using sentence frames in Spanish and English.

TEXTS READ IN THE DISCIPLINARY WATER UNIT

Alexander, C. (2004). *Water Detectives*. Rigby.
Bydlowski, D., Kline, C., & Ribits, F. (2010). *The Rain Song*. Retrieved from *www.youtube.com/watch?v=Yw275056JtA*.
Cole, J., & Degen, B. (1996). *El autobus mágico se salpica todo*. Scholastic.
Frost, H. (2004). *El ciclo del agua*. Capstone Press.
GetGreenGlobal. (2010). *Día de la tierra*. Retrieved from *www.youtube.com/watch?v=pEJC5DxTynQ&NR=1*.
Jerome, K. (2003). *Protecting the Planet*. National Geographic.
Ring, S. (1999). *Looking at Clouds*. Newbridge Educational Publishers.
Thompson, G. (2002). *Kids Care for the Earth*. National Geographic.
Vaughan, M. (1997). *Clouds*. Shortland Publications.
Weaver, J., & Weaver, B. (2004). *Earth Day*. National Geographic.

Note. From Mercuri and Ebe (2011, p. 80).

GUIDELINES FOR DEVELOPING DISCIPLINARY LITERACY INSTRUCTION

If you do not have access to an already established disciplinary literacy program, then I suggest that you work with your school and grade-level colleagues to develop and implement your own program. Stahl and I (Stahl & García, 2022) provide ideas on how to do this. First, we recommend that grade-level teachers create a large chart on butcher paper or online through a shared Google document that lists your current English language arts/literacy, science, and social studies units. In addition, each grade-level team should double-check to see how their units address their state standards in literacy, English language arts, science, and social studies, indicating areas that need updating. Next, we recommend that all the school's grade-level teams meet to share their charts so that duplicate topics or topics that overlap are identified, and you can make decisions about which grades should cover which topics. Then, each grade level needs to decide how many disciplinary areas you will integrate. If you already are conducting thematic instruction that combines literacy/English language arts with science or social studies, then I recommend that you begin by expanding and improving your thematic instruction. Form 11.1, at the end of the chapter, provides a unit template that you and other grade-level teachers can use to design disciplinary literacy units.

Tips for Implementing Disciplinary Literacy Instruction with Bilingual Students According to Language-Proficiency Levels

When you plan the implementation of disciplinary literacy instruction with emergent bilingual and dual-language students, you should take into account the students' language-proficiency levels. If you teach Spanish–English bilingual students, you can use the WIDA English language development (2020) and Spanish language development and language arts standards (2013, 2023b).

Use of Translanguaging

The point of disciplinary literacy instruction is to improve bilingual students' learning of academic content and literacy performance, not their use of a particular language. So, when implementing disciplinary literacy instruction, you should translanguage when it improves your communication with your students. I also advise you to accept your students' translanguaging. In addition, you and your students should read, write about, and discuss L1 and L2 texts tied to the disciplinary theme, as occurred in the Mercuri and Ebe (2011) example.

Provision of Discussion Supports

When I worked with second-grade and fourth-grade bilingual teachers on implementing dialogic cognitive strategy instruction (G. García et al., 2021), I learned the importance of teachers supporting their students' small-group discussions. Assigning students specific roles to play in discussion groups helps to initiate and maintain authentic discussions. Also, some bilingual students may need to be taught how to interpret requests for further elaboration and how to qualify opinions. Showing emergent bilingual students videos of successful small-group student discussions is helpful. Asking them to develop and implement rules for small-group student-led discussions also can result in effective student-led discussions.

CONCLUDING REMARKS

Disciplinary literacy instruction is an effective way to increase the language development and academic learning of emergent bilingual and dual-language students. When it includes student discussion and hands-on activities, it essentially becomes sheltered instruction because it integrates listening, speaking, reading, and writing, provides multiple opportunities for students to see and use the same vocabulary, and gives students the opportunity to see the instruction or end-result of the instruction in action.

Although teachers of bilingual students already have a lot to do in their classrooms, the improved language development and learning outcomes reported for disciplinary literacy instruction make its implementation worth the effort. Therefore, I encourage you to work with other grade-level teachers to incorporate disciplinary literacy instruction into your classroom instruction.

However, to make sure that your bilingual students develop the necessary literacy skills, I also recommend teaching beginning literacy, general comprehension strategies (i.e., dialogic strategy instruction), and writing separately. You can reference and reinforce the comprehension strategies and what your students know about writing during your disciplinary literacy instruction.

FORM 11.1. Unit Template for Disciplinary Literacy Instruction

# of Days	Topic	Content Disciplines	Texts	Writing Focus

Big Ideas—Ideas that cut across disciplines, such as "change, exploration, freedom, power, justice, and so forth" (Stahl & García, 2022, p. 55).

Essential Questions—Open-ended questions that engage students so that they want "to learn more about the topic. . . . When writing essential questions, teachers should ask themselves, 'What should my students remember and be able to do, or reflect on, a year from now?'" (Stahl & García, 2022, p. 55).

Essential Vocabulary (5–8 words per text)—"Taught, tested throughout and at conclusion of unit" (Stahl & García, 2022, p. 55).

Dialogic Cognitive Strategies and Test Structures to Be Taught and/or Practiced (Choose cognitive strategies and text structures that will help students to comprehend the texts in the unit.)

Standards:

Disciplinary:

Reading Standards:

Writing Standards:

Speaking/Listening Standards:

Skills: What do students need to know and do to attain the standards for the unit?

Disciplinary (Content) Objectives: ("What are the observable, measurable learning outcomes of the unit?") (Stahl & García, 2022, p. 56; see Echevarria, Vogt, & Short, 2017, to write disciplinary and language objectives)

Language Objectives:

Adaptations for Different Language Proficiency Levels:

ASSESSMENTS:

PROJECTS:

FIELD TRIPS:

Note. Adapted with permission from Stahl and García (2022). Copyright © 2022 The Guilford Press.

The Language and Literacy Assessment of Bilingual Students

GUIDING QUESTIONS

- What is the standards-based reform movement in the United States?
- What are authentic assessments?
- What are the advantages of formative assessments?
- What are summative assessments?
- What are the differences among norm-referenced, criterion-referenced, and standards-based assessments?
- Why do schools use interim assessments?
- What are the federal test requirements for emergent bilingual students?
- What unique assessment issues affect the literacy evaluation of bilingual students?
- Why should schools employ a comprehensive assessment system with bilingual students?

Ms. Jones is a newly certified bilingual education teacher who is scheduled to teach a sixth-grade, one-way DL class of Spanish-speaking emergent bilingual students. She and the school principal just reviewed her roster for this year's incoming class. The principal said that the majority of the students in her class had completed fifth grade at the DL school last year, so she should ask the DL fifth-grade teachers about the students' L1 and L2 language and literacy performance. The principal also gave her a list of the students' scores on the English language proficiency test and the state English language arts test that they took last spring and on the Logramos reading test in Spanish that they took at the end of the school year.

However, six new emergent bilingual students transferred into the school from other states. Ms. Jones is concerned that she does not know very much about them. Although they will take the required English language proficiency test for all entering students at the beginning of the school year, the principal said that it will be a while before the school gets their test scores.

The principal recommended that Ms. Jones use authentic and formative assessments to learn about the new students' L1 and L2 language and literacy performance. Ms. Jones has never heard of authentic and formative assessments. She decided to ask the DL school coordinator about them.

This chapter begins by describing the standards-based reform movement in the United States and the role of standards in student assessment and instruction. Next, the types of assessments that bilingual teachers use to plan their students' instruction are introduced—authentic and formative assessments. Authentic assessments show how students enact the actual tasks being evaluated, such as reading and writing. Formative assessments inform bilingual teachers' instruction, and show how individual students respond to instruction. Then, the types of formal (published or commercial) assessments that school personnel employ to evaluate the language and literacy progress of bilingual students are described. A review of the federal assessment requirements for current and former emergent bilingual students is provided. Next, bilingual issues that affect bilingual students' literacy evaluation are discussed. The chapter concludes with a review of recommended assessment practices for bilingual students.

THE STANDARDS-BASED REFORM MOVEMENT

Unlike other countries, the United States does not have a national curriculum. State and local governments, not the federal government, are in charge of what is taught in public schools and provide most of the public school funding. During 2019–2020, the federal government provided only 8% of all funds to public schools (NCES, 2023a). One way that the federal government controls what happens in public schools is requiring states to apply for federal funds through competitive grants.

To improve the academic performance of students in public schools, educational policymakers and researchers supported the development of common academic standards (called the Common Core State Standards or

CCSS) to guide the instruction and assessment of public school students in English language arts and mathematics (NGA Center for Best Practices & CCSSO, 2010). The CCSS identify what students at specific grade levels should perform and know in English language arts and mathematics. To motivate states to adopt the CCSS for student instruction and assessment, the federal government not only awarded competitive points for federal funding to those states that required the CCSS, but also provided funding for the development of assessments tied to the CCSS (G. García & Lang, 2018).

Although the federal government no longer requires states to implement the CCSS, if they want federal funding, states still have to develop and use college- and career-ready standards to guide their student instruction and assessment. As of 2017, 35 states still were using the CCSS to guide their English language arts and mathematics instruction and assessments, while 11 states decided to develop their own standards and assessments (New America, n.d.). The standards reform movement also recommends that teachers use formative assessments tied to state standards to evaluate individual students' language and literacy performance and to inform their instruction (Alvarez, Ananda, Walqui, Sato, & Rabinowitz, 2014). In addition, per the Every Student Succeeds Act (ESSA, 2015), every state that receives federal funds is required to develop and implement English language development standards to guide the English instruction and assessment of emergent bilingual students.

AUTHENTIC LANGUAGE AND LITERACY ASSESSMENTS

To estimate the new DL students' Spanish and English language and literacy performance, I recommend that Ms. Jones, whom you met in the chapter vignette, conduct several authentic assessments. Authentic assessments require students to perform the actual tasks being evaluated. Ms. Jones should collect and analyze samples of the new students' L1 and L2 talk and their L1 and L2 reading and writing. To analyze the students' performance, she should ask the DL coordinator for copies of the sixth-grade English and Spanish report cards.

Oral Interviews in the L1 and L2

I recommend that Ms. Jones begin by conducting conversational interviews in the L1 and L2 with each student. A conversational interview is designed to get the students to talk about themselves. She should ask the students how well they think they currently speak, read, and write in the L1; what they like to do in school; what they did the previous day at home; and what they hope to do the next day at home. As the student talks during the interview, Ms. Jones should quickly circle any key points that she hears or observes on the report card rubric. Before another student is interviewed, she should write a brief summary of the student's L1 oral performance. Then, she should staple the circled report card rubrics to the summary, make sure the student's name is on the materials, date them, and store them in a secure place.

Next, she should use the same procedures to conduct a conversational interview with each student in their L2 about how well they speak, read, and write in the L2; what they like to do at home, what they did last summer; and what they hope to do during the upcoming weekend. Again, it helps to have a list of report card rubrics to circle as students talk. I also recommend that Ms. Jones write brief summaries of each student's talk in the L2; staple the circled standards or report card categories with the summary, put their name and date on the materials, and store them in a secure place.

L1 and L2 Writing

The procedures that Ms. Jones will use to estimate the new students' L1 and L2 writing are linked to their L1 and L2 reading. Prior to conducting the assessments, Ms. Jones should select and copy several short L1 and L2 texts (about 250–300 words each) at different reading levels for students to read aloud. Next, she should read each text and write a graphic organizer for the text according to its text structure (story map for narrative texts and relevant expository text structures for informational texts; see Chapter 5). Below each of the graphic organizers, she should list a few comprehension questions for each text, leaving space for her to write the students' answers. Then, she should make copies of the graphic organizers.

Next, Ms. Jones should ask each student to select one of the short L1 texts to read aloud and discuss. After the student selects the text, she should have them write a three-sentence or longer L1 explanation of why they chose the text. This will be part of their L1 writing sample.

After they read the text and complete the reading assessment activities (see below), Ms. Jones should give them the texts they read aloud and their initial writing samples and ask them to add written explanations about whether the texts were good choices. She should include the student's name on the respective writing sample, date it, and collect it for later analysis.

The procedures for collecting the L2 writing samples are the same as for the L1 writing samples, except that Ms. Jones should speak in the L2 and ask students to read and write in the L2. Again, she needs to include the student's name on the respective writing sample, to date it, and to collect it for analysis.

Ms. Jones can use the biliteracy squared writing rubrics in Spanish and English (Escamilla et al., 2014, pp. 99–100) to analyze and summarize the students' writing in each language or the report card rubrics. If none of the above are available, she can do her own writing analyses and summaries.

L1 and L2 Reading

The procedures that Ms. Jones uses to estimate the new students' L1 and L2 reading are identical. She needs to have copies of the texts and of the textual analyses with the graphic organizers and comprehension questions on them, so that she can use them to record students' answers. Then, as each student reads the selected text aloud, she should document any oral reading errors on a copy of the text. I recommend that she circle skipped words, insert added words, and underline mispronounced words. Then, she should briefly summarize how fluently and accurately students orally read.

After each student reads the text aloud, Ms. Jones should ask the student comprehension questions about the text and write their answers to the questions on the printed text analysis. Then, if she has time, she should ask the students to pretend that they are telling a friend who did not read the text all about the text. She should use the graphic organizer on the textual analysis to record what the student retold and forgot to retell. I recommend circling what they retold and drawing a line through what they forgot to retell. If they have an unusual interpretation of the text, I would briefly note this on the textual analysis.

At the end of the L1 reading assessment, Ms. Jones should have the following for each student: the student's oral reading errors on a printed copy of the text, the student's answers to the comprehension questions, and what the student included and omitted in the retelling. Before asking the student to read in the other language, she should briefly review her findings and write a brief summary of the student's reading, putting the student's name and date on it. Then, she should store it for future reference.

FORMATIVE ASSESSMENTS

Formative assessments are part of the standards-based reform movement in the United States (Alvarez et al., 2014; Heritage, 2010; Osmundson, 2011). When classroom teachers plan their literacy instruction, they are supposed to link their instruction to state standards and identify formative assessments. Formative assessments reveal how students approach and complete classroom instructional activities tied to state standards, as well as show students' individual responses to their teachers' instruction (G. García

& DeNicolo, 2016). Teachers are supposed to use what they learn from formative assessments to inform their subsequent instruction. Formative assessments can occur daily, weekly, and/or monthly, and be implemented in English, Spanish, and other languages. Sometimes, teachers at the same grade level develop common formative assessments that all the teachers utilize. For more information on how to plan and implement common formative assessments, see Stahl and García (2022).

Formative assessments tied to state standards are useful because in addition to revealing how the individual student's work addresses the state standards, they show how the student responds to your instruction. They also provide you with diagnostic information that you can use to provide explicit feedback to your students (Perie, Gong, & Marion, 2009). Alvarez et al. (2014) explain that "formative assessment is a continuous cycle that entails gathering evidence of and judging student learning; providing feedback to students about their learning; and using assessment data to adjust subsequent instruction as needed" (p. 2). To track each student's progress, you need to make sure that each student's name is on the formative assessment work and that the work is dated and stored in a folder or file drawer so that it is accessible.

Formative assessments in Spanish or the partner language also resolve a problem that many DL teachers and teachers of emergent bilingual students face. There are few formal (published) partner-language assessments that DL teachers can use to monitor the partner language progress of their students. In DL classrooms, the Spanish language and literacy development of two types of students (i.e., native-Spanish speakers and English-dominant students) should be assessed. Formative assessments provide a way to evaluate the language and literacy development of DL students in the partner language.

When published standards are not available in the partner language, then you can use the categories and rubrics on your school's partner-language report card to keep track of individual students' progress. When I worked with elementary Spanish–English DL teachers on formative assessments (G. García & Lang, 2018), one of them created a chart for each student, in which she posted the specific competence or skill (e.g., accurate oral reading; writing of a narrative with a beginning, middle, and end; accurate use of the past tense) that she was supposed to assess for the report card. Then, when she saw a student demonstrate a competence or skill during the grading period, she indicated the date of her observation on the chart.

Examples of Formative Assessments

Many instructional activities discussed in earlier chapters in this book can be turned into formative assessments. A practical aspect of formative assessments is that they do not take additional time away from instruction (Osmundson, 2011; Shepard, 2009). However, teachers need to purposefully plan the assessments, collect data for each student, put students' names on the assessment materials, date them, and store them in a secure place. Among other activities, the following can be used as formative assessments:

- Students' drawing and/or writing about what they learned during disciplinary literacy instruction (e.g., a drawing of how a light bulb works; a drawing of the water cycle).
- Written summaries of what students read.
- Written responses to what they read.
- Completion of story maps for interactive teacher read-alouds or independent reading.
- Completion of expository graphic organizers to show comprehension of expository texts.
- Use of signal/clue words to complete expository frames.
- Use of unprompted dictation to show taught language structures.
- Independent writing according to the genre taught.
- Oral reading of texts.
- Retelling of texts read.
- Answering of comprehension questions that involve different types of inferences.
- Use of cognitive strategies to discuss comprehension of texts.

Analysis of Formative Assessments

Effective use of formative assessments involves analysis of how your students completed the instructional activities. For example, when students write summaries of what they read, you need to analyze the completeness of the summaries. You can use a story map for narrative texts and graphic organizers that match the text structures in expository texts. When students orally retell what they read, you can use retelling charts that match the type of text and its text structure, such as Forms 12.1 and Form 12.2 (see the end of this chapter). Dating and storing your analysis of the formative assessments for each student allows you to track each student's progress.

Student Self-Evaluation

Formative assessments include asking students to self-evaluate their own work, so that they are aware of their performance and the purpose of their instruction (Stahl & García, 2022). When teachers use formative assessments, they periodically hold brief (3- to 10-minute) conferences with individual students to review their reading and/or writing performances. You can vary the frequency of the conferences according to your students' reading/writing performance; that is, you can hold more conferences for the poor readers and writers and fewer conferences for the strong readers and writers.

Before holding the conference, teachers typically ask each student to complete a self-evaluation form. On the form, students reflect on their current performance, identify what they think the teacher wants them to do to improve their performance, and show what the students think they should do (G. García & Lang, 2018). When the teacher meets with the student, they review the completed form together, discuss the student's progress, and specify goals for the student and teacher for the next time period. Form 12.3 provides a student self-evaluation tool that you can use for a student–teacher reading conference, while Form 12.4 provides a student self-evaluation tool that you can use for a student–teacher writing conference. Both forms can be found at the end of this chapter.

A self-evaluation formative assessment that I found useful were exit slips (G. García & Lang, 2018). I implemented exit slips with a group of teachers (grades K–5) who were participating in professional staff development on formative assessments. They, in turn, used exit slips with their students.

To implement exit slips, you give each student a quarter to a half-sheet of paper. You ask them to write what they learned and understood about their instruction or what they did not learn or did not understand (Stahl & García, 2022). The purpose is communication, so students should be allowed to use invented spelling and translanguaging. The teachers with whom I collaborated liked using the exit slips because their students actually used them to explain what they understood or did not understand.

Student Peer Evaluation

Formative assessments also should include peer evaluation so that students learn to work with each other (Osmundson, 2011). Before implementing peer evaluations, Heritage (2007) suggests that you make sure that you have established "classroom norms of students' listening respectfully to one another, responding positively and constructively, and of appreciating different skill levels among peers" (p. 144). I observed a first-grade DL teacher support peer assessment in her classroom. She posted a magnetic poster in her room, which listed the topic her class was working on, and two questions in Spanish with space below them: "¿Puedes ayudarme? (Can you help me?) ¿Necesitas ayuda? (Do you need help?)" (G. García & Lang, 2018, p. 20). Students who wanted help, put magnets with their names on them beneath the first question, while students who could provide help put their name magnets beneath the second question. Then, the teacher gave the students time to work together.

FORMAL ASSESSMENTS

Most schools use two types of formal or published assessments to evaluate the language and literacy performance of bilingual students: summative and interim assessments. Summative assessments include tests that evaluate the performance of large numbers of students according to other students, criteria, or standards. Interim assessments provide progress-monitoring information. Interim assessments usually are commercially developed measures that schools employ periodically to evaluate aspects of students' language and literacy performance.

Summative Assessments

Summative is a good name for this type of assessment because the assessment does not tell why students perform the way they do on it. Instead, this type of assessment summarizes the student's assessment performance at a particular point in time. Summative assessments also are called large-scale assessments because they typically are group administered to large numbers of students. They are standardized in that their instructions, formats, and procedures are uniform. Summative assessments can be norm-referenced, criterion-referenced, or standards-based.

Norm-Referenced Summative Assessments

When summative assessments are norm-referenced, individual student scores indicate how the student performed on the assessment compared to other students. For instance, if a student receives a norm-referenced score of 70%, then this means that the student scored better than 70% of the other students who took the test. Norm-referenced assessments are designed to separate student performance according to a bell curve, with most of the students obtaining scores at the mean and smaller numbers of students obtaining scores above or below the mean (Stahl & García, 2022). Norm-referenced assessments sample student performance. The Gates–MacGinitie Reading Tests (MacGinitie, MacGinitie, María, & Dreyer, 2000) are norm-referenced summative, reading-comprehension assessments in English. *Logramos* (Houghton Mifflin Harcourt, 2014) is a norm-referenced summative reading-comprehension assessment in Spanish.

Criterion-Referenced Summative Assessments

Criterion-referenced summative assessments evaluate student performance according to how well students attain certain criteria. A score of 70% means that the student attained 70% of the criteria being measured. End of unit basal reading tests often are criterion-referenced, as is the National Assessment of Educational Progress (NAEP) (NCES, 2023b).

Description of NAEP. NAEP provides summative, criterion-referenced, English assessments in mathematics, reading, and science for students in the fourth, eighth, and twelfth grade (NCES, 2023b). Students in eighth and twelfth grade also take NAEP assessments in writing and other academic areas. NAEP assessments are the only publicly funded national tests in the United States. They are mandated by the United States Congress and are often called the nation's report card.

NAEP administers a summative, criterion-referenced, English reading comprehension assessment for students in fourth grade (NCES, 2023b). The scores on NAEP summarize student performance for the designated group. For example, representative samples of students from specific regions of the United States, states, and ethnic/racial and linguistic groups (i.e., current and former emergent bilingual students) participate in the NAEP reading comprehension assessment. However, no one student participates in the entire assessment. The score for an average student from a designated region and/or ethnic/racial and linguistic group is a composite score. Student performance is reported according to average scale scores (0–500) and criteria that indicate how the average student performed at the basic, proficient, or advanced level on NAEP. The NAEP basic score means that the student partially attained the content and skills for the grade level; a proficient score means that the student demonstrated solid mastery of the content and skills; and an advanced score means that the student demonstrated high-level mastery of the content and skills.

NAEP Reading Scores for Emergent Bilingual Students. Although the average NAEP reading comprehension scale scores for emergent bilingual fourth graders were lower in 2022 (190) than in 2019 (191), the difference was not statistically significant (NCES, 2023b, 2023c). The NAEP scores for both years were significantly higher than in previous years (e.g., in 2000, the average score was 167, and in 2013 it was 187), but significantly lower than the 2022 average scale score for nonemergent bilingual students (220). However, the percentage of emergent bilingual fourth graders who performed at or above the proficient level improved from 9% in 2019 to 10% in 2020.

Standards-Based Assessments

Assessments based on standards are described as standards-based. On a standards-based summative assessment, students' scores are not compared to those of other students. Instead, they indicate how well the students' test performance met or did not meet the standards. If a student receives a 70% score, it means that the student met 70% of the standards on the test.

States that receive federal funds currently are required to use a standards-based assessment annually with public school students in English language arts and a standards-based language proficiency test with emergent bilingual students (New America, n.d.). For both types of assessments, states have to develop or choose the standards and use assessments tied to the standards.

Interim Assessments

Companies or universities develop interim assessments; they can be norm-referenced or criterion-referenced. The scoring procedures are uniform, and interim assessments can be used to track student progress (Stahl, Flanigan, & McKenna, 2020). Schools typically use interim assessments to indicate students' reading and instructional levels at different times during the school year (Stahl & García, 2022). Interim assessments include computer-adapted tests, informal reading inventories, decoding tests, and reading comprehension measures. They are sometimes available in Spanish.

EXAMPLES OF SPANISH AND ENGLISH INTERIM ASSESSMENTS

- The *Developmental Reading Assessment 3* (DRA 3) (Beaver & Carter, 2019)/ *Evaluación del desarrollo de la lectura 2* (EDL 2) (Ruiz & Cuesta, 2000). These criterion-referenced assessments evaluate individual students' decoding and reading comprehension. The English version identifies students' reading levels in K through the middle grades, while the Spanish version identifies students' reading levels in K through sixth grade. Both assessments measure students' reading growth and identify students' reading strengths and challenges.
- *Dynamic Indicators of Basic Early Literacy Skills* (*DIBELS*)/*Indicadores Dinamicos del Éxito en la Lectura* (IDEL) (University of Oregon, 2024). DIBELS/IDEL are 1-minute decoding and fluency measures for students in K–8 in English or Spanish. School personnel can download DIBELS/IDEL for free but have to pay to have the tests scored.

FEDERAL ASSESSMENT REQUIREMENTS FOR CURRENT AND FORMER EMERGENT BILINGUAL STUDENTS

When states receive federal funds, school district personnel must administer a survey to the parents or guardians of all entering children to determine if the children are emergent bilingual students (United States Department of Education, Office of English Language Acquisition [OELA], 2016). If the parents/guardians report on the survey that their children speak another language in the home, then the children will take a screening assessment to determine if they are eligible for bilingual or ESL services. When they are enrolled in bilingual or ESL classrooms, their English proficiency and English language arts progress, along with other academic areas, also will be assessed and monitored annually while they are in the programs and for each of four years after they have exited from bilingual or ESL programs (ESSA, 2015).

Home Language Survey

Most states and school districts use a home language survey to identify which students are eligible for bilingual or ESL services. When students first enter a school district (within 30 days), the students' parents or guardians are asked to complete a survey that indicates which languages the students first acquired, understood, employed, and where (home, community, school) (United States Department of Education, OELA, 2016). If the parents or guardians do not speak English well enough to participate in the English survey, then they are supposed to receive the survey and accompanying information in a language they do speak. Based on the survey answers, district personnel decide which students are likely to be emergent bilingual students and should be administered the state-approved English language proficiency screener or assessment to determine their placement in bilingual/ESL services. Parents or guardians of entering students are supposed to receive the assessment results as soon as possible so that they can decide if they want to accept or reject bilingual/ESL services for their children.

Standards-based English Language Proficiency Assessments

Title III of the Elementary and Secondary Education Act, as amended by the Every Student Succeeds Act [ESSA] in 2015, requires that states establish and implement a statewide, uniform process for identifying, monitoring, and exiting emergent bilingual students from relevant services (United States Department of Education, OELA, 2016). The federal government requires states that receive federal funds to administer a standards-based English language proficiency assessment to potential emergent bilingual students, to ongoing emergent bilingual students, and to students who exited from bilingual/ESL services within the last two to four years. The English language proficiency assessment evaluates students' English speaking, listening, reading, and writing performance according to state standards for emergent bilingual students' English language development. The assessment also should be tied to English language development benchmarks developed by (or approved by) the state to show students' English progress. In addition, the assessment needs to be statistically valid (i.e., it evaluates what it says it measures) and reliable (students receive consistent scores when the test is repeated).

Given the work involved in developing English language standards, benchmarks, and a valid and reliable language proficiency assessment tied to the standards, most states joined consortia to develop the state standards and assessment and to score the assessment. Two state-wide consortia that develop and score English language proficiency assessments are the World Class Instructional Design and Assessment (WIDA, 2020) and the English Language Proficiency Assessment for the 21st Century (ELPA21; Rangel-Pacheco & Witte, 2020). Four states (Arizona, California, New York, and Texas) decided to develop their own standards and assessments, and two states (Mississippi and Connecticut) use another type of language proficiency assessment: LAS Links (n.d.).

World Class Instructional Design and Assessment (WIDA)

Thirty-five states participate in WIDA (2020). WIDA has an online and paper English proficiency screener to identify newly enrolled emergent bilingual students eligible for bilingual/ESL services and an English language proficiency exam called Assessing Comprehension and Communication in English State-to-State (ACCESS 2.0) (WIDA, 2023). ACCESS 2.0 is a standards-based English language proficiency assessment. It evaluates the English proficiency of emergent bilingual students according to English language development standards for social and instructional purposes, as well as for English language arts, mathematics, science, and social studies. Students receive a score of 1 to 6 (entering to reaching) in each of the areas, with a score of 1 meaning the student is a beginning learner of English and a score of 5 or higher meaning the student is proficient in English. When students receive a composite score of 4.5 or higher, then they can be reclassified (i.e., they will no longer be considered emergent bilingual) and moved into all-English classrooms.

In addition to the English language proficiency assessment, WIDA provides "can do" descriptors to aid teachers' language instruction in English (WIDA, 2020) and Spanish (WIDA, 2023b). The "can do" descriptors identify what types of L2 support and instruction to provide students at different levels of language proficiency to promote their social and instructional language development and language development in language arts, mathematics, science, and social studies.

English Language Proficiency Assessment for the Twenty-First Century

Eight states belong to the English Language Proficiency Assessment consortia for the Twenty-First Century (ELPA21, n.d.). ELPA21 is an online standards-based assessment that evaluates emergent bilingual students' English reading, writing, speaking, and listening. It includes a screening test for newly enrolled emergent bilingual students and a summative assessment to monitor the English progress of emergent bilingual students at the end of every school year. It scores students on a scale of 1–5 in speaking, listening, reading, and writing, with a total composite score. Students who receive a composite score of 2 or below are ranked "emerging English learners"; those whose composite scores are above 2 but below 4 are ranked "progressing English learners"; and those whose composite scores are 4 or higher are ranked "proficient English learners." Students can be reclassified and moved out of bilingual or ESL services into all-English classes with composite scores of 4 or higher.

State English Language Arts Tests

After emergent bilingual students have completed one full year of public school instruction in the United States, they are required to participate in the same standards-based, state tests in English language arts required of native-English-speaking students once per year in third through eighth grade and once in high school (New America, n.d.; United States Department of Education, 2016). The tests are supposed to be tied to the state standards in English reading comprehension and language arts, which were developed for monolingual English speakers. The federal government requires that the school and grade-level scores be disaggregated so that scores for emergent bilingual students are reported every year and for each year up to four years after the students are reclassified or exited from bilingual or ESL services. The scores for emergent bilingual students who have been in bilingual/ESL programs for five years or more also should be reported.

ASSESSMENT DILEMMAS AND BIASES

Students' reading comprehension is difficult to evaluate because comprehension primarily involves invisible mental processes (Stahl & García,

2022). The reading comprehension assessments utilized with students are designed to show what they know and can do related to reading comprehension. However, when the assessments are developed for monolingual English speakers, using them with emergent bilingual and DL students is problematic because they do not identify all that emergent bilingual and DL students know and can do (G. García & DeNicolo, 2016; O. García & Flores, 2013).

Relationship between Limited English Proficiency and English Reading Comprehension?

It is impossible to know how much of the English reading test performance of emergent bilingual students reflects their developing English proficiency or their actual English reading comprehension (AERA, APA, & NCME, 2014; G. García, McKoon, & August, 2008). One way to estimate their English reading comprehension is to compare their performance on an English reading comprehension test with their performance on an L1 reading comprehension test (Hopewell & Escamilla, 2014).

In recognition of the L1 role, federal law currently requires that emergent bilingual students be assessed in the language they know best, usually their L1, before receiving special education services (Individuals with Disabilities Act, [IDEA] 2015). Current federal law also allows states and school districts to develop and use L1 reading comprehension assessments with emergent bilingual students for up to three years (ESSA, 2015, Section 1111(b)(2)(B)(ix)), and in some cases up to five years.

Few states provide reading comprehension tests in Spanish or other L1 languages. WIDA provides Spanish language and language arts standards to guide the assessment and instruction of Spanish-speaking bilingual students, including those in Spanish–English DL programs (WIDA, 2013, 2023b). It also includes can-do descriptors for the instruction of Spanish speakers at different proficiency levels. However, WIDA does not publish a Spanish language proficiency assessment.

Limited Participation in Norming and Standardization Samples

A problem that occurs with summative and interim assessments is that they usually do not include very many, if any, emergent bilingual students in their norming or standardization samples. Norming or standardization samples are used to determine a typical performance range for the population being tested. If few emergent bilingual students are in the samples, then their performance is not taken into account when the typical score is determined or described (New America, n.d.). When emergent bilingual students' background and vocabulary knowledge differ from those of monolingual English-speaking students in the norming sample, then cultural and linguistic testing biases occur (G. García, 1991; G. García et al., 2008).

Minimal Accommodations Allowed with English Reading Comprehension Tests

Although the federal government allows states to provide testing accommodations when emergent bilingual students are tested in English (ESSA, 2015), few accommodations are permitted for English reading comprehension assessments. For instance, when emergent bilingual students participate in mathematics tests in English, they often are allowed to use bilingual glossaries or dictionaries for unknown English words, to hear the questions read aloud and to read the questions in their L1 or to provide their answers in the L1 (New America, n.d.; Pennsylvania Department of Education, 2024). However, none of these currently are allowed with standards-based English reading comprehension tests because of the perceived overlap in language arts skills assessed on the tests and included in the accommodations.

No Accepted Use of Translanguaging

Although emergent bilingual students may translanguage or use all their linguistic resources, when they respond to comprehension questions in their bilingual or DL classrooms, or when they write (Lee & García, 2021), translanguaging is not allowed on the summative and interim English assessments of reading comprehension and writing. The test taker is viewed as monolingual, not bilingual. When I used Spanish to read the instructions and multiple-choice questions on an English reading test to Spanish-speaking fifth and sixth graders, I found that the students performed better than when they had to read the instructions and answer choices in English (G. García, 1991).When emergent bilingual students are forced to use only English on reading comprehension tests and writing assessments, an incomplete picture of their literacy development typically is obtained.

Lack of Fit between CCSS in Language Arts and Appropriate Instruction for Bilingual Students

A serious problem with the CCSS (NGA Center for Best Practices & CCSSO, 2010) is that they were developed for monolingual English-speaking students (G. García, 2012; O. García & Flores, 2013). Yet, many states use the CCSS to guide the instruction and assessment of all students, including bilingual students.

The CCSS initially discussed emergent bilingual students in a 2⅓ page supplement, entitled Application for English learners (CCSS, 2014). However, the supplement ignored important research findings about the English reading performance of Spanish–English bilingual students (G. García, 2012). For example, it failed to acknowledge that Spanish-speaking Latinx students who were taught to read in Spanish and English outperformed on English reading measures those who were only taught in English (Francis et al., 2006). Instead, authors of the supplement tended to take a special-needs view of emergent bilingual students, recommending individual diagnosis and instructional practices.

In a study of how two districts implemented the CCSS with emergent bilingual students, my colleague and I discovered that it was important for district personnel to include bilingual experts in the decisions about which of the CCSS standards to emphasize with emergent bilingual students (DeNicolo & García, 2014). For example, based on the expertise of the bilingual coordinators in one district, district staff allowed the bilingual staff in a 90-10 DL program to ignore one of the CCSS language arts standards, which read: "Blend and segment onsets and rimes of single-syllable spoken words (/g/-/oat/)" (RF.K.2c). They were allowed to ignore this standard because it was inappropriate for Spanish reading instruction, which the DL students received before they received English reading instruction.

Since the publication of the initial supplement, other authors have critiqued or explained how the CCSS should be implemented with emergent bilingual students (Duguay, Massoud, Tabaku, Himmel, & Sugarman, 2013; O. García & Flores, 2013). Because not all the standards designed for monolingual English speakers are appropriate for bilingual students, when school district personnel consider the implementation of the CCSS or state standards with emergent bilingual and DL students, I urge them to listen to national and local bilingual education experts, including their bilingual staff. They also can refer to the San Diego County Office of Education's (2012, December) standards publication, which lists English and Spanish standards appropriate for emergent bilingual students.

RECOMMENDED ASSESSMENT PRACTICES

Most bilingual educators recommend that schools use a comprehensive assessment system with bilingual students. A comprehensive assessment system involves all three types of assessments: summative, interim, and formative. As mentioned above, the federal government requires the use of language and literacy summative assessments in English with current and former emergent bilingual students and literacy summative assessments with English-dominant DL students. Many schools that serve Spanish–English emergent bilingual students and DL students also administer a Spanish summative literacy assessment (e.g., *Logramos*) toward the end of each school year. The summative assessments show how students' language and/or literacy performance compares to those of other students.

To monitor Spanish–English bilingual students' biliteracy progress during the school year, schools often use interim assessments in Spanish and English at the beginning and middle of the school year, such as the EDL2 in Spanish (Ruiz & Cuesta, 2000) and the DRA3 in English (Beaver & Carter, 2019). DIBELS/IDEL (University of Oregon, 2024) are primarily timed decoding and fluency measures, so I do not recommend using them to monitor bilingual students' reading comprehension. If you use DIBELS/IDEL, I recommend that you do not time bilingual students' oral reading or ask emergent bilingual students to decode nonsense words.

Formative assessments in English and the partner language are important because they not only reveal information about bilingual student's actual ongoing language and literacy performance, but also reveal how bilingual students respond to your instruction. They are the only assessment that involves self-assessment.

It is important to remember that bilingual students often think about and interact with texts by using all their linguistic resources (G. García & Godina, 2017). Therefore, to get a more complete picture of bilingual students' literacy development, it is important to encourage them to translanguage when participating in formative assessments. Facilitating their use of translanguaging strategies (e.g., explaining their reading by using all their languages) is especially important. In a study with fifth- and sixth-grade Spanish-speaking students, I found that the students demonstrated increased comprehension of English test passages when I read the questions to them in Spanish and encouraged them to translanguage to explain their answers (G. García, 1991).

Also, when possible, you need to assess bilingual students' literacy development in all the languages that they use. Hopewell and Escamilla (2014) recommend that school personnel use a "holistic bilingual perspective" to assess bilingual students' reading comprehension. A holistic bilingual perspective involves measuring bilingual students' reading comprehension in all their languages and comparing their reading comprehension performance in the languages to those of other bilingual students from the same language and cultural backgrounds. When they did this for Latinx bilingual students who participated in biliteracy squared (Escamilla et al., 2014), they found that the students performed at grade level in Spanish but about one grade below grade level in English. In biliteracy squared, Spanish–English bilingual students receive their early literacy instruction in Spanish, but do not receive their formal literacy instruction in English until third grade. Given the sequence of reading instruction that the students received in the two languages, Hopewell and Escamilla considered this developmental trajectory to be normal for the Spanish–English bilingual students.

CONCLUDING REMARKS

Although bilingual students typically participate in more formal assessments than monolingual English speakers (G. García & DeNicolo, 2016), the formal assessments generally do not reveal what teachers of current and former emergent bilingual and DL students need to know to facilitate their students' bilingual and biliteracy development. This is one of the major reasons that I encourage teachers of bilingual and DL teachers to use formative assessments in the students' L1 and L2.

Bilingual school personnel also need to be involved in district decisions about which standards and assessments to emphasize with current and former emergent bilingual and DL students. It is imperative that school personnel knowledgeable about bilingualism and biliteracy participate in district assessment and standards decisions. Hopefully, your advocacy and participation will result in improved decisions about the education and assessment of current and former emergent bilingual and DL students.

FORM 12.1. Narrative Retelling Record Sheet

Student's name: Date:

Text or chapter title: Page numbers:

Language of text:

Language(s) used by student for retelling:

Unprompted (U) or Prompted (P)	Key Parts of Narrative	Yes/No	Comments
	Title		
	Type of narrative (genre)		
	Setting		
	Main character(s)		
	Other characters		
	Initiating problem or goal		
	Episodes or events to address the problem or attain the goal		
	How the problem was resolved or goal attained		
	Narrative ending		

Note. Adapted with permission from Stahl and García (2022). Copyright © 2022 The Guilford Press.

FORM 12.2. Expository Retelling Record Sheet

Student's name: Date:

Text or chapter title: Page numbers:

Language of text:

Language(s) used by student for retelling:

Unprompted (U) or Prompted (P)	Key Parts of Expository Text	Yes/No	Comments
	Title		
	Type of expository text		
	Text structure(s)		
	Use of text structure clue/ signal words in retelling		
	Main ideas		
	Supporting details (subordinate ideas)		
	Inclusion of major vocabulary		
	Appropriate inferences		
	Erroneous inferences or erroneous information		

Note. Adapted with permission from Stahl and García (2022). Copyright © 2022 The Guilford Press.

FORM 12.3. Student-Teacher Reading Conference Form

Name: Date:

Reading Language:

Points from last conference to review:

Student goal:

Teacher goal:

Next goals:

Note. Adapted with permission from Stahl and García (2022). Copyright © 2022 The Guilford Press.

FORM 12.4. Student–Teacher Writing Conference Form

Name: Date:

Writing Language:

Points from last conference to review:

Student goal:

Teacher goal:

Next goals:

Note. Adapted with permission from Stahl and García (2022). Copyright © 2022 The Guilford Press.

Conclusion

Pulling It All Together

If you just completed reading this book, you might be wondering, "OK, now what? How do I pull all this together to accelerate the literacy progress of elementary bilingual students?" This Conclusion addresses your questions. It specifies what teachers should emphasize to accelerate the literacy performance of current and former emergent bilingual students and dual-language students.

The Conclusion is divided into three parts. The first part focuses on assessment and instructional activities applicable to bilingual students of all ages. The second part emphasizes assessment and instructional activities that promote the beginning L1 and L2 language and literacy performance of bilingual students. The third part discusses assessment and instructional activities that promote the more advanced L1 and L2 language and literacy performance of bilingual students.

ASSESSMENT AND INSTRUCTIONAL ACTIVITIES FOR ALL GRADE LEVELS

Formative Assessment

I recommend that you work with other bilingual teachers to develop formative assessments that you can use during your ongoing classroom instruction so that you can see how your students are responding to your instruction. Then, you should adjust your instruction and use of instructional activities according to your students' varied performance. Chapter 12 provides information on how to use formative assessments.

Develop a Unitary View of Reading and Writing

As teachers of bilingual students, one of your aims should be to help your students to develop a unitary view of reading and writing across their languages so that they automatically use all that they know about literacy when employing literacy in either language. It is difficult for bilingual students to do this if they are not exposed to literacy in both languages.

When you focus on literacy instruction in one language, remember to also provide your students with opportunities to use the noninstructed language. You can do this by encouraging your students to read independently in both languages, by providing them with interactive teacher read-alouds in both languages, by assigning them to write summaries and responses to the read-alouds in both languages, and by occasionally providing them with dictations in the noninstructed language.

Also, not all bilingual students will automatically use comprehension strategies that are taught or used in one language when reading in the other language. Therefore, you should model and remind your students that the comprehension and vocabulary strategies they learn in one language can be used in the other language.

Improve Bilingual Students' Knowledge and Use of Vocabulary

When there are unfamiliar words in the books you read aloud to your students or in the books that students read, you need to figure out which words warrant explicit vocabulary instruction. When the words do not have long-term uses, then you can teach them for the moment by providing your students with sheltered, child-friendly definitions or by telling them the L1 meanings of the words. However, if they are words that students will need to know in the future or that they can use to figure out other words, then you should provide them with explicit vocabulary instruction. As explained in Chapter 10, if you want your students to learn and use the new vocabulary, then over three to five days you should provide them with multiple exposures to the words and multiple opportunities to actively use them. Typically, you only provide explicit, extensive vocabulary instruction for five to eight words per text.

Increase Student Engagement and Discussion of Texts

Implementing literature circles with multicultural texts is one way to increase bilingual students' engagement and discussion of texts. Asking bilingual students to draw and/or write their responses to texts they read before discussing them in the whole class or small groups usually leads to improved participation and discussion. Bilingual students also should be allowed to use either language and to translanguage when sharing and writing their responses.

Provide Sheltered Instruction and Strategic Use of Translanguaging during L2 Instruction

Even when bilingual students have moved beyond beginning L1 or L2 instructional activities, it still is important to shelter their L2 instruction and to strategically use translanguaging to make your instruction comprehensible. When you combine language instruction with academic instruction or employ content-based language instruction, I also advise you to post and review content and language objectives so that the focus of your instruction is clear to you and your students.

Include Explicit Language Instruction in Content-Based Language Instruction

One of the most effective ways to teach bilingual students language and academic content is content-based language instruction. However, this does not mean that you should not provide your students with some explicit language instruction in the L1 and L2. The experience of French immersion students in Canada showed that simply being immersed in a language for learning did not result in their knowing grammatical constructs that native speakers would know. Modeled writing and dictation are two ways to teach languages explicitly so that bilingual students not only learn the constructs but also apply them.

ASSESSMENT AND INSTRUCTIONAL ACTIVITIES TO PROMOTE BEGINNING L1 AND L2 LANGUAGE AND LITERACY DEVELOPMENT

The instructional activities described in this section are appropriate for bilingual students in grades K–2. They also are appropriate for older bilingual students who are learning to read and write for the first time in the L1 or L2.

Use of Authentic Assessments

Based on my collaborative work with a first-grade, Spanish–English, DL teacher, I suspect that kindergartners and first graders and beginning L1 and L2 learners will begin the school year with a wide range of oral language and literacy skills. For example, at the beginning of the school year, one student in the DL first grade could write two- to three-page stories in three languages—English, Spanish, and Russian. However, other students only wrote a string of indecipherable letters in Spanish, which was their L1. Therefore, I suggest that you begin the school year by conducting short authentic assessments of the students' L1 and L2 oral language and reading and writing performance.

How to Deal with Unknown Vocabulary

When possible, I would avoid unknown words in bilingual students' English phonics instruction or reading of decodable and leveled texts. If that is impossible, then you will need to teach the meanings of the unknown words to your students. If you do not do this, then your bilingual students may not understand that the purpose of decoding is to understand the words read aloud.

Asking your students to develop their own bilingual dictionaries is a good way for them to keep track of the words that they are learning. One way to do this is to give them notebooks in which you ask them to reserve three pages for each letter of the alphabet in the language that you are teaching. Then, model how they should list the words in alphabetical order in the notebook and how to write the definitions. Be sure to encourage them to use translanguaging when they write the definitions.

Cognate Recognition

The identification of cognates is a translanguaging strategy that you can introduce to Spanish–English bilingual students as early as first grade to aid their vocabulary development. A first-grade DL teacher with whom I collaborated taught her first graders how to recognize Spanish–English cognates in mathematics, reading, science, and social studies. She first posted and reviewed a definition of cognates and cognate examples. Then, when students saw a cognate, she asked them to raise their hands and to say the cognate. If it was accurate, she then added it to the list of posted examples. If it was inaccurate or a false cognate, she briefly explained why it was not a cognate.

Comprehension Instruction

As early as first grade, you can use interactive teacher read-alouds to instruct students on how to do the following while reading (Shanahan et al., 2010; Stahl & García, 2015):

- Make inferences.
- Answer and ask questions about texts.

- Use story maps and simple informational text structures (e.g., descriptive and sequence) to understand and recall texts.
- Visualize or make a picture in their heads of what they heard read or are reading.
- Summarize or retell important information in texts (see Chapter 7).

You can accompany your teacher read-alouds with think-alouds to demonstrate how your students should monitor their comprehension and utilize fix-up strategies. Fix-up strategies include slowing down their reading when they encounter difficult vocabulary or a difficult section of the text, reading ahead and then back to the point they do not understand, and rereading a difficult section (Stahl & García, 2015). When you work with students in small groups, you should have them practice monitoring and applying fix-up strategies when they read.

Beginning in second grade, comprehension strategy instruction should be introduced through teacher read-alouds. I recommend that you use the GRR (see Chapter 8) to model strategy instruction, asking your students to work in pairs or individually at their desks on the strategies that you teach and model. As explained in Chapter 8, by mid-second grade, students should practice using strategies while reading and discussing narrative and expository texts in student-led discussion groups (three times for 30 minutes/week).

If your students already have learned how to comprehend texts in their L1 or L2, then you do not need to repeat all the comprehension instructional activities with them. You should review the comprehension activities and remind your students that they can use what they learned about comprehension in one language while reading in the other language.

Thematic Instruction

Thematic instruction helps to increase bilingual students' background and vocabulary knowledge by combining literacy, science, social studies, and/or mathematics instruction. For example, if your second-grade class is studying animal habitats, you can include mathematics instruction and literacy instruction in your study of science. Thematic instruction has the potential to accelerate bilingual students' learning because students encounter the same topic and vocabulary repeatedly across different academic domains.

INSTRUCTIONAL ACTIVITIES THAT PROMOTE MORE ADVANCED L1 AND L2 LITERACY DEVELOPMENT

Once students have developed the foundations for reading and writing, they are ready for instruction that increases their comprehension of narrative and expository texts, aids their evaluation and appreciation of the craft of writing, and focuses on writing in different genres, increasing their academic language and vocabulary knowledge and using reading and writing to advance their academic learning. You can refer to your state standards for information about the types of knowledge, skills, and strategies that should be developed in more advanced literacy learners.

Comprehension of Narrative and Expository Texts

Teachers should remind bilingual students of the comprehension strategies that they already learned and implemented in the earlier grades and in the other language. In addition, teachers should use the GRR (Pearson & Gallagher, 1983; see Chapter 8) to introduce new comprehension strategies. Typically, more advanced readers are taught the following strategies:

- how to determine and activate background knowledge appropriate for a respective text.
- how to employ context to figure out unknown vocabulary or difficult parts of a text.
- how to make different types of inferences, including how to apply information in the text to comprehend or do something outside the text.
- how to identify and use sophisticated text structures (story grammars for different types of narrative genres—for example, fables, mysteries, science fiction; cause and effect, and problem solution for expository texts).
- how to use graphic organizers to comprehend narrative and nonfiction narrative texts and to recall the main ideas and subordinate ideas in expository texts.
- how to recognize figurative language, such as similes and metaphors.

Academic Language and Vocabulary instruction

Texts now are sufficiently complex to require explicit academic language instruction. I found that fourth graders who were strong readers in Spanish, their L1, but grade-level or below grade-level readers in English did not always know how to identify the speaker in dialogue sequences in English texts (G. García, 1998). They also tended to skip information presented in independent clauses and dependent clauses when they explained what they read. They probably would have benefited from teacher think-alouds and paired practice on how to identify who is speaking in English dialogues and how to recognize and use information in independent and dependent clauses to comprehend English texts. It is likely that bilingual students also will benefit from instruction on polysemous words.

As long as bilingual students are motivated to learn and practice affixes (i.e., prefixes, root words, and suffixes), teaching them how to use affixes should improve their text comprehension and use of vocabulary in their writing. Because many Spanish–English cognates involve affixes (e.g., *civilización* and civilization), I encourage you to combine affix instruction with cognate instruction.

More Advanced Cognate Instruction

Beginning with third-grade students, you can ask them to identify the word parts that are the same in cognate pairs and the word parts that are different. As described earlier in the book (see Chapter 10), a DL, Spanish–English third-grade teacher with whom I collaborated used cognates to help her students improve their spelling in their writing by indicating when they had misspelled a word that was a cognate (G. García et al., 2020). Her students seemed to have internalized the cognate patterns and applied what they knew about cognate relationships in Spanish and English, to correct their misspellings.

My colleagues and I conducted research with fourth-grade bilingual Latinx students showing that few of the students employed cognates when reading English texts (Nagy et al., 1993). However, when I provided fourth-grade bilingual Latinx students with extensive Spanish–English cognate instruction and worked with them individually on how to use cognates when they read English informational texts, then they independently used cognates to figure out unknown English words when reading (G. García et al., 2020). My conclusion is that bilingual students as young as fourth grade can use cognates when reading in English, but they first need explicit instruction and practice on how to do this while reading.

Use of Translanguaging

A fourth-grade teacher of bilingual students, who spoke only English and who was implementing dialogic strategy instruction, reported that the emergent bilingual students in her class participated more when she let them translanguage when meeting in small groups (G. García et al., 2021). When the groups primarily included L1 speakers, she tried to place a bilingual student who spoke both English and the students' L1 in each of the groups. She then asked the student who spoke English to share with her and the class what the group worked on, learned, or wanted to share.

Similarly, bilingual students' oral participation often increases when they are encouraged to write their responses to texts before being asked to share them orally with the whole class or in small groups. Allowing them to write in their language of choice or to translanguage usually results in more writing than limiting their writing to only one language.

Disciplinary Literacy Instruction

Although many state standards do not include disciplinary literacy instruction in language arts, science, social studies, or mathematics until sixth grade, implementing a version of it with bilingual students in third grade and above is one way to accelerate their learning. Because disciplinary literacy instruction focuses on how experts in the disciplinary field think, read, and write, it is a more sophisticated version of thematic instruction.

When you combine literacy instruction with disciplinary instruction, then students are introduced to the vocabulary and ways of reading, thinking, and writing in the respective discipline. Students do not have to make the connections across the different fields because the fields already have been integrated. It also is advantageous for bilingual students to receive disciplinary literacy instruction in both their languages, similar to thematic instruction across different classroom contexts (e.g., all-English, ESL, bilingual). However, if you present disciplinary literacy instruction in English and the partner language, be sure to extend your students' knowledge and skill development; do not repeat their instruction.

CONCLUDING REMARKS

I hope this book has been helpful to you. The Appendix shows which instructional activities are appropriate for beginning L1 and L2 readers and writers and for more advanced L1 and L2 readers and writers. I wish you all the best as you diligently work to accelerate the language and literacy performance of bilingual students in the United States.

APPENDIX

Instructional Activities for Beginning and Advanced Bilingual Readers and Writers		
Activities	Appropriateness for Beginning Readers and Writers in L1 or L2	Appropriateness for Advanced Readers and Writers in L1 or L2
Rhymes and songs	Always	Sometimes
Morning message	Always	Sometimes
Interactive teacher read-alouds	Always	Always
Interactive teacher read-aloud with text structure and strategy instruction	Toward end of first year and beyond	Expand to include new text structures, strategies, explicit vocabulary, and academic language instruction
Dictation	Always	Sometimes
Shared reading	Always	Sometimes
Lotta Lara	Always	Sometimes
Shared writing (e.g., modeled writing, language experience approach)	Always	Sometimes
Beginning reading instruction in partner language or decoding and sight-word reading instruction in English	Until learned	No to beginning reading instruction but yes to continued sight-word instruction
Guided reading instruction	Depends on reading performance	No
Teacher-led small-group instruction	When guided reading instruction no longer needed	Yes
Independent reading, writing, word work during guided reading or teacher-led small-group instruction	Always	Independent reading and writing work—Yes

(continued)

Cognate instruction and practice	First grade and beyond	Yes
Explicit vocabulary instruction	Always	Yes
Student-led strategy discussion groups	Mid-second grade and beyond	Yes
Thematic instruction	Always	Yes, unless you are doing disciplinary literacy instruction
Literature circles	Second grade and beyond	Yes
Disciplinary literacy instruction	No	Third grade and beyond
Adapted writing workshop and conferences	Second grade and beyond	Yes
Whole-class advanced comprehension, cognate, language, writing, and/or vocabulary instruction	No	Yes

References

Acosta, J., Williams, J., III, & Hunt, B. (2019). Dual language program models and English language learners: An analysis of the literacy results from a 50/50 and a 90/10 model in two California schools. *Journal of Educational Issues, 5*(2), 1–12.

Ada, A. F. (1990). *Abecedario de los animales*. Planeta.

Ada, A. F. (2016). *Todo es canción: Antología poética* (Everything is a song: Poetry anthology). Santillana.

Adger, C. T., Wolfram, W., & Christian, D. (2007). *Dialects in schools and communities* (2nd ed.). Routledge.

Adkins, J. (2013). *What if you met a cowboy?* Roaring Book Press.

Akhondi, M., Malayeri, F. A., & Samad, A. A. (2011). How to teach expository text structure to facilitate reading comprehension. *The Reading Teacher, 64*, 368–372.

Alderson, J. C. (1984). Reading in a foreign language: A reading problem or a language problem? In J. C. Alderson & A. H. Urquhart (Eds.), *Reading in a foreign language* (pp. 1–24). Longman.

Alvarez, L., Ananda, S., Walqui, A., Sato, E., & Rabinowitz, R. (2014, February). *Focusing formative assessment on the needs of English language learners*. WestEd. Retrieved January 7, 2024, from *www.westEd.org*.

American Educational Research Association, American Psychological Association, & National Council on Measurement in Education. (1999). *Standards for educational and psychological testing 1999*. Author.

American Educational Research Association, American Psychological Association, & National Council on Measurement in Education. (2014). *Standards for educational and psychological testing 2014*. Author.

American Reading Company. (2023). Retrieved from *www.americanreading.com*.

Anderson, R. C., & Freebody, P. (1983). Reading comprehension and the assessment and acquisition of word knowledge. *Advances in Reading Language Research, 2*, 231–256.

Arizona Department of Education. (2014, December). *Structured English immersion models of the Arizona English Language Learner Task Force.* Retrieved from *www. azed.gov.*

Arkolaki, E. (2022). *Nelly's Box—La boîte de Nelly: A bilingual children's book in French and English.* Independently published.

Armbruster, B. B., & Anderson, T. H. (1985). Producing "considerate" expository text: Or easy reading is damned hard writing. *Journal of Curriculum Studies, 17*(3), 247–274.

Armbruster, B. B., Lehr, F., & Osborne, J. (2006). *The research building blocks for teaching children to read: Put reading first (kindergarten through grade 3)* (3rd ed.). National Institute for Literacy, the Partnership for Reading.

Ashton-Warner, S. (1963). *Teacher.* Simon & Schuster.

Associated Press. (2021, March 16). *Racial diversity in children's books grows, but slowly.*

Au, K. H. (2016). Culturally responsive instruction: Application to multiethnic, multilingual classrooms. In L. Helman (Ed.), *Literacy development with English Learners: Research-based instruction in grades K–6* (pp. 20–42). Guilford Press.

Au, K., & Jordan, C. (1981). Teaching reading to Hawaiian children: Finding a culturally appropriate solution. In H. T. Trueba, G. P. Guthrie., & K. Au (Eds.), *Culture and the bilingual classroom: Studies in classroom ethnography* (pp. 139–152). Newbury.

August, D. A., Calderón, M., & Carlo, M. (2002). *Transfer of skills from Spanish to English: A study of young learners. Report for practitioners, parents and policy makers.* Center for Applied Linguistics.

August, D. A., & Shanahan, T. (Eds.). (2006). *Developing literacy in second-language learners: Report of the National Literacy Panel on language minority children and youth.* Erlbaum.

Awde, N., & Samano, P. (1986). *The Arabic alphabet: How to read and write it.* Kensington Publishing Group.

Baker, S., Lesaux, N., Jayanthi, M., Dimino, J., Proctor, C. P., Morris, J., et al. (2014). *Teaching academic content and literacy to English learners in elementary and middle school* (NCEE 2014-4012). National Center for Education Evaluation and Regional Assistance (NCEE), Institute of Education Sciences, U.S. Department of Education. Retrieved from *http://ies.ed.gov/ncee/wwc/publications_reviews.aspx.*

Banks, J. A. (2019). *An introduction to multicultural education* (6th ed.). Pearson.

Bauer, E. B. (2000). Code-switching during shared and independent reading: Lessons learned from a preschooler. *Research in the Teaching of English, 35*(1), 101–130.

Baumann, J., Edwards, E. C., Boland, E. M., Olejnik, S., & Kame'enui, E. (2003). Vocabulary tricks: Effects of instruction in morphology and context on fifth-grade students' ability to derive and infer word meanings. *American Educational Research Journal, 40*(2), 447–494.

Bear, D. R., & Smith, R. E. (2016). The literacy development of emergent bilinguals: What do we know about each student's literacy development? In L. Helman (Ed.), *Literacy development with English learners: Research-based instruction in grades K–6* (2nd ed., pp. 109–108). Guilford Press.

Beatty, A. (2013). *Rosie Revere, the engineer (questionneering)*. Harry N. Adams.

Beaver, J., & Carter, M. (2019). *Developmental reading assessment (DRA)* (3rd ed.). Pearson.

Beck, I. L., McKeown, M. G., & Kucan, L. (2002). *Bringing words to life: Robust vocabulary instruction*. Guilford Press.

Beeman, K., & Urow, C. (2012). *Teaching for biliteracy: Strengthening bridges between languages*. Brookes.

Bennett, R. (2023). Toward a theory of socioculturally responsive assessment. *Educational Assessment, 28*(2), 83–104.

Bernhardt, E. B. (2011). *Understanding advanced second language reading*. Routledge.

Bingham, K. (2012). *Z is for moose*. Greenwillow.

Blachowicz, C. L. Z. (1986). Making connections: Alternatives to the vocabulary notebook. *Journal of Reading, 29*, 643–649.

Blum, I. (2021). *Fly, little bird—Vole, petit oiseau: Bilingual children's picture book English–French with pics to color* (Kids Learn French). Independently published.

Boardman, A., & Lasser, C. J. (2016). Using strategy instruction to promote reading comprehension and content learning. In C. P. Proctor, A. Boardman, & E. H. Hiebert (Eds.), *Teaching emergent bilingual students: Flexible approaches in an era of new standards* (pp. 99–118). Guilford Press.

Boland, P. (2021, October 14). *What is the difference between Mandarin and Cantonese?* Retrieved September 20, 2023, from *www.thoughtco.com*.

Brandl, K. (2009). *Communicative language teaching in action: Putting principles to work* (2nd ed.). Cognella.

Bravo, M. (2016). Situating the English Language Arts Common Core Standards in science: Enhancing access to language for emergent bilingual students. In C. P. Proctor, A. Boardman, & E. H. Hiebert (Eds.), *Teaching emergent bilingual students: Flexible approaches in an era of new standards* (pp. 179–194). Guilford Press.

Brisk, M. E., Kaveh, Y. M., Scialoia, P., & Timothy, B. (2016). Writing arguments: The experience of two mainstream teachers working with multilingual students. In C. P. Proctor, A. Boardman, & E. H. Hiebert (Eds.), *Teaching emergent bilingual students: Flexible approaches in an era of new standards* (pp. 138–156). Guilford Press.

Brodeur, D. R. (1998). Thematic teaching: Integrating cognitive and affective outcomes in elementary classrooms. *Educational Technology, 38*(6), 37–43.

Brown, M. (2013). *Marisol McDonald Doesn't Match/Marisol McDonald no combina*. Lee & Low Books.

Brown, M. (2015). *Maya's blanket. La manta de Maya,* Lee & Low Books.

Calderón, M., August, D., Slavin, R., Duran, D., Madden, N., & Cheung, A. (2005). Bringing words to life in classrooms with English-language learners.

In E. H. Hiebert & M. L. Kamil (Eds.), *Teaching and learning vocabulary: Bringing research to practice* (pp. 115–136). Erlbaum.

California Department of Education. (1993, November). *A report on specially designed academic instruction in English (SDAIE).* Prepared by the working group of the Commission on Teacher Credentialing and the California Department of Education.

Calkins, L. M. (1987). *The writing workshop: A world of difference.* Heinemann.

Camlibel, Z. C., & García, G. (2012). Zehra's story. Becoming biliterate in Turkish and English. In E. B. Bauer & M. Gort (Eds.), *Early biliteracy development: Exploring young learners' use of their linguistic resources* (pp. 111–131). Routledge.

Canagarajah, S. (2011). Codemeshing in academic writing: Identifying teachable strategies of translanguaging. *Modern Language Journal, 95*(3), 401–417.

Canale, M., & Swain, M. (1980). Theoretical bases of communicative approaches to second language teaching and testing. *Applied Linguistics, 1*(1), 1–47.

Carle, E. (2016). *The very hungry caterpillar's ABCs.* World Publishing Company.

Carlo, M. S., August, D., & Snow, C. E. (2005). Sustained vocabulary-learning strategy instruction for English learners. In E. H. Hiebert & M. L. Kamil (Eds.), *Teaching and learning vocabulary: Bringing research to practice* (pp. 137–153). Erlbaum.

Castañeda v. Pickard [648 F.2d 989 (5th Cir., 1981)]. Retrieved July 5, 2022, from *www2.ed.gov.*

Catalyzing Comprehension through Discussion and Debate. (2023). *CCDD: WordGen Elementary. www.serpinstitute.org.* Retrieved February 12, 2023, from *www.serpinstitute.org.*

Catalyzing Comprehension through Discussion and Debate. (2024a). *Advancing academic language for all.* Retrieved January 27, 2024, from *www.serpinstitute.org.*

Catalyzing Comprehension through Discussion and Debate. (2024b). *CCDD: SoGen for Grade 6.* Retrieved January 24, 2024, from *www.serpinstitute.org.*

Catalyzing Comprehension through Discussion and Debate. (2024c). *CCDD: WordGenWeekly.* Retrieved January 2, 2024 from *www.serpinstitute.org.*

Cazden, C. (1988). *Classroom discourse: The language of teaching and learning.* Heinemann.

Cervantes-Soon, C. G., Dorner, L., Palmer, D., Heiman, D., Schwerdtfeger, R., & Choi, J. (2017). Combating inequalities in two-way language immersion programs: Toward critical consciousness in bilingual education spaces. *Review of Research in Education, 41*, 401–427.

Cervetti, G. N., Barber, J., Dorph, R., Pearson, P. D., & Goldschmidt, P. G. (2012). The impact of an integrated approach to science and literacy in elementary school classrooms. *Journal of Research in Science Teaching, 49*, 631–658.

Cervetti, G. N., Pearson, P. D., Palincsar, A. S., Afflerbach, P., Kendeou, P., Biancarosa, G., et al. (2020). How the Reading for Understanding Initiative's research complicates the Simple View of Reading invoked in the Science of Reading. *Reading Research Quarterly, 55*(1), S161–S172.

Chamot, A. U., & O'Malley, J. M. (1986). The cognitive academic language learning approach: A model for linguistically diverse classrooms. *Elementary School Journal*, *96*(3), 259–273.

Chamot, A. U., & O'Malley, J. M. (1987). The cognitive academic language learning approach: A bridge to the mainstream. *TESOL Quarterly, 21*, 227–249.

Chamot, A. U., & Robbins, J. (2005). *The CALLA model: Strategies for ELL student success.* Workshop for Allentown City School District. Retrieved from *www.http:calla.ws.*

Cheung, H., McBride-Chang, C., & Wing, Y-C. B. (2016). Reading Chinese. In R. M. Joshi & P. G. Aaron (Eds.), *Handbook of orthography and literacy* (pp. 421–439). Routledge.

Choi, B. (2023). *Chinese characters: When and how to introduce to kids.* Chalk Academy. Retrieved September 25, 2023 from *www.chalkacademy.com.*

Choi, H.-M. (2018). *Beautiful short stories in English and Korean: Bilingual/dual language picture book for beginners.* New Ampersand.

Choi, L., & Choi, E. (2021). *Dim sum, please!* (Mandarin ed.). Independently published.

Choi, Y. (2003). *The name jar.* Dragonfly Books.

Civil Rights Act of 1964. Public Law 88–352, 78 Stat. 241, enacted July 2, 1964.

Clark, E. R., Flores, B. B., Smith, H. L., & González, D. A. (2016). *Multicultural literature for Latino bilingual children: Their words, their world.* Rowman and Littlefield.

Clarke, M. A. (1980). The short-circuit hypothesis of ESL reading—Or when language competence interferes with reading performance. *Modern Language Journal*, *64*(2), 203–209.

Collier, L. (2013, November). Teaching complex texts: A guide. *The Chronicle Council,* pp. 6–9.

Collier, V. P., & Thomas, W. P. (2017). Validating the power of bilingual schooling: Thirty-two years of large-scale, longitudinal research. *Annual Review of Applied Linguistics, 37,* 1–15.

Common Core State Standards (CCSS). (2014). *Application for English learners.* Retrieved from *www.tesol.org.*

Connor, U. (2002). New directions in contrastive rhetoric. *TESOL Quarterly, 16*(4), 493–510.

Cortina, R., Makar, C., & Mount-Cors, M. F. (2015). Dual language as a social movement: Putting languages on a level playing field. *Current Issues in Comparative Education, 17*(1), 5–16.

Coxhead, A. (2000). A new academic word list. *TESOL Quarterly, 34*(2), 213–238.

Crosson, A. C. (2016). Supporting linguistically diverse students to develop deep, flexible knowledge of academic words. In C. P. Proctor, A. Boardman, & E. H. Hiebert (Eds.), *Teaching emergent bilingual students: Flexible approaches in an era of new standards* (pp. 82–98). Guilford Press.

Crosson, A. C., & McKeown, M. G. (2016). How effectively do middle school learners use roots to infer the meaning of unfamiliar words? *Cognitive Instruction*, *34,* 1–24.

Cummins J. (1976). The influence of bilingualism on cognitive growth: A synthesis of research findings and explanatory hypotheses. *Working Papers on Bilingualism, 9*, 1–43.

Cummins, J. (1981). The role of primary language development in promoting educational success for language minority students. In Office of Bilingual Bicultural Education, *Schooling and language minority education: A theoretical framework* (pp. 3–49). California State Department of Education.

Cummins, J. (2000). *Language, power, and pedagogy. Bilingual children in the crossfire*. Multilingual Matters.

Cummins, J. (2008). *Putting language proficiency in its place: Responding to critiques of the conversational/academic language distinction*. Retrieved May 23, 2008, from *www.iteachilern.com/cummins/converacademlangdisti.html*.

Cunningham, P. M. (2000). *Phonics they use: Words for reading and writing* (3rd ed.). Longman.

Cunningham, P. M. (2017). *Phonics they use: Words for reading and writing* (7th ed.). Pearson.

Daniels, H. (2002). *Literature circles: Voice and choice in book clubs & reading groups*. Stenhouse.

David, M. K., & Norazit, L. (2000, Spring/Summer). Selection of reading texts: Moving beyond content schemata. *Literacy across Cultures, 3*(2), 11–17.

de la Luz Reyes, M. (1991). A process approach to literacy using dialogue journals and literature logs with second language learners. *Research in the Teaching of English, 25*(3), 291–313.

DeNicolo, C. P., & Fránquiz, M. E. (2006). "Do I have to say it?": Critical encounters with multicultural children's literature. *Language Arts, 84*(2), 157–170.

DeNicolo, C. P., & García, G. E. (2014). Examining policies and practices: Two districts' responses to federal reforms and their use of language arts assessments with emerging bilinguals (K–3). *63rd Yearbook of the Literacy Research Association*, 229–242.

DeNicolo, C. P., Yu, M., Crowley, C. B., & Gabel, S. L. (2017). Reimagining critical care and problematizing sense of school belonging as a response to inequality for immigrants and children of immigrants. *Review of Research in Education, 41*, 500–530.

Dien, T. H. (2004). Language and literacy in Vietnamese American communities. In B. Pérez (Ed.), *Sociocultural context of language and literacy* (2nd ed., pp. 137–177). Erlbaum.

Domke, L. (2020). Clarity, culture, and complications: An analysis of Spanish–English dual-language concept books. *Journal of Children's Literature, 46*(1), 23–36.

Domke, L. M. (2022). Children translating when reading dual-language books. *Journal of Literacy Research, 54*(3), 247–271.

Dorros, A. (1997). *Abuela*. Puffin.

Duesbery, L., Werblow, J., & Twyman, T. (2011). *The effect of the Seeds of Science/Roots of Reading curriculum (planets and moons unit) for developing literacy through science in fifth grade*. Unpublished report to the National Science Foundation.

Duguay, A., Massoud, L., Tabaku, L., Himmel, J., & Sugarman, J. (2013). *Implementing the Common Core for English Learners: Responses to common questions*. Center for Applied Linguistics.

Duke, N., & Cartwright, K. (2021). The science of reading progresses: Communicating advances beyond the simple view of reading. *Reading Research Quarterly, 56*(51), 525–544.

Durgunoğlu, A. Y. (2002). Cross-linguistic transfer in literacy development and implications for language learners. *Annals of Dyslexia, 52*, 189–204.

Durgunoğlu, A. Y., Nagy, W. E., & Hancin-Bhatt, B. J. (1993). Cross-language transfer of phonological awareness. *Journal of Educational Psychology, 85*(3), 453–465.

Dutro, S., Nuñez, R. M., & Helman, L. (2016). Explicit language instruction: A key to academic success for English learners. In L. Helman (Ed.), *Literacy development with English learners: Research-based instruction in grades K–6* (2nd ed., pp. 43–77). Guilford Press.

Eastman, P. D. (2000). *The alphabet book (Bright and early board books)*. Random House Books for Young Readers.

Echevarria, J., Vogt, M. E., & Short, D. (1999). *Making content comprehensible for English language learners: The SIOP model*. Prentice-Hall.

Echevarria, J., Vogt, M. E., & Short, D. (2004). *Making content comprehensible for English learners: The SIOP model*. (2nd ed.). Pearson Allyn and Bacon.

Echevarria, J., Vogt, M. E., & Short, D. (2017). *Making content comprehensible for English learners: The SIOP model* (5th ed.). Pearson Allyn and Bacon.

Edelsky, C. (1986). *Writing in a bilingual program: Habia una vez*. Ablex.

Edutainment, T., & Al Amani. (2021). *Learn to write Arabic letters and numbers: Great learning fun for boys and girls from 4 years old*. Independently published.

English Language Proficiency Assessment for the 21st Century (ELPA21). (n.d.). Retrieved January 31, 2024, from *www.elpa21.org*.

Escamilla, K., Geisler, D., Hopewell, S., & Ruiz, O. (2007, March). *Transitions to biliteracy: Beyond Spanish and English*. Paper presented at the annual meeting of the American Educational Research Association, Chicago.

Escamilla, K., Hopewell, S., Butvilofsky, S., Sparrow, W., Soltero-Gonzalez, L., Ruiz-Figueroa, O., & Escamilla, M. (2014). *Biliteracy from the start: Literacy squared in action*. Caslon.

Estrellita. (2023). Every child deserves a shining start. Retrieved from *www.estrellita.com*.

Every Student Succeeds Act (ESSA), 20 U.S.C. § 6301. (2015). Retrieved from *www.congress.gov/bill/114th-congress/senate-bill/1177*.

Fleming, C. (2016). *Giant squid*. Roaring Book Press.

Flores, N. (2020). From academic language to language architecture: Challenging raciolinguistic ideologies in research and practice, *Theory into Practice, 59*(1), 22–31.

Ford, K., & Palacios, R. (2015). Early literacy instruction in Spanish: Teaching the beginning reader. Retrieved September 27, 2023, from *www.colorincolorado.org*.

Fountas, I. C. (2012). *Sistema de evaluación de la lectura, Grados K–2, Niveles, A-N.* [Reading evaluation system, grades K–2, levels, A–N]. Heinemann.

Fountas, I., & Pinnell, G. S. (2010). *The Fountas & Pinnell Benchmark Assessment System Series* (2nd ed.). Heinemann.

Fountas, I. C., & Pinnell, G. S. (2011). *The continuum of literacy learning, grades PreK–8.* Heinemann.

Fox, M. (1992). *Hattie and the Fox.* Aladdin.

Francis, D. J., Lesaux, N. K., & August, D. (2006). Language of instruction. In D. August & T. Shanahan (Eds.), *Developing literacy in second-language learners: Report of the National Literacy Panel on language minority children and youth* (pp. 365–414). Erlbaum.

Freeman, Y. S., & Freeman, D. E. (2009). *La enseñanza de la lectura y la escritura en español y en inglés en clases bilingües y de doble inmersión.* [Teaching reading and writing in Spanish and English in bilingual and dual language classrooms]. (Segunda edición revisada). Heinemann.

Freeman, Y. S., & Freeman, D. (2023). *Teaching reading and writing in Spanish and English in bilingual and dual language classrooms.* Heinemann.

Freire, J., & Valdez, V. E. (2017). Dual language teachers' stated barriers to implementation of culturally relevant pedagogy. *Bilingual Research Journal, 40*(1), 55–69.

Freire, P. (1970). *Pedagogy of the oppressed.* Penguin Books.

Gallagher, M. A., Barber, A. T., Beck, J. S., & Buehl, M. M. (2019). Academic vocabulary: Explicit and incidental instruction for students of diverse backgrounds. *Reading & Writing, 35*(2), 84–102.

Garcia, A. (2020, January 27). A new era for bilingual education in California. *Kappan.* Retrieved from *kappanonline.org.*

García, G. E. (1991). Factors influencing the English reading test performance of Spanish-speaking Hispanic children. *Reading Research Quarterly, 26*(4), 371–392.

García, G. E. (1992). Taking an emic perspective. *Topics in Language Disorders, 12*(3), 54–66.

García, G. E. (1998). Mexican-American bilingual students' metacognitive reading strategies: What's transferred, unique, problematic? *National Reading Conference Yearbook, 47*, 253–263.

García, G. E. (2000). Bilingual children's reading. In M. L. Kamil, P. B. Mosenthal, P. D. Pearson, & R. Barr (Eds.), *Handbook of reading research* (Vol. 3, pp. 813–834). Erlbaum.

García, G. E. (2003). The reading comprehension development and instruction of English language-learners. In A. P. Sweet & C. E. Snow (Eds.), *Rethinking reading comprehension* (pp. 30–50). Guilford Press.

García, G. E. (2012, April). *Common Core State Standards (K–5) and English learners/bilingual research findings.* Paper presented at English Learners Panel, annual convention of International Reading Association.

García, G. E., & DeNicolo, C. P. (2016). Improving the language and literacy assessment of emergent bilinguals. In L. Helman (Ed.), *Literacy development with English learners: Research based instruction in grades k–6* (2nd ed., pp. 78–108). Guilford Press.

García, G. E., & Godina, H. (2017). A window into bilingual reading: The bilingual reading practices of fourth-grade, Mexican American children who are emergent bilinguals. *Journal of Literacy Research, 49*(2), 273–301.

García, G. E., & Lang, M. (2018). The link between standards and dual language teachers' Spanish literacy instruction and use of formative assessments. *Bilingual Research Journal, 41*(2), 167–186.

García, G. E., & Lang, M. G. (2023). A longitudinal study of strengths, challenges, and inequities in a Spanish–English dual-language program. *Bilingual Research Journal, 46*(1–2), 9–24.

García, G. E., & Nagy, W. (1993). Latino students' concept of cognates. In D. J. Leu & C. K. Kinzer (Eds.), *Examining central issues in literacy research, theory, and practice. Forty-second Yearbook of the National Reading Conference* (pp. 367–373). National Reading Conference.

García, G. E., McKoon, G., & August, D. (2008). Language and literacy assessment. In D. August & T. Shanahan (Eds.), *Developing reading and writing in second-language learners: Lessons from the report of the National Literacy Panel on Language Minority Children and Youth* (pp. 251–274). Erlbaum.

García, G. E., Sacco, L. J., & Guerrero-Aria, B. E. (2020). Cognate instruction and bilingual students' improved literacy performance. *The Reading Teacher, 73*(5), 617–625.

García, G. E., Taylor, B. M., Pearson, P. D., Bray, T. M., Primeaux, J., & Mora, R. A. (2021). Improvements in teachers' reading comprehension instruction and bilingual students' reading test performance in high-poverty schools. *The Elementary School Journal, 121*(3), 357–384.

García, O. (2009). *Bilingual education in the 21st century: A global perspective.* Wiley-Blackwell.

García, O., & Flores, N. (2013). Multilingualism and Common Core State Standards in the United States. In S. May (Ed.), *The multilingual turn: Implications for SLA, TESOL, and bilingual education* (pp. 147–166). Routledge.

García, O., Johnson, S. I., & Seltzer, K. (2017). *The translanguaging classroom: Leveraging student bilingualism for learning.* Caslon.

García, O., & Kleifgen, J. (2018). *Educating emergent bilinguals: Policies, programs, and practices for English Learners* (2nd ed). Teachers College Press.

García, O., Kleifgen, J., & Falchi, L. (2008). From English language learners to emergent bilinguals. *Equity Matters: Research Review #1.*

García, O., & Lin, A. M. Y. (2017a). Extended understandings of bilingual and bilingual education. In O. García, A. M. Y. Lin, & S. May (Eds.), *Bilingual and multilingual education* (3rd ed., pp. 1–20). Springer.

García, O., & Lin, A. M. Y. (2017b). Translanguaging in bilingual education. In O. García, A. M. Y. Lin, & S. May (Eds.), *Bilingual and multilingual education* (3rd ed., pp. 117–130). Springer.

Gee, J. P. (1991). Sociocultural approaches to literacy (literacies). *Annual Review of Linguistics, 12*, 31–48.

Genesee, F., Geva, E., Dressler, C., & Kamil, M. (2006). Synthesis: Cross-linguistic relationships. In D. August & T. Shanahan (Eds.), *Developing literacy in second-language learners: Report of the National Literacy Panel on language-minority children and youth* (pp. 153–174). Erlbaum.

Genesee, F., & Riches, C. (2006). Literacy: Instructional issues. In F. Genesee, K. Lindholm-Leary, W. M. Saunders, & D. Christian (Eds.), *Educating English language learners: A synthesis of research evidence* (pp. 109–175). Cambridge University Press.

Genzuk, M. (2011). *Specially Designed Academic Instruction in English (SDAIE) for language-minority students*. Center for Multilingual, Multicultural Research Digital Paper Series. Center for Multilingual, Multicultural Research, University of Southern California. Retrieved from *www.usc.edu/dept/education/CMMR/DigitalPapers/SDAIE_Genzuk.pdf*.

Gersten, R., Baker, S. K., Shanahan, T., Linan-Thompson, S., Collins, P., & Scarcella, R. (2007). *Effective literacy and English language instruction for English Learners in the elementary grades: A practice guide* (NCEE 2007-4011). National Center for Education Evaluation and Regional Assistance, Institute of Education Sciences, U.S. Department of Education. Retrieved from *http://ies.ed.gov/ncee/wwc/publications/practiceguides*.

Gibbons, P. (2015). *Scaffolding language, scaffolding learning* (2nd edition). Heinemann.

Go Abroad China. (2019, May 21). *Most common Chinese character list*. Retrieved from *http://goabroadchina.com*.

Goldenberg, C. (1992–1993). Instructional conversations: Promoting comprehension through discussion. *The Reading Teacher, 46*(4), 316–326.

Goldenberg, C. (2011). Reading instruction of English language learners. In M. Kamil, P. D. Pearson, E. B. Moje, & P. Afflerbach (Eds.), *The handbook of reading research* (Vol. 4, pp. 684–710). Routledge.

Goldenberg, C., Tolar, T., Reese, L., Francis, D., Ray, A., & Mejia-Arauz, R. (2014). How important is teaching phonemic awareness to children learning to read in Spanish. *American Educational Research Journal, 51*(3), 604–633.

Goldman, S. R., Snow, C., & Vaughn, S. (2016). Common themes in teaching reading for understanding: Lessons from three projects. *Journal of Adolescent and Adult Literacy, 60*(3), 255–264.

González, N., Moll, L. C., & Amanti, C. (2005). *Funds of knowledge: Theorizing practices in households, communities, and classrooms*. Erlbaum.

Goodenow, C., & Grady, K. E. (1993). The relationship of school belonging and friends' values to academic motivation among urban adolescent students. *The Journal of Experimental Education*, 62(1), 60–71.

Gort, M. (2019). Developing bilingualism and biliteracy in early and middle childhood. *Language Arts, 96*(4), 229–243.

Gough, P., & Tunmer, W. (1986). Decoding, reading, and reading disability. *Remedial and Special Education, 7*(1), 6–10.

Gravelle, M. (1996). *Supporting bilingual learners in schools*. Trentham Books.

Great Schools Partnership. (2013, August 29). Academic language. In *The glossary of education reform*. Retrieved from *www.edglossary.org*.

Grosjean, F. (1982). *Life with two languages: An introduction to bilingualism*. Harvard University Press.

Grosjean, F. (2010). *Bilingual: Life and reality*. Harvard University Press.

Hale, S., & Hale, D. (2015). *The princess in black*. Candlewick.

Halliday, M. A. K. (1978). *Language as social semiotic: The social interpretation of language and meaning.* Edward Arnold.

Halliday, M. A. (1993). Towards a language-based theory of learning. *Linguistics and Education, 5*, 93–116.

Hamman-Ortiz, L., & Palmer, D. (2020). Identity and two-way bilingual education: Considering student perspective: Introduction to the special issue. *International Journal of Bilingual Education and Bilingualism, 26*(1), 1–6.

HarperCollins Children's Books. (2024). *The adventures of Paddington: My first letters book.* HarperCollins Children's Books.

Harris, V. J. (1993). *Teaching multicultural literature in grades k–8.* Christopher Gordon.

Heath, S. B. (1983). *Ways with words: Language, life and work in communities and classrooms.* Cambridge University Press.

Hecht, T. (2016). *The nocturnals: The mysterious abductions.* Fabled Films Press.

Heller, M. (1999). *Linguistic minorities and modernity: A sociolinguistic ethnography.* Longman.

Helman, L. (2016). Opening doors to texts: Planning effective phonics instruction with emergent bilinguals. In L. Helman (Ed.), *Literacy development with English learners: Research-based instruction in grades K–6* (2nd ed., pp. 164–181). Guilford Press.

Heritage, M. (2010). *Formative assessment and next-generation assessment systems: Are we losing an opportunity?* Council of Chief State School Officers.

Herman, L. (2016). Effective instructional practices for emergent bilinguals. In L. Helman (Ed.), *Literacy development with English learners: Research-based instruction in grades K–6* (2nd ed., pp. 309–328). Guilford Press.

Herman, S. (2017). *Messi: A boy who became a star.* CreateSpace Independent Publishing Platform.

Hernandez, H. (2000). *Multicultural education: A teacher's guide to linking context, process, and content* (2nd ed.). Pearson.

Herrera, S. G., Perez, D. R., & Escamilla, K. (2010). *Teaching reading to English language learners: Differentiated literacies.* Allyn & Bacon.

Hiebert, E. H. (2023, September 25). Thinking through research and the science of reading. *Kappan: Connecting education research, policy, and practice, 105*(2), 37–41.

Hiebert, E. (2024). Enhancing opportunities for decoding and knowledge building through beginning texts. *The Reading Teacher, 77*(6), 965–974.

Hill, J. D., & Björk, C. L. (2008). *Classroom instruction that works with English Language Learners.* Nebraska ELL Professional Development Cohort in partnership with the North Central Comprehensive Center and McREL International.

Ho, C. S.-H., & Bryant, P. (1997). Learning to read Chinese beyond the logographic phase. *Reading Research Quarterly, 32*(3), 276–289.

Holdaway, D. (1982). Shared book experience: Teaching reading using favorite books. *Theory into Practice, 21*(4), 293–300.

Hoover, W. A., & Gough, P. B. (1990). The simple view of reading. *Reading and Writing: An Interdisciplinary Journal, 2*(2), 127–160.

Hopewell, S., & Escamilla, K. (2014). Struggling reader or emerging biliterate student? Reevaluating the criteria for labeling emerging bilingual students as low achieving. *Journal of Literacy Research, 46*(1), 68–89.

Hornberger, N. H. (1989). Continua of biliteracy. *Review of Educational Research, 59*(3), 271–296.

Hornberger, N. H. (1990). Creating successful learning contexts for bilingual literacy. *Teachers College Record, 92*(2), 212–229.

Houghton Mifflin Harcourt. (2014). *Logramos*. Author.

Howard, E. R., Lindholm-Leary, K. J., Rogers, D., Olague, N., Medina, J., Kennedy, et al. (2018). *Guiding principles for dual language education* (3rd ed.). Center for Applied Linguistics.

Howard, E. R., Sugarman, J., & Coburn, C. (2006). *Adapting the Sheltered Instruction Observation Protocol (SIOP) for two-way immersion education: An introduction to the TWIOP*. Center for Applied Linguistics.

Howell, T. (2003). *A is for airplane/A es para avión* (Multilingual edition). Cooper Square.

Hsiang, T. P., Graham, S., Wong, Z., Wong, C., & Skar, G. B. (2022). Teaching Chinese characters to students in grades 1 to 3 through emerging rote instruction during the Covid-19 pandemic. *Reading & Writing, 35*(8), 1975–2014.

Hussar, B., Zhang, J., Hein, S., Wang, K., Roberts, A., Cui, J., et al. (2020). *The condition of education 2020* (NCES 2020-144). U.S. Department of Education. National Center for Education Statistics. Retrieved July 11, 2024, from *https://nces.ed.gov/pubsearch/pubsinfo. asp?pubid=2020144.*

Hymes, D. (1972a). Introduction. In C. Cazden, V. P. John, & D. Hymes (Eds.), *Functions of language in the classroom* (xi–xvii). Teachers College Press.

Hymes, D. (1972b). Models of the interaction of language and social life. In J. Gumperz & D. Hymes (Eds.), *Directions in sociolinguistics: The ethnography of communication* (pp. 35–71). Basil Blackwell.

Illinois State Board of Education. (2022). Retrieved July 5, 2022. from *www.isbe.net.*

Individuals with Disabilities Education Act. (IDEA), 20 U.S.C. § 1400. (2004).

International Literacy Association. (2018). *Literacy leadership brief: Explaining phonics instruction: An educators' guide*. Author.

Jiban, C. (2022, January 25). The science of reading explained. Retrieved from *www.isbe.net.*

Jiménez, R. T., David, S., Fagan, K., Risko, V. J., Pacheco, M., Pray, L., et al. (2015). Using translation to drive conceptual development for students becoming literate in English as an additional language. *Research in the Teaching of English, 49*(3), 248–271.

Jiménez, R. T., García, G. E., & Pearson, P. D. (1995). Three children, two languages, and strategic reading: Case studies in bilingual/monolingual reading. *American Educational Research Journal, 32,* 31–61.

Jiménez, R. T., García, G. E., & Pearson, P. D. (1996). The reading strategies of bilingual Latina/o students who are successful English readers: Opportunities and obstacles. *Reading Research Quarterly, 31*(1), 90–112.

Johnson, D. D., Pittelman, S. D., & Heimlich, J. E. (1986). Semantic mapping. *The Reading Teacher, 39,* 778–782.

Johnson, D. W., & Johnson, R. (1989). *Cooperation and competition: Theory and research.* Interaction Book Company.

Juliá, L. M., & Montalvo, L. A. (2020). *El ABC de la comida Puertorriqueña: The ABC's of Puerto Rican food.* Luli Bilingual Books.

Kamil, M. L., Borman, G. D., Dole, J., Kral, C. C., Salinger, T., & Torgesen, J. (2008). *Improving adolescent literacy: Effective classroom and intervention practice: A practice guide (NCEE No. 2008-4027).* National Center for Education Evaluation and Regional Assistance, Institute of Educational Sciences, U.S. Department of Education.

Kaplan, R. B. (1972). *The anatomy of rhetoric: Prolegomena to a functional theory of rhetoric: Essays for teachers.* Center for Curriculum Development.

Katz, S. B. (2020). *The story of Ruth Bader Ginsburg: A biography book for new readers.* Callisto Kids.

Kidditube Arabic. (2024, June 28). YouTube.

Kieffer, M. J., & Lesaux, N. K. (2007). Breaking down words to build meaning: Morphology, vocabulary, and reading comprehension in the urban classroom. *The Reading Teacher, 61*(2), 134–144.

Klass, P. (2017, February 21). Language lessons start in the womb. *New York Times.* Retrieved July 1, 2023, from *www.NYTimes.com.*

Klingner, J. K., & Vaughn, S. (1996). Reciprocal teaching of reading comprehension strategies for students with learning disabilities who use English as a second language. *The Elementary School Journal, 96*(3), 275–293.

Klingner, J. K., & Vaughn, S. (1999). Promoting reading comprehension, content learning and English acquisition through Collaborative Strategic Reading. *The Reading Teacher, 52*(7), 738–747.

Klingner, J. K., & Vaughn, S. (2000). The helping behaviors of fifth graders while using Collaborative Strategic Reading in ESL content classes. *TESOL Quarterly, 34*(1), 69–98.

Kole, N. (2003). *Native-language supported reading instruction: A VALID framework.* Unpublished doctoral dissertation, Kansas State University, Manhattan, KS.

Krashen, S. (1981). *Second language acquisition and second language learning.* Pergamon Press.

Krashen, S. (1982). *Principles and practice in second language acquisition.* Pergamon Press.

Krashen, S. (1985).*The input hypothesis: Issues and implications.* Longman.

Krashen, S., & Terrell, T. D. (1983). *The natural approach (Language acquisition in the classroom).* Alemany Press.

Kucer, S. B., & Silva, C. (1999). The English literacy development of bilingual students within a transition whole-language curriculum. *Bilingual Research Journal, 23*(4), 345–371.

Lachtman, O. D. (1995). *Pepita speaks twice/Pepita habla dos veces.* Arte Público Press.

Lam, H. C. (2011). A critical analysis of the various ways of teaching Chinese characters. *Electronic Journal of Foreign Language Teaching, 8*(1), 57–70.

Lambert, W. E. (1981). Bilingualism and language acquisition. *Annals of the New York Academy of Sciences, 379,* 9–22.

Lang, M. G. (2019). *Border inspections in a dual-language second grade classroom in a small urban community.* Unpublished doctoral dissertation, University of Illinois at Urbana-Champaign.

LAS links. (n.d.). Data Recognition Corporation. Retrieved January 28, 2024, from *www.laslinks.com.*

Lau Remedies. (2022). Retrieved June 11, 2022, from *https://web.stanford.edu.*

Lau v. Nichols [414 U.S. 563 (1974)].

Lebanese Arabic Institute. (2023). *The Arabic alphabet: A guide to the phonology and orthography of Modern Standard Arabic and Lebanese Arabic.* Retrieved September 13, 2023, from *www.lebanesearabicinstitute.com.*

Lee, C. (2021). Third-grade students' responses to multicultural children's literature during post-reading activities. *The Dragon Lode, 39*(2), 14–26.

Lee, C., & García, G. E. (2020).Unpacking the oral translanguaging practices of Korean-American first graders, *Bilingual Research Journal*, *43*(1), 32–49.

Lee, C., & García, G. E. (2021). Understanding Korean-American first graders' written translanguaging practices. *Linguistics and Education, 66*, 100998.

Lems, K., Miller, L. D., & Soro, T. M. (2017). *Building literacy with English Language Learners: Insights from linguistics* (2nd ed.). Guilford Press.

Lesaux, N. K., Crosson, A. C., Kieffer, M. J., & Pierce, M. (2010a). Uneven profiles: Language minority learners' word reading, vocabulary, and reading comprehension skills. *Journal of Applied Developmental Psychology, 31*(6), 475–483.

Lesaux, N. K., Kieffer, M. J., Faller, E., & Kelley, J. (2010b). The effectiveness and ease of implementation of an academic vocabulary intervention for linguistically diverse students in urban middle schools. *Reading Research Quarterly, 45*(2), 198–230.

Li, J. (2020). *Mulan: the story of the legendary warrior told in English and Chinese.* Shanghai Press.

Lightblown, P., & Spada, N. (2011). *How languages are learned* (3rd ed.). Oxford University Press.

Lindholm-Leary, K. J. (2001). *Dual language education.* Multilingual Matters.

Lindholm-Leary, K. J., & Hernández, A. M. (2011). Achievement and language proficiency of Latino students in dual language programmes: Native English speakers, fluent English/previous ELLs and current ELLs. *Journal of Multilingual and Multicultural Development, 32*, 531–545.

Lobel, A. (1983). *Mouse soup.* HarperCollins.

Long, M. H. (1981). Input, interaction, and second language acquisition. *Annals of the New York Academy of Sciences, 379*, 259–278.

Long, M., & Porter, R. (1985). Group work, interlanguage talk and second language acquisition. *TESOL Quarterly, 19*, 207–228.

López-Robertson, J. (2012). "Está página me recordó": Young Latinas using personal life stories as tools for meaning making. *Bilingual Research Journal, 35*(2), 217–233.

López-Velásquez, A. M., & García, G. E. (2017). The bilingual reading practices and performance of two Hispanic first-graders. *Bilingual Research Journal, 40*(3), 246–261.

Lubliner, S., & Grisham, D. L. (2017). *Translanguaging: The key to comprehension for Spanish-speaking students and their peers*. Rowman & Littlefield.

Lubliner, S., & Hiebert, E. H. (2011). Analysis of English–Spanish cognates as a source of general academic language. *Bilingual Research Journal, 34*(1), 76–93.

Lucero, A. (2014). Teachers' use of linguistic scaffolding to support the academic language development of first-grade emergent bilingual students. *Journal of Early Childhood Literacy, 14*(4), 534–561.

MacGinitie, W. H., MacGinitie, R. K., Maria, K., & Dreyer, L. G. (2000). *Gates-MacGinitie Reading Tests*. Author.

MacLeod, E. (2014). *Bunny the brave war horse: A true story*. Kids Can Press.

Manyak, P. C., Baumann, J. F., & Manyak, A. M. (2018). Morphological analysis instruction in the elementary grades: Which morphemes to teach and how to teach them. *The Reading Teacher, 72*(3), 289–300.

Marcus, L. (2012). *Show me a story! Why picture books matter. Conversations with 21 of the world's most celebrated illustrators*. Candlewick Press.

Mariscal, G. (2017). *El abecedario de Lucía (El mundo de Lucía)*. CreateSpace Independent Publishing Platform.

Marisco, K. (2018). *Sybil Ludington's Revolutionary War story*. Lerner.

Marshall, L. W. (2016). *Rainbow weaver/Tejadora del arcoíris*. Lee & Low.

Martin, B., & Carle, E. (1992). *Brown bear, brown bear, what do you see?* Holt.

Martin-Beltrán, M. (2010). The two-way language bridge: Co-constructing bilingual language learning opportunities. *The Modern Language Journal, 94*(2), 254–277.

Martínez-Roldán, C. M. (2005). The interplay between context and students' self-regulation in bilingual literature discussions: A case study. In J. Cohen, K. T. McAlister, K. Rolstad, & J. MacSwain (Eds.), *Proceedings of the 4th International Symposium on Bilingualism* (1501–1521). Cascadilla Press.

Martínez-Roldán, C. M., & López-Robertson, J. M. (1999–2000). Initiating literature circles in a first-grade bilingual classroom. *The Reading Teacher, 53*(4), 270–281.

Marzollo, J. (2012). *I spy little letters*. Cartwheel Books.

Massachusetts State Board of Education. (2022). Retrieved July 6, 2022, from *www.doe.mass.edu*.

Matsuyama, U. K. (1983). Can story grammar speak Japanese? *The Reading Teacher, 36*(7), 666–669.

McCarthey, S. J., & García, G. E. (2005). English language learners' writing practices and attitudes. *Written Communication, 22*(1), 36–75.

Mercuri, S., & Ebe, A. E. (2011). Developing academic language and content for emergent bilinguals through a science inquiry unit. *Journal of Multilingual Education Research, 2*(6), 81–102.

Mercuri, S., & Musanti, S., with Rodríguez, S. (2021). *La enseñanza en el aula bilingüe: Content, language, and biliteracy*. [Teaching in the bilingual classroom]. Caslon.

Meyer, B. J. F. (1985). Chapter III: Signaling the structure of text. In D. H. Jonassen (Ed.), *The technology of text* (pp. 64–89). Educational Technology.

Miranda, L. M. (2008). *In the Heights*. Directed by T. Kail. Richard Rodgers Theatre.

Mitchell, C. (2019, November 27). Massachusetts law paves the way for more bilingual education. *Education Week*.

Mo, K. (2019, May 14). New law changes how English Language Learners are taught. But what comes next? Retrieved June 14, 2022, from *www.cronkite-news.azpbs.org*.

Moll, L. C. (2001). The diversity of schooling: A cultural-historical approach. In M. de la Luz Reyes & J. J. Halcón (Eds.), *The best for our children: Critical perspectives on literacy for Latino students* (pp. 13–28). Teachers College Press.

Moll, L. C., Saez, R., & Dworin, J. E. (2001). Exploring biliteracy: Two student case examples of writing as social practice. *The Elementary School Journal, 101*, 435–450.

Montaño-Harmon, M. R. (1991). Discourse features of written Mexican Spanish: Current research in contrastive rhetoric and its implications. *Hispania*, *74*(2), 417–425.

Montero, M. K., & Kuhn, M. R. (2016). English learners and fluency development: More than speed and accuracy. In L. Helman (Ed.), *Literacy development with English learners: Research-based instruction in grades K–6* (2nd ed., pp. 182–205). Guilford Press.

Morpugo, M. (2013). *An elephant in the garden: Inspired by a true story*. Square Fish.

Munsch, R. (1980). *The paper bag princess*. Annick Press.

Munsch, R. (2018). *The paper bag princess*. Annick Press.

Nagy, W. E., García, G. E., Durgunoğlu, A., & Hancin, B. (1993). Spanish–English bilingual children's use and recognition of cognates in English reading. *Journal of Reading Behavior*, *25*(3), 241–259.

Najarro, I. (2021, November 3). The complicated picture of English Language Learners' progress during the pandemic. *Education Week*.

Naqvi, R., Thorne, K. J., Pftischer, C. M., Nordstokke, D. W., & McKeough, A. (2013). Reading dual language books: Improving early literacy skills in linguistically diverse classrooms, *Journal of Early Childhood Research, 11*(1), 3–15.

Nation's Report Card. (2022). Retrieved from *www.nationsreportcard.gov/reading/nation/groups/?grade=4*.

National Academies of Sciences, Engineering, and Medicine. (2018). *How people learn II: Learners, contexts, and cultures*. National Academies Press.

National Assessment Governing Board. (NAGB) (2017). *Reading framework for the 2017 National Assessment of Educational Progress*. U.S. Department of Education.

National Assessment Governing Board. (2023). *Reading framework for the 2026 National Assessment of Educational Progress*. U.S. Department of Education. Retrieved January 28, 2024, from *www. nagb.gov*.

National Center for Education Statistics. (2020). *The condition of education:*

Reading performance. U.S. Department of Education. Retrieved from *http://nces.ed.gov/programs/coe/indicator_cnb.asp*.

National Center for Education Statistics. (2023a). *Common core data*. Institute of Education Sciences, U.S. Department of Education.

National Center for Education Statistics. (2023b). *The condition of reading: Reading performance*. U.S. Department of Education. *http://nces.ed.gov/programs/coe/indicator_cnb.asp*.

National Center for Education Statistics. (2023c). *National Assessment of Educational Progress (NAEP), 2019 and 2022 reading assessments*. U.S. Department of Education.

National Center for Education Statistics. (2023d). Racial/ethnic enrollment in public schools. *Condition of education*. U.S. Department of Education. Retrieved January 28, 2023, from *https://nces.ed.gov/programs/coe/indicator/cge*.

National Center for English Language Acquisition, Office of English Language Acquisition. (NCELA, 2019–2020). The top languages spoken by English learners in the U.S, 2019–2020. Retrieved September 18, 2023, *www.NCELA.ed.gov*.

National Council for the Social Studies. (2013). *The college, career, and civic life (C3) framework for social studies state standards*. Author.

National Governors Association Center for Best Practices & Council of Chief State School Officers (CCSO). (2010). *Common Core State Standards*. Author.

National Institute of Child Health and Development (NICHD). (2000). *Report of the National Reading Panel. Teaching children to read: An evidence-based assessment of the scientific research literature on reading and its implications for reading instruction: Reports of the subgroups* (NIH Publication No. 004754). U.S. Government Printing Office.

New America. (n.d.). Retrieved from *www.newamerica.org*.

Next Generation Science Standards Lead States. (2013). *Next generation science standards: For states, by states*. National Academies Press.

Nhin, M., (2020). *Bruce Lee: A kid's book about pursuing your passions*. Grow Grit Press.

Nickolaisen, D. (n.d.). *Specially designed academic instruction in English (SDAIE)*, pp. i–xiii. Retrieved from *https://people.ucsc.edu/~ktellez/sdaie-easy.pdf*.

Northwest Education Association. (2023). Retrieved January 28, 2024, from *www.nwea*.

Ogle, D. (1986). K-W-L: A teaching model that develops active reading of expository text. *The Reading Teacher, 39*, 564–570.

Oro, B. (2017). *Día a día, letra a letra, de la A a la* Z. BEASCOA.

Orta, R. Q. (2020). *Puerto Rico en ABC*. Independently published.

Osmundson, E. (2011, February 8). Effective use of classroom formative assessments for the CCSS. In the *Common Core State Standards: Planning for effective implementation*. Symposium conducted at the Northwest Comprehensive Center of Education, Portland, OR.

Ovando, C. M., & Combs, M. C. (2018). *Bilingual and ESL classrooms: Teaching in multicultural contexts* (6th ed.). Rowman & Littlefield.

Padrón, Y. N. (1992). The effect of strategy instruction on bilingual students' cognitive strategy use in reading. *Bilingual Research Journal, 16*(3–4), 35–51.

Palincsar, A. S., & Brown, A. I. (1984). Reciprocal teaching of comprehension-fostering and comprehension-monitoring activities. *Cognition and Instruction*, 2, 117–175.

Palincsar, A. S., & Brown, A. I. (1986). Interactive teaching to promote independent learning from texts. *The Reading Teacher, 39*, 771–777.

Palincsar, A. S., Fitzgerald, M. S., DellaVecchia, G. P., & Easley, K. M. (2020). *The integration of literacy, science, and engineering in prekindergarten through fifth grade.* The National Academies Press.

Parrish, T. B., Merickel, A., Pérez, M., Linquanti, R., Socías, M., Spain, A., et al. (2006). *Effects of the implementation of Proposition 227 on the education of English learners: K–12 findings from a five-year evaluation.* American Institutes for Research and WestEd.

Paterson, K. (2008). *Bridge to Terabithia.* HarperTeen.

Paul, M. (2015). *One plastic bag: Isatou Ceesay and the recycling women of the Gambia.* Milbrook Press.

Pearson, P. D., & Gallagher, M. C. (1983). The instruction of reading comprehension. *Contemporary Educational Psychology, 8*(3), 317–344.

Pearson, P. D., & Johnson, D. D. (1978). *Teaching reading comprehension.* Holt, Rinehart, & Winston.

Pennsylvania Department of Education. (2024). *Accommodation guidelines for English Learners (ELs). 2024 PSSA and Keystone Exams.* Author. Retrieved January 29, 2024, from *www.education.pa.gov.*

Peregoy, S. F., & Boyle, O. F. (2000). *Reading, writing and learning in ESL: A resource book for teaching K–12 English Learners.* Pearson.

Perie, M., Gong, B., & Marion, S. (2009). Moving toward a comprehensive assessment system: A framework for considering interim assessments. *Educational Measurement Issues and Practices, 28*(3), 5–13.

Pica, T. (1987). Second-language acquisition, social interaction, and the classroom. *Applied Linguistics, 8*, 3–21.

Proctor, C. P., Boardman, A., & Hiebert, E. H. (Eds.). (2016). *Teaching emergent bilingual students: Flexible approaches in an era of new standards.* Guilford Press.

Punset, A., & Serrano, L. (2014). *La casa de las letras.* BEASCOA.

Raimes, A. (1998). Teaching writing. *Annual Review of Applied Linguistics, 18*, 142–167.

RAND Reading Study Group. (2002). *Reading for understanding: Toward a R & D program in reading comprehension.* Science & Technology Policy Institute; RAND Education.

Rangel-Pacheco, A., & Witte, A. L. (2020*). English Language Proficiency Assessment for the 21st Century (ELPA21): An NeMTSS Research Brief.* Nebraska Multi-tiered System of Support (NeMTSS).

Raphael, T. E. (1982). Question-answering strategies for children. *The Reading Teacher, 36* (November), 186–190.

Rawls, W. (1996). *Where the red fern grows.* Yearling.

Rayner, C. (2007). *Augustus and his smile.* Little Tiger Press.

Reading Rockets. *www.readingrockets.org.*

Riordan, R. (2006). *The lightning thief (Percy Jackson and the Olympians, book 1).* Disney Hyperion.

Rolstad, K., Mahoney, K., & Glass, G. V. (2005). The big picture: A meta-analysis of program effectiveness research on English language learners. *Educational Policy, 19*(4), 572–594.

Romance, N. R., & Vitale, M. R. (2001). Implementing an in-depth expanded science model in elementary schools: Multi-year findings, research issues, and policy implications. *International Journal of Science Education, 23*(4), 373–404.

Rose, F. (2020). *A day with grandpa.* Mantra Lingua.

Ruiz, O., & Cuesta, V. (2000). *Evaluación del Desarrollo de la Lectura (EDL).* [Developmental Reading Assessment]. Celebration Press.

Rutherford-Quach, S., Torre Gibney, D., Kelly, H., Ballen Riccards, J., Garcia, E., Hsiao, M., et al. (2021). *Bilingual education across the United States.* CCNetwork.

Sachar, L. (2000). *Holes (Hole series).* Yearling.

San Diego County Office of Education. (2012, December). *Common Core Language Arts/Literacy Standards in Spanish.* Author.

Santamans, I. P. (2017). *Abecedario escondido.* Editorial Juventud, S. A.

Saunders, W. M., & Goldenberg, C. (1999). Effects of instructional conversations and literate logs on limited and fluent-English-proficient students' story comprehension and thematic understanding. *The Elementary School Journal, 99*(4), 277–301.

Saunders, W. M., & Goldenberg, C. (2010). Research to guide English language development instruction. In D. Dolson & L. Burnham-Massey (Eds.), *Improving education for ELs: Research-based approaches* (pp. 21–82). California Department of Education Press.

Savignon, S. J. (1983). *Communicative competence: Theory and classroom practice.* Addison-Wesley.

Saville-Troike, M. (2006). *Introduction to second-language acquisition.* Cambridge University Press.

Schwartz, S. (2020, March 13). "Decodable" books: Boring, useful, or both? *EducationWeek.*

Shanahan, C., & Shanahan, T. (2014). Does disciplinary literacy have a place in elementary school? *The Reading Teacher, 67*(8), 636–639.

Shanahan, T., & Beck, I. (2006). Effective literacy teaching for English language learners, In D. August & T. Shanahan (Eds.), *Developing literacy in second language learners: Report of the National Literacy Panel on language minority children and youth* (pp. 415–488). Erlbaum.

Shanahan, T., Callison, K., Carriere, C., Duke, N. K., Pearson, P. D., Schatschneider, C., et al. (2010). *Improving reading comprehension in kindergarten through 3rd grade: A practice guide (NCEE 2010-4038).* National Center for Education Evaluation and Regional Assistance, Institute of Education Sciences, U.S. Department of Education.

Shepard, L. (2009). Commentary: Evaluating the validity of formative and interim assessments. *Educational Measurement: Issues and Practice, 28*(3), 32–37.

Silverman, R. D., Proctor, C. P., Harring, J. R., Doyle, B., Mitchell, M. A., & Meyer, A. G. (2013). Teachers' instruction and students' vocabulary and comprehension: An exploratory story with English monolingual and Spanish–English bilingual students in grades 3–5. *Reading Research Quarterly 49*(1), 31–60.

Silverstein, S. (2014). *Where the sidewalk ends*. HarperCollins.

Slavin, R. E., & Cheung, A. (2005). A synthesis of research on language of reading instruction for English language learners. *Review of Educational Research, 75*(2), 247–284.

Snow, C. E., Lawrence, J. F., & White, C. (2009). Generating knowledge of academic language among urban middle school students. *Journal of Research in Educational Effectiveness, 2*, 325–344.

Snow, C. E., & Sweet, A. P. (2003). Reading for comprehension. In A. P. Sweet & C. E. Snow (Eds.), *Rethinking reading comprehension* (pp. 1–11). Guilford Press.

Song, S. (2017). Narrative structures in Korean folktales: A comparative analysis of Korean and English versions. *Topics in Linguistics, 18*(2), 1–23.

Soto, G. (1996). *Qué montón de tamales! (Too many tamales!)*. Penguin Random House.

Sotomayor, S. (2018). *Pasando páginas: La historia de mi vida (Turning pages: The story of my life*). Philomel Books.

Spencer, C. M. (1990). Comparison and contrast of Spanish and English discourse Styles. Deseret Language and Linguistic Society Symposium: *16*(1), Article 8. Retrieved from *https://scholarsarchive.byu.edu/dlls/vol16/iss1/8*.

Stahl, K. A. D., Flanigan, K., & McKenna, M. C. (2020). *Assessment for reading comprehension* (4th ed.). Guilford Press.

Stahl, K. A. D., & García, G. E. (2015). *Developing reading comprehension: Effective instruction for all students in preK–2 (the essential library of preK–2 literacy)*. Guilford Press.

Stahl, K. A. D., & García, G. E. (2022). *Expanding reading comprehension in grades (3–6): Effective instruction for ALL students*. Guilford Press.

Stauffer, R. G. (1965). A language experience approach. In J. A. Kerfoot (Ed.), *First grade reading programs, perspectives in reading No. 5*. International Reading Association.

Stead, T. (2014). Nurturing the inquiring mind through the nonfiction read-aloud. *The Reading Teacher, 67*(7), 488–495.

Steele, J. L., Slater, R. O., Zamarro, G., Miller, T., Li, J., Burkhauser, S., et al. (2017). Effects of dual-language immersion programs on student achievement: Evidence from lottery data. *American Educational Research Journal, 54*(1), 282S–306S.

Steffensen, M. S., Joag-Deve, C., & Anderson, R. C. (1979). A cross-cultural perspective on reading comprehension. *Reading Research Quarterly, 15*(1), 10–29.

Stewart, M. (2014). *Feathers: Not just for flying*. Charlesbridge.

Street, B. (2003). The implications of the "New Literacies Studies" for literacy education. In S. Goodman, J. Maybin, & N. Mercer (Eds.), *Language, literacy, and education: A reader* (pp. 77–88). Trentham Books.

Sugarman, J., & Lazarin, M. (2020). *Educating English Learners during the*

COVID-19 pandemic: Policy ideas for states and school districts. Migration Policy Institute. Retrieved January 11, 2023, from *Migrationpolicy.org.*

Swain, M. (2000). French immersion research in Canada: Recent contributions to second-language acquisition and applied linguistics. *Annual Review of Applied Linguistics, 20,* 199–212.

Swain, M., & Lapkin, S. (1995). Problems in output and the cognitive processes they generate. A step toward second language learning. *Applied Linguistics, 16,* 371–391.

Tales, T. (2011). *A Is for Apple* (Smart Kids Trace and Flip). Tiger Tales.

The Thinking Muslim. (2023). *www.thethinkingmuslim.com.*

Thwaite, A. (2019). Halliday's view of child language learning: Has it been misinterpreted?. *Australian Journal of Teacher Education, 44*(5) 42–56. Retrieved from *http://dx.doi.org/10.14221/ajte.2018v44n5.3.*

Tolkien, J. R. R. (2002). *The hobbit.* HarperCollins.

U.S. Department of Education. (2016). *Every Student Succeeds Act: Assessments under Title 1, Part A and Title 1, Part B: Summary of final regulations.* Author. Retrieved from *www2.ed.gov.*

U.S. Department of Education, Office of English Language Acquisition. (2015). *Dual language education programs: Current state policies and practices.* Author.

U.S. Department of Education, Office of English Language Acquisition. (2016). *Home language survey.* Author.

U.S. Department of Education, Office of English Language Acquisition. (2022). *Our nation's English learners: What are their characteristics?* Author. Retrieved June 13, 2022, from *www2.ed.gov.*

Urow, C., & Beeman, K. (n.d.). *El dictado adaptado* [Adapted dictation]. Retrieved from *www.TeachingForBiliteracy.com.*

Valdés, G. (1996). *Con respeto: Bridging the distances between culturally diverse families and schools.* Teachers College Press.

Valdés, G. (2004). Between support and marginalization: The development of academic language in linguistic minority children. *International Journal of Bilingual Education and Bilingualism, 7,* 102–132.

Valenzuela, A. (1999). *Subtractive schooling: U.S.–Mexican youth and the politics of caring.* New York State University of New York Press.

Van Allsburg, C. (2018). *Jumanji.* Clarion Books.

Velasco, P., & García, O. (2014). Translanguaging and the writing of bilingual learners. *Bilingual Research Journal, 37*(1), 6–23.

Vygotsky, L. S. (1978). *Mind in society: The development of higher psychological processes.* Harvard University Press.

Walsh, R. (2015, February 25). From text complexity to considerate text. Retrieved December 8, 2023, from *www.russonreading.blogspot.com.*

Wang, J., & Herman, J. (2005). *Evaluation of Seeds of Science/Roots of Reading project: Shoreline Science and Terrarium Investigations.* CRESST. Retrieved from www.scienceandliteracy.org/PDFs/CRESST_Final_Report.pdf

White, E. B. (1952). Charlotte's web. Harper & Brothers.

Wiley, T. G. (1996). *Literacy and language diversity in the United States.* Center for Applied Linguistics and Delta Systems.

Wilkinson, I. A. G., & Son, E. H. (2011). A dialogic turn in research on learning and teaching to comprehend. In K. Kamil, P. D. Pearson, E. B. Moje, & P. Afflerbach (Eds.), *The handbook of reading research* (Vol. IV., pp. 359–387). Routledge.

Williams, C. (1994). *Arfarniad o dduliau dysgu ac addysgu yng nghyd-destun addysg uwchrad ddwyleithog* [An evaluation of teaching and learning methods in the context of bilingual secondary education]. [Unpublished doctoral thesis, University of Wales].

Williams, C. P., & Marcus, M. (2021, August 11). *Pandemic response to pandemic recovery: Helping English learners to succeed this fall and beyond.* Migration Policy Institute. *Migrationpolicy.org.* Retrieved January 11, 2023.

Willis, A. I., García, G. E., Barrera, R. B., & Harris, V. J. (Eds.). (2002). *Multicultural issues in literacy research and practice.* Routledge.

Wolfram, W. (1991). *Dialects and American English.* Prentice Hall.

World-Class Instructional Design and Assessment. (2013). *The Spanish language development standards, K–12* (2013 edition). Wisconsin Center for Education Research and the Board of Regents of the University of Wisconsin System.

World-Class Instructional Design and Assessment. (2020). *WIDA English language development standards framework, 2020 edition: Kindergarten–grade 12.* Board of Regents of the University of Wisconsin System.

World-Class Instructional Design and Assessment. (2023a). *Assessing comprehension and communication in English state-to-state (ACCESS for ELLs).* Wisconsin Center for Education Research and the Board of Regents of the University of Wisconsin System.

World-Class Instructional Design and Assessment. (2023b). *Marco de los estándares del desarrollo auténtico del lenguaje español de WIDA: Kinder al 12o grado.* [WIDA's Spanish language development standards: Kindergarten to 12th grade]. Junta de Regentes del Sistema de la Universidad de Wisconsin.

Wright, T. S., & Domke, L. M. (2019). The role of language and literacy in K–5 science and social studies standards. *Journal of Literacy Research, 51*(1), 529.

Wu, X., & Anderson, R. C. (2007). Reading strategies revealed in Chinese children's oral reading. *Literacy Learning & Teaching, 12*(1), 47–72.

Zaidi, R. (2020). Dual-language learners: Enhancing engagement and language awareness. *Journal of Literacy Research, 52*(3), 269–292.

Index

Note. *t* or *f* following a page number indicates a table or a figure.

D

E

F

G

Q

R

S

T